God, Grades, and Graduation

God, Grades, and Graduation

Religion's Surprising Impact on Academic Success

ILANA M. HORWITZ

OXFORD
UNIVERSITY PRESS

OXFORD
UNIVERSITY PRESS

Oxford University Press is a department of the University of Oxford. It furthers the University's objective of excellence in research, scholarship, and education by publishing worldwide. Oxford is a registered trade mark of Oxford University Press in the UK and certain other countries.

Published in the United States of America by Oxford University Press
198 Madison Avenue, New York, NY 10016, United States of America.

Library of Congress Cataloging-in-Publication Data
Names: Horwitz, Ilana M., author.
Title: God, grades, and graduation : religion's surprising impact on academic success / Ilana M. Horwitz.
Other titles: God, grades and graduation
Description: New York : Oxford University Press, [2022] |
Includes bibliographical references and index.
Identifiers: LCCN 2021037314 (print) | LCCN 2021037315 (ebook) |
ISBN 9780197534144 (Hardback) | ISBN 9780197534168 (eBook) | ISBN 9780197534175
Subjects: LCSH: Church and education—United States. | Academic achievement—United States. | Child rearing—Religious aspects. |
Parenting—Religious aspects. | Families—Religious aspects. | Success.
Classification: LCC LC111 .H6 2022 (print) | LCC LC111 (ebook) |
DDC 261.80973—dc23
LC record available at https://lccn.loc.gov/2021037314
LC ebook record available at https://lccn.loc.gov/2021037315

DOI: 10.1093/oso/9780197534144.001.0001

1 3 5 7 9 8 6 4 2

Printed by Sheridan Books, Inc., United States of America

To my mom, Cecilia Straznik

Contents

Figures

Preface

Some people write books about questions they have long wrestled with. In her book *When God Talks Back: Understanding the American Evangelical Relationship with God*, anthropologist Tanya Luhrmann describes her long-standing curiosity about how people develop a God-centered existence stemming from observing her deeply conservative Christian family members. "I have lived these questions . . . my cousins played in a world I did not understand," Luhrmann says. Similarly, sociologist Vern Bengtson also grew up in a highly religious family, with 33 born-again Christian family members. His own family story kindled his research interests, including his most recent book, *Families and Faith: How Religion Is Passed Down across Generations*. Many books about religion are written by people who are religious, experienced a profound personal religious change, or feel so strongly opposed to religion that they feel compelled to argue against it.

I do not fall into any of these camps. Having spent my childhood living in Russia under a communist regime that forbade free expression of religion, I didn't even know what religion was until I was an early adolescent. I had no interest in the lives of Conservative Christians until I was well into my thirties, having been born a Jew and growing up in a family that didn't openly practice their faith. I do not recall my family ever talking with me about being Jewish or celebrating any Jewish holidays. The few Jewish rituals my parents observed in Russia were done in secret, and I wasn't aware of them. It was only when we came to the United States that we started to slowly engage in Jewish practices, largely because I started attending non-Orthodox Jewish private schools and taught my parents about what we as Jews were "supposed" to do. Consequently, I developed a social circle that was filled with other Jewish teenagers, few of whom would have described themselves as intensely religious. While my kids do attend a Jewish school, it is primarily for social and cultural reasons rather than for religious ones. Like many Jews, I feel fairly agnostic about God. How, then, did I come to write a book about intensely religious Christian teenagers?

In 2013, I moved into Escondido Village, which houses many of Stanford's student families. It is an idyllic living arrangement, with attached houses organized around large playgrounds that serve as the epicenter of community life. Sitting on these playgrounds with my own child, I discovered that many of my neighbors organized much of their lives around their Christian commitments. They piled into their cars on Sunday mornings for church, gathered at home every night to eat dinner and teach their children biblical stories, and decorated their homes with religious symbols.

At the time I was a graduate student in sociology and education, and I spent much of my time thinking about how race, social class, and gender shaped educational outcomes. But as I spoke with my neighbors, I kept wondering whether their religious upbringing played a role in their academic trajectories. What was patently clear was that religion was not something that happened just on Sunday; these individuals lived and breathed their faith. And it wasn't just my neighbors—a lot of Americans organized their lives around religion. According to Pew's 2015 Religious Landscape study, half of American adults said religion was "very" important and prayed at least once a day, with two-thirds of respondents reporting they believed in God with absolute certainty. Thus, it seemed logical to me that people's religious upbringing might play a role in their educational journeys.

I decided to do a little digging and see what the research said but surprisingly came up empty handed. Not a single book spoke to my interests, and aside from a few dozen articles, I found very little about how religion shapes young people's academic outcomes. When I considered just how influential religion has been in the United States, I found this gap shocking. I started to dig deeper, intrigued by what I wasn't discovering. This book is my attempt to begin to fill that gap.

Over the years I have told a lot of people about my research. I usually got one of two reactions. One camp of people would look at me dubiously, hesitantly trying to tell me I was barking up the wrong tree. Like many academics, many of these people had grown up in highly liberal and secular areas, completely unaware of how religious Americans really are. They were shocked when I told them that the United States was the most devout country among other rich nations. The second camp were people who were religious themselves or had grown up religious. They were excited to share their personal stories but did so quietly at the risk of breaking the norms of university life where being "too" religious was a bit taboo. I will never forget how one colleague, who was biracial and came from a low-income family, told me that of all of the challenges she faced when she chose to attend an Ivy League college, her parents' antimaterialistic religious beliefs were the biggest obstacle.

I am writing this book for both of these camps—those who either haven't thought about religion's role in academic success and those who have been too nervous to talk about it. Plenty of sociologists and education scholars have written about other social factors like race, social class, and gender that shape academic success. But how religious upbringing intersects with educational outcomes has gone largely unexplored.

I am also writing this book for those who are interested to learn how religion shapes the various facets of the lives of ordinary Americans. A great deal of research has documented how religion influences people's happiness, health, labor market outcomes, and social networks. By focusing on religion and schooling, this book helps explain how many of the downstream outcomes of being religious come to be.

I am also writing this book for the millions of Americans who work as religious leaders and teach at Christian schools and colleges. Understanding the experiences of students with deeply held religious commitments is central to their mission. Finally, I am also writing this book for parents who are constantly thinking about how they want to raise their children religiously and/or academically. They deserve a clear picture of what my subtitle says: religion's surprising impact on academic success.

How religion intersects with academic outcomes is surprising, or at least it was to me. I suspect they will be for others, and that people will feel either elated and livid—or both—about the conclusions that the data led me to make. That I suspect won't come as a surprise: religion, as is well known, can be divisive. But my goal is neither to champion nor denigrate religion, but rather to understand how it intersects with the educational journeys of American teenagers and young adults. The results are fascinating and revealing all at once. Because if there is one truth that shines clearly from my research, it's that despite the separation of church and state, teenagers don't check their religious commitments at the school door.

Acknowledgments

If you had asked me in my teenage years, or even in my twenties, what kind of career I imagined for myself, becoming an academic would have never appeared on the list. I did not know any academics growing up, and I imagined their jobs to be quite boring and lonely. Frankly, I was never a big fan of sitting in a classroom, and I hated academic reading. I saw myself as a "people person," and I wanted to be entrepreneurial. But my teachers and mentors at Stanford helped me fall in love with research and scholarship. They encouraged me to think about big ideas and to see patterns in social behavior that I hadn't ever recognized. I realized that most K–12 schooling, and even most undergraduate education, rewards people who are good at *consuming* information. I was never very good at this, which is probably why I found school to be boring and irrelevant. But as a doctoral student at Stanford, my job was now to *produce* information. The shift from being a passive consumer to active producer of information changed my life. It piqued my curiosity in a way I never thought possible. This book was born out of this curiosity. I am indebted to so many mentors who helped me get to this point.

First, I owe enormous gratitude to Ari Y. Kelman, my doctoral advisor at Stanford University. Ari prompted me to re-evaluate my understanding of religion in many unexpected yet productive ways. At the same time, he always made me feel capable. On several occasions, usually while reading dense theoretical texts, I wanted to give up on academia. Ari sat with me for hours to help me make sense of the material, and always believed in me. He read everything I wrote thoroughly and consistently gave constructive feedback. He supported my study of religion in America, recognizing that it would help me become a better scholar of American Jews. I am fairly certain that I would not have stayed in academia, nor written this book, if it were not for Ari's mentorship.

I was also mentored by some of the greatest scholars of education and sociology. My dissertation advisors—Sean Reardon, Chiqui Ramirez, and Mitchell Stevens—taught me how to analyze data, how to structure compelling arguments, and how to navigate the hidden curriculum of the academy. Other Stanford faculty also influenced my work in significant ways. David Labaree, whose 1997 article about education as a public and private good completely changed my view of education, has been one of my greatest mentors, reading drafts of my book proposal and manuscript. David's confidence in my writing and in my ideas was profoundly encouraging. I also received incredible mentorship from Sam Wineburg, who also encouraged me to write this book and taught me that good writing should be free of academic jargon. At Stanford, I received rigorous training in quantitative research methods at the Stanford Center for Education Policy (CEPA) through a fellowship from the Institute of Education Sciences. I would not have been able to pursue this quantitative training were it not for the support of Eric Bettinger. At CEPA, my interest in religion was anomalous, but Eric supported my ideas, advising me to diversify the risk and reward portfolio of my research projects. This project was certainly on the riskier end, so thank you, Eric, for the great advice. I am also grateful to other Stanford faculty members who have played an instrumental role in teaching me and supporting my work, including but certainly not limited to Anthony Antonio, Sanne Smith, Denise Pope, Guadalupe Valdez, Ann Porteus, Florencia Torche, Brigid Barron, Michelle Jackson, and Tom Ehrlich.

Ben Domingue played a pivotal role in this book and my self-concept as a scholar. Ben was initially skeptical about my finding that intensely religious teens fared better academically. His legitimate skepticism led us to collaborate on a project (along with Kathleen Mullan Harris) in which we examined whether more religious siblings fared better academically than their less religious sibling (they did). This study, which we published in Social Science Research, helped me feel confident that a book about religion's role in academic success was a book worth writing. Perhaps more importantly, Ben encouraged me to be persistent. After one particularly painful journal rejection, Ben told me that Mark Granovetter's seminal "The Strength of Weak Ties" article was initially rejected from the American Sociological Review (and was later accepted in the American Journal of Sociology). Instead of giving up, I saw that some great ideas have slow starts. Thank you Ben for giving me the courage to persist.

Lee Shulman, who mentored me throughout his retirement from Stanford, was an invaluable source of support. Lee and I met regularly—often weekly—in his office over coffee. He pushed me to be question driven rather than data driven in my research and taught me that good research methods are only valuable when you have an interesting research question. Because of Lee's advice, I began to walk around with a more curious mind, looking for big-picture puzzles. It was this mindset that made me intrigued about my neighbors' religious commitments, and whether they were related to their educational journeys. That intrigue is what spawned this book.

It was also because of a fortuitous meeting with Lee in 2015 that I met Chris Smith. Chris mentioned that he, along with Lisa Pearce, had directed the most comprehensive study of the religious lives of American teenagers, which included an oversample of American Jews. I jumped at the chance to analyze the data, and I am grateful to the National Study of Youth and Religion (NSYR) team who made it possible. Chris and Lisa supported my project throughout its various stages and helped make this book a reality. I am especially grateful to Sara Skiles, who spent countless hours matching the NSYR data to the National Student Clearinghouse (NSC). This book would not be what it is without Sara's support.

Over the last several years, I have met several sociologists and scholars of religion outside of Stanford who have been remarkable mentors and collaborators. Willa Johnson, Jeremy Uecker, Richard Flory, Tim Clydesdale, David Sikkink, Tomas Jimenez, Jon Levisohn, and Steve Weitzman each gave me advice about the world of book publishing and provided input at various stages of the project. I am especially grateful to John W. Meyer, Melissa Wilde, Robert Putnam, and Phil Zuckerman, who gave me feedback on different sections of the book.

I was also fortunate to be part of an incredible book writing group with Landon Schnabel, Helana Darwin, and Elizabeth Mount—all of whom were also writing their first books at the time. This book has benefitted tremendously from their insights and support.

My colleagues at the Stanford Center on Longevity (SCL), where I have been the Education Fellow for the past 2 years, have been amazing. They have given me the time and space to work on this book and helped me think more deeply about how education and learning happen along the life course. Many of my views about the life course were developed at the SCL.

This book would also not be possible without an incredibly dedicated, brilliant, and collaborative team of 23 research assistants, two of whom were PhD students, 20 undergraduates, and one postbaccalaureate at Mission College: Valeria Rincon, Corey Lamb, Merrell Guzman, Amy Zhou, Maddy Fish, Alexess Sosa, Jonathan Tang, Michelle Ibarra, Minha Khan, Lora Supandi, Corey Lamb, Muhammad Dhafer Muhammad Faishal, Forrest Dollins, Sarah Lee, Lucero Carrasco, Saray Bedoya, Michael Massey, Casie Chavez, Adam Acevedo, Natalie Milan, Jennifer Osugi, Krystal Laryea, and Kaylee Matheny. Kaylee played a particularly important role in bringing this book to fruition. She has supported my research for several years, eventually becoming an expert in the NSYR data herself.

In the summer of 2020, 12 of my undergraduate researchers worked with me full time. In addition to writing memos, they helped me analyze data that were specific to several key questions that this book tackles. Working in teams, they dove into one of three substantive areas and analyzed data for a particular subset of interviewees. Minha Khan, Lora Supandi, Corey Lamb, and Muhammad Dhafer Muhammad Faishal helped me understand why working-class abiders fared better academically than nonabiders (Chapter 4). Forrest Dollins, Sarah Lee, and Lucero Carrasco helped me understand why the academic performance of atheists was not significantly different from abiders (Chapter 5). Saray Bedoya, Michael Massey, Michelle Ibarra, Casie Chavez, and Adam Acevedo helped me understand how abiders' religious commitments changed as they entered adulthood (Chapter 6). Natalie Milan and Jennifer Osugi also helped me see that poor abiders do not see as much of an academic boost because they face overwhelmingly difficult obstacles in several domains of their life that spill over into the academic domain. My research assistants also read earlier drafts of book chapters and provided exceptionally insightful input. A special thank you to Saray Bedoya, Sarah Lee, and Forrest Dollins, who read the entire manuscript and provided invaluable feedback.

Presenting this research at several conferences each year helped me sharpen my thinking and arguments. I am especially grateful to the American Educational Research Association (AERA), the Society for the Scientific Study of Religion (SSSR), the Association for the Sociology of Religion (ASR), the Association for Jewish Studies (AJS), the Association for Studies in Higher Education (ASHE), Sociology of Education Association (SEA), the American Sociological Association (ASA), and the Notre Dame Scholars of Religion conference for providing space for me to work out my ideas and helping me connect with colleagues outside of Stanford.

My officemates during graduate school, the "five-fifths" team, including Angela Johnson, Ericka Weathers, David Song, Ben Stenhaug, and Diana Mercado-Garcia, provided much needed social and emotional support during the early years of this research. I am grateful to my colleagues at the GSE, especially CEPA, the Race and Religion and Ethnicity Group that I cofounded with Tamara Gilkes, and the Sociology and Education network, where I workshopped many of these ideas. My colleagues in Jewish Studies—Elayne Weissler-Martello, Jeremiah Lockwood, Erin Johnston,

Abiya Ahmed, Marva Marom, Caitlyn Brust, Hannah Kober, and Shoshana Olidort—have also cheered me along every step of the way and helped me wrestle with many ideas.

Over the years, I received funding from several organizations that made this book project possible: the Jim Joseph Foundation, the Wexner Foundation, the Stanford Graduate School of Education, and the Institute of Education Sciences.

As I conclude this book project, I am also wrapping up a decade-long adventure at Stanford University. Stanford has taught me a great deal about what good education looks like, and the great insights that come from student-faculty collaborations. I will carry these lessons with me into my new role as an Assistant Professor and the Fields-Rayant Chair in Contemporary Jewish Life at the Suzanne and Stuart Grant Center for the American Jewish Experience at Tulane University.

Much of this book was written during the COVID-19 pandemic. Working from my small Stanford apartment proved to be quite difficult. I am grateful to Ivor and Jess Castelino, who welcomed me into their farm cottage for several weekends of uninterrupted writing (and biking!). On top of the pandemic, the California wildfires in fall 2020 forced us to pull our children out of school and leave the Bay Area. I am beyond grateful to my in-laws, Liz and Allan Horwitz, my mother, Cecilia Straznik, and my stepfather, Vitaly Fridman, who provided housing and took care of my children so that I could focus on writing significant chunks of this book.

Cynthia Read, my editor at Oxford University Press, believed in this project from the very beginning. I am fortunate to have found such a fantastic press to work with.

My editor, Olson, went above and beyond to see this book through, from start to finish. He helped me organize my thoughts, made my arguments clearer, and trimmed unnecessary details. Olson, thank you for making my ideas shine.

My children have grown up with one central idea of what their mom does all day: "Mommy writes." Araya (now 8) and Mikayla (5) have been incredibly supportive and patient, often saying to my husband, "Let's give Mommy time to write! She needs to finish her book!" While they are disappointed by the lack of pictures and abundance of big words, I hope that they come to find as much joy in writing as I do.

And finally, to my husband, Robbie, who has been my biggest cheerleader. From the very beginning when I got into Stanford, Robbie encouraged me to go, even though I didn't think I'd succeed. Along the way, he has supported me in more ways than I can name. Academia is full of surprises, and Robbie has celebrated my wins and lamented my losses. He gave me feedback on my writing, always catching places where I used confusing academic jargon, and he spent countless hours caring for our two young children so that I had the time and space to work. Robbie, this book would not have been possible without you by my side every step of the way.

Introduction

Americans don't agree on a lot of things these days, but there is consensus over one issue: education matters. Regardless of race, ethnicity, social class, gender, sexual orientation, religion, or political stance, Americans largely agree that it's important to complete as many years of education as we can. It doesn't mean that everyone carries out this ideal, but it is still something most Americans strive for and encourage their kids to do.

Our intuition about the importance of education is grounded in reality. Going to college means more job opportunities, more economic security, better health, and longer lives.[1] For example, of the 16 million jobs created in 2019, only 19% could be obtained with just some college education, and a mere 0.003% were available to those with only a high school diploma.[2] Education is also directly linked to higher pay. In 2019, Americans who had dropped out of high school earned about $31,000. Those with a high school diploma earned over 25% more—about $40,000—and graduates with some college education or an associate degree earned on average an additional $5,000. But the biggest pay bump comes with a college diploma: Americans with a bachelor's degree earned about $66,000, and advanced degree holders earned about $81,000.[3] Compared to a high school dropout, Americans with a bachelor's degree have enough additional earnings to buy themselves a new car every year.

Education doesn't just lead to more jobs and higher earnings. It also leads to healthier and longer lives. American men who drop out of high school live for about 72 years. Those with a high school diploma gain an additional 4 years to live till 76, while those with some college education get another year of life. But like with earnings, the biggest longevity bump comes with a 4-year college degree: those with a bachelor's degree live into their eighth decade.[4] The evidence is clear: the longer we stay in school, the more we will earn and the longer we will live.

The quantity of education isn't all that matters. Quality does, too. Selectivity is one key indicator of the quality of a college,[5] and research suggests that selective colleges confer more benefits on those that attend than less selective schools. Graduating from a selective college provides a roughly 20% earnings advantage relative to graduating from a less selective college. These earnings seem to increase over the early stages of the careers of graduates.[6] In addition to the economic benefit, those from more selective institutions are more likely to earn graduate degrees,[7] tend to feel better about their social and economic circumstances,[8] and have better mental health[9] and physical health.[10]

Class and College

Unfortunately, not everyone has an equal chance of enjoying the benefits that come from attending a selective college because our education system is deeply stratified by social class (i.e., socioeconomic status [SES]).[11] Individuals have unequal educational opportunities based on their parents' education levels, occupation, and income.[12] Here is just one example of how much social class matters: children from the top SES quartile were four times as likely to obtain a bachelor's degree than children from the bottom SES quartile (60% vs. 15%).[13] There is no doubt that the road to college, especially a selective college, is much smoother for those who come from more affluent and educated families.[14] The farther down on the socioeconomic ladder you go, the bumpier and steeper the climb becomes to attending a selective college.

Social class wasn't always such a strong predictor of college completion and economic mobility. As political scientist Robert Putnam describes in his 2015 book, *Our Kids: The American Dream in Crisis*,[15] children from all social class backgrounds used to have a good shot of doing better than their parents. But in the twenty-first century, affluent children have many advantages that compound to make their academic trajectories easier. Here are just a few of the reasons why affluent kids get ahead. By 18 months of age, toddlers from disadvantaged families are already several months behind more advantaged children in language proficiency because their parents have been talking to them and reading to them since they were babies.[16] They tend to live in well-resourced neighborhoods with a strong social infrastructure[17] where they have access to playgrounds, libraries, and safe outdoor spaces. They tend to go to well-funded public schools because their parents live in places with high property taxes. They participate in more extracurricular activities.[18] They have more familial and geographic stability, which means they rarely need to transfer between schools and sever social ties. And they interact with lots of other adults.

I could go on and on, but the point is clear: for children whose parents are part of the professional class—those who are in the top quarter of the socioeconomic distribution—the road to college is a well-paved highway with only a few twists and turns. For these children, any off-ramps that would divert them from arriving at their destination are few and far between, and a few bad grades in high school or even a suspension won't prevent them from finding an on-ramp back to the highway, allowing them to continue their journey to college.

But for children whose parents are working and even middle class, the road to college is more like a bumpy road that is uphill and has several off-ramps. They live in under-resourced neighborhoods with poor social infrastructure. Parents often work several jobs or in the evenings, giving teenagers more opportunity to fall into risky behaviors that knock them off the road to college. Parents are either unable to be home for dinner or are often just too worn out to converse deeply with their children. If nonaffluent kids get a few bad grades in high school or get suspended, it is much more likely they will take an exit ramp diverting them from the path toward college. For those whose parents are poor, the road is in even worse shape, with potholes scattered across the surface. Driving on such a road makes it even more likely that teenagers will wind up in a ditch not of their own making because of their social class. The farther down you go on the socioeconomic ladder, the harder and steeper the road you have to climb to get to college.

Just how steep is this climb? So steep that only 16 of every 100 kids whose parents have a high school diploma complete college. The other 84 are rerouted somewhere along the way, usually because of circumstances beyond their control. The odds increase a bit for those kids whose parents had some college education: for every 100 of them, 28 complete college. But for those whose parents are college educated, the odds skyrocket. For every 100 of them, 60 earn a bachelor's degree.

~

John was one student I encountered in my research whose road to college was uphill, making him statistically unlikely to have reached his destination. As a 16-year-old, he lived with his parents, brother, and four dogs in a city 1 hour north of Jackson, Mississippi. John's parents each had a vocational certificate and together earned about $35,000 a year. His father owned an auto-repair shop while his mother worked as a bookkeeper and substitute teacher. Based on their income, education, and occupation, John's family fell squarely into America's working class—a group of Americans who have been having an especially hard time making it to college and are now faring economically worse than their parents' generation.[19]

John attended public school, where he played football, lifted weights, and was in the band. In the summers, he played on a summer basketball league, and on the weekends, he went fishing and hunting with his grandparents. For fun, he and his friends rode their four-wheeler trucks around town, and to earn some money he mowed people's lawns. From the outside John appeared to be a wholly normal teenager, and indeed like his professional- and middle-class peers he aspired to go to college and make a decent living. But because of his social origins, it was unlikely that John would make it to college or finish if he did.

Yet there was something different about John—or to be more accurate, something different about his particular road to college. Unlike many working-class kids who struggle to make it through high school, John was on track to graduate. He was not a top student by any means—his report card was filled with Bs and Cs. But many of his working-class male counterparts were faring much worse, often failing several classes. John was not apathetic about school. He was unsatisfied with his grades and tried to improve them, but academics didn't come easily to him. Still, John knew it was important to do well in school and that college was crucial for his ability to earn a living.

For John, doing well in school was not just a matter of getting good grades. It was also about behaving well—respecting his teachers and being kind. On top of this, he was exceptionally self-disciplined, especially compared to other working-class boys. When interviewed, John revealed that he didn't drink, use drugs, or attend any parties where beer or even smoking were present: "There's a lot of opportunity, but I just don't do it." Substance abuse was very prevalent in his community, and he had already seen several people die. John's self-discipline and compliant behavior were evident in other ways, too. He didn't listen to rap because it has too much cursing nor watch any movies with a lot of violence, and he didn't even mind that his parents forbade him from doing so. He says the only thrill-seeking activity he engages in is hunting. His mantra in life pretty much sums up his behavior: "Respect your elders, do good things, and always treat other people the way you want to be treated."

This outlook has gotten him farther in life than one might expect. After graduating high school in 2006, John enrolled full time in his local community college. He didn't have an easy time of it and took several breaks, but his self-discipline helped him persist. By 2013 he had completed enough courses to become an EMT, and by 2015 he earned an associate degree. He hoped to one day complete a bachelor's, but he had already done better than would have been predicted based on his social origins and the struggles that working men like him have been facing since the early part of this century.

Teenagers like John are often pointed to as examples of the indelible role that character and personal responsibility plays in a student's ultimate ascent up the educational ladder. But a closer look at his story reveals that instead of an "up by your bootstraps" narrative of grit and determination, John—and other boys like him—benefited from a set of "concealed" guardrails that kept him on track when many of his peers fell by the wayside. What were those guardrails that helped John graduate high school and persist long enough through community college to earn an associate degree?

Bringing Up Baby

When I began this research, I thought a lot about how John's upbringing may have influenced his academic trajectory. What did childrearing look like in John's house? I had been intrigued by the role of childrearing ever since reading the work of sociologist Annette Lareau, who demonstrated how social class influenced childrearing strategies and how these childrearing strategies subsequently influenced children's dispositions in school.[20] In her book *Home Advantage,* Lareau argued that social class matters to children's schooling because parents' childrearing strategies continue to influence children even after they leave home and enter school. Lareau's data led her to identify two distinct childrearing strategies: "concerted cultivation," which she found prevalent in professional-class homes, and "natural growth," which she found to be prevalent in poor and working-class homes.

Professional-class parents who take a "concerted cultivation" approach seek to develop their children's talents through organized leisure activities. Life is hectic, with the children and parents racing from one structured activity to another activity. Children's activities are accorded so much importance that they stipulate families' entire schedules. Children are also much more embedded in parents' social worlds than are poor and working-class children. They spend a lot of time accompanied by adults, which allows them to develop a more robust vocabulary. Professional-class parents encourage their children to question authority and advocate for themselves. Consequently, more privileged students come to see interactions with teachers as opportunities for reward. When it comes to interacting with teachers, they feel entitled to their attention and seek out support proactively and persistently.[21]

The story of what happens for working-class and poor families couldn't be more different. In working-class and poor families who tend to use the "natural growth" approach, parents do not structure their children's daily activities and are not especially interested in taking part in children's interests. Rather, they let children play on their own. Children end up spending a lot of unstructured time with peers and extended family members. This grants children an autonomous world in which they are free to explore their own social worlds where they work out their problems on their own or with peers. Parents communicate with children by issuing directives rather than engaging in negotiations, and they encourage children to trust and obey people in authority positions. In contrast to privileged children who see interactions with teachers as opportunities for reward, less privileged children tend to see interactions with teachers as opportunities for reprimand. When it comes to interacting with teachers, they feel deferential and seek out support patiently and politely.[22]

While John's socioeconomic background means that his parents don't subscribe to the concerted cultivation approach, a closer look at his upbringing reveals that it didn't fit neatly into Lareau's model of the natural growth approach either. Attempts to align John's upbringing within her framework for children of his socioeconomic class leaves out a critical part of his experience and arguably the most important part of his narrative about how he wound up attending college. What's missing from the story is God.

Absent from most socioeconomic analyses of America is the fact that it is a very religious country—the most devout country among rich Western democracies.[23] And typically left out of the class-based story about adolescents is the astonishing fact that about one in four teenagers has a deep relationship with God. Their relationship with God is reinforced over and over again because they are socially embedded in church communities during some of the most important years of child development. Yet the current narratives that we have about American adolescents raised by their parents and sitting in our schools do not reflect their religious upbringing.

While the separation of church and state means that religion and education are technically separate domains, could it be that teenagers' relationship with God still seeps through the schoolhouse doors? *God, Grades, and Graduation* is an argument that this is exactly what happens—in surprising and unexpected ways.

John was raised by Protestant parents who attended their local Church of Christ, which is generally considered an Evangelical church. A hallmark of these types of churches is that they affirm the orthodox teaching of the person of Christ as the sole rule of faith. The idea that Christ is a person is not just a rhetorical move by these churches—it infuses every element of their work. John attends his church every week and oftentimes twice. He is also active in his church youth group, which he says he "gets a lot out of." All of this involvement has reinforced the church's teachings, leading John to come to think of Christ as someone he strives to emulate. When asked about people they admire or want to be like, most teenagers answer by referring to somebody famous like an actor, musician, or athlete, or they reference a family member. But John and teenagers like him consistently point to Jesus: "I want to be more like Christ and try to live a full, faithful life," he said when interviewed. How did John come to believe that who he most wanted to "be like" was Jesus Christ?

By observing how his parents and others in his religious community behaved, John learned to see and hear God for himself. He sees God as "the master" and someone he "can talk to and tell personal things." It's not just that John admired God—he orientates his entire life around God. His purpose in life is "to be as righteous as God and to act in a way that's pleasing to him." As a 16-year-old, making God happy is what he most wants to accomplish.

John's attitude about God is not surprising given the social world he is growing up in. Part of belonging to a social world means behaving and thinking like the people who inhabit that world. In John's world, God is in the air. People center their life around God, and belonging means following suit. Sociologists like Pierre Bourdieu describe how children are so profoundly shaped by their social and cultural surroundings that they come to embody them to the point where it is even evident in their posture. John's posture reflected the religious sensibilities he had developed as a result of his upbringing in much the same way that children develop sensibilities that reflect their social class position. He looks to religion as an instruction manual for life: "I think it's [religion] a good thing 'cause it teaches you how to live your life better ... it helps you in your troubled ways."

~

Brittany was another student I encountered who on closer investigation did not neatly fit into Lareau's framework of social class and childrearing. Outwardly Brittany seemed like just the sort of teen who was the product of the childrearing logic of concerted cultivation. She was a 16-year-old girl living in Washington State raised by professional-class parents. Her father had a bachelor's degree and worked as a certified public accountant while her mother was an elementary school teacher with some graduate-level course-work. Together her parents earned about $95,000 in 2003, making them a typical professional-class family. Brittany was also an excellent student, doing even better than her peers from similar class backgrounds. She earned straight As, and during her sophomore year she was elected to the class cab-inet and was inducted into the school's honors society. She shared at the time that it is "very" important to do well in school, and she was confident in her ability to do so: "I always want to do well and I know that I always will do well ... I've had a 4.0 since seventh grade and I care about keeping it." In her senior year she took challenging classes like AP Biology and later scored a 4 on the exam. Outside of class she wrote for her school's literary magazine. In short, by all indications Brittany seems poised not just to go to college but to attend a selective one.

But a close look reveals that Brittany differs from her professional-class peers because she isn't fixated on going to a selective college at all. As Brittany explains, where she went to college didn't matter to her: "I didn't have a dream school. I really didn't care that much." In her senior year she only applies to one school—a moderately selective regional college a short hour away. Given Brittany's academic track record in high school, she could have aimed for a more selective college. Compared to her professional-class peers, she had performed better in high school but made a less ambitious decision about higher education. As scholars would say, she "undermatched" by attending a less selective college than she could have gotten into. Undermatching tends to happen to less affluent students, but Brittany is squarely in the professional class. Yet her actions run counter to what we would expect of someone raised under the logic of concerted cultivation. Why did she not consider more se-lective colleges?

Because her life purpose had nothing to do with going to a selective college or having a professional career. Instead, Brittany's goals in life are centered around God and being altruistic:

[My purpose is] to serve God and try to show Him to other people. And also just to love people. Because the people are all that are left when everyone else is gone, their immortal soul . . . I think that I'm here to take care of people in some way . . . I think that I could help anyone—just to make people smile, to make their lives a little bit easier. And I think I'm going to be a teacher, something like that, but it doesn't really matter.

Brittany saw religion at the core of who she is: "It's not like I think it through, and go, religion. It's part of my basic personality at this point." For Brittany, feeling close to God meant "living the way that He would want me to." The beliefs that Brittany holds about herself, which sociologists and psychologists refer to as her self-concept, are driven by her conviction that she is living her life for God. Such a self-concept fundamentally alters how she behaves, and in particular the kind of aspirations she held for herself as an adolescent. As she remarked, "I can't really believe in God and His truths without having that affect how I act and how I live."

To some readers, Brittany's fervent embrace of religion might sound hyperbolic, designed to impress those listening to her. But this does not appear to be the case, because Brittany readily admitted to some struggles. Like typical teenagers, Brittany acknowledged that it was hard to wake up in the morning to attend church. But she was grateful that her parents forced her to go because the messages she heard in church helped "build her faith" and "confirm what I believe." Brittany also admitted that reading the Bible is challenging at times, but she still found it valuable: "God speaks through the Bible, so when you pray and you ask for answers, sometimes it's in the text." Brittany's self-concept was so deeply interwoven with her religious outlook that she even chose to attend a different church than her parents because she felt like it was a better fit with her beliefs.

John and Brittany's religious fervor is not an anomaly. Their descriptions may sound foreign to some readers who either are not religious themselves or do not have deeply religious friends, and the notion that kids today are intensely religious is perhaps hard to jibe with the largely secular nature of mainstream adolescent culture. But in fact, religion is alive and well in the United States.

America's New Religion

What do I mean by religion in the twenty-first century? Understanding being religious today requires distinguishing between religious *traditions* and religious *intensity*. An individual's religious tradition refers to which of the huge number of religious faiths they belong to, including the various denominations and other subgroupings within those faiths. To borrow Robert Putnam and David Campbell's analogy, religious tradition is the "flavor" of one's religion. My work centers on the broad flavor of Christianity because it is the most prevalent religion in America,[24] with 65% of Americans identifying as Christians, including Evangelical Protestants, Mainline Protestants, Black Protestants, Catholics, and members of the Church of Jesus Christ of Latter-day Saints.[25] But my focus in this book is on religious intensity rather than a particular denomination within the broader tradition of Christianity.

I am especially curious about Christians who are deeply religious—who display high degrees of "religiosity" as measured by how they say they behave and what they say they believe. I foreground the role of religious intensity because this is where the most profound polarization exists in the current American landscape. As Robert Putnam and David Campbell describe in their landmark study of religion, *American Grace*, the flavor of religion used to matter much more than intensity. In the decades following World War II, religious tensions were primarily between religious traditions, especially between Catholics and Protestants. At that time, millions of Americans who were not deeply religious still flocked to religious institutions on Sunday mornings based on their denominational affiliation. But the American religious landscape has changed dramatically.[26] We live in a time when religious intensity matters more than religious flavor—a time when an Evangelical may find more in common with an Ultra-Orthodox Jew and a conservative Catholic than with a Mainline Protestant.

Religious intensity could mean a lot of different things, so in 2018 Pew decided to investigate this issue more deeply. They found that about 3 in 10 Americans (28%) have an active and reciprocal relationship with God in which they talk to God and God talks back. And about the same percentage of people (27%) think that God determines what happens to them "all the time." These individuals typically emphasize the role of faith in their daily lives, feel close to God, attend religious services at least weekly, pray by themselves on a regular basis, and look to God and scripture for guidance. This degree of religious intensity cuts across the classic distinctions of religious traditions: about 50% of these religiously intense teens identify as Conservative Protestants, 15% are Black Protestants, 12% are Mainline Protestants, 14% are Catholics, and 6% belong to the Church of Jesus Christ of Latter-day Saints.[27]

Some readers of this book probably cannot think of many (if any) people who are intensely religious, and perhaps they see America as on an inevitable march toward secularism. And it is true that studies consistently show that the share of Americans who identify with Christianity is declining while the share of Americans who say they have no religion (including self-described atheists, agnostics, and those who religiously identify as "nothing in particular") is growing. The percentage of Americans who say they believe in God with absolute certainty has also decreased in recent years, from 71% in 2007 to 63% in 2014.[28]

But it turns out that people who believe that religion is on its way out in America tell us more about them than about religion, revealing that they are "strangers in their own land."[29] About 75% of the residents of southeastern states like Arkansas, Louisiana, and South Carolina are deeply religious.[30] In midwestern states like Wyoming, Nebraska, and Indiana and mid-Atlantic states like Virginia, about 55% of the population are deeply religious. In Western states that are often thought of as more secular like California, Oregon, and Washington, about 45% of residents are still deeply religious. Even in the least religious states like Massachusetts, Vermont, and Maine, about one in three adults is deeply religious.

Although average rates of religiosity in America are declining and people are increasingly identifying as religiously unaffiliated,[31] the percentage of Americans who are deeply religious has not budged.[32] In 2017, sociologists Landon Schnabel and Sean Bock examined religious change between 1989 and 2016 using data from the General Social Survey across three groups: the most intensely religious, the least religious, and those in between. They found intense religiosity has remained largely unchanged from the 1970s to the present. In their words, "rather than religion fading into irrelevance as the secularization thesis would suggest, intense religion—strong affiliation, very frequent practice, literalism, and evangelicalism—is persistent and, in fact, only moderate religion is on the decline in the United States." In other words, there still is a sizable part of the population that is deeply religious. What's changed are the religious sentiments of those postwar Americans who were not deeply religious to begin with but still flocked to religious institutions on Sunday mornings.

The reality is that America is a country where approximately 6 in 10 adults report praying at least daily. A country where 3 in 10 adults think the Bible is the literal word of God.[33] And a country where Americans fill the pews of megachurches every Sunday.[34] And for these Americans their religious beliefs and behaviors are not relegated solely to their private lives. It affects how they vote, where they choose to live, which causes they donate their money to, and even who their friends are.[35]

Of course, adults are not the only ones who are highly religious—their children are religious, too. As sociologist Christian Smith shows in his book on religious parenting, religious views are passed down intergenerationally, and almost all religious children are raised by parents who are themselves religious.[36] That doesn't mean that all children who were raised religious choose to stay religious as they grow up, but it's rare to find a child who came to be religious without following the example of their parents. Having grown up in religious families, John and Brittany are just two of the millions of American teenagers who orientate their life around their faith. About one-quarter of adolescents in America fit this description in 2003, the period around which most of my data come. Schnabel and Bock show that things have not changed for adults since that time, but have they changed for teenagers?

In the spring of 2019, the Pew Research Center surveyed a nationally representative set of 1,811 teens and parents (one parent and one teen from each household).[37] Teens in the study were between 13 and 17, the same age as the teens I studied in this book. Pew didn't ask nearly as many questions to gauge teens' religious commitments as the sources I use, but they did collect data on the four most common and traditional indicators of religiosity: the self-assessed importance of religion in one's life, religious attendance, prayer, and belief in God. Although the questions were not phrased identically as the survey instruments used in this book, they still give an approximate sense of where teens fall in terms of their religious practices and beliefs.

These statistics suggest that the proportion of teenagers with intense religious commitments has not decreased as dramatically as people might imagine, given the constant headlines about religious decline—in fact, religious intensity in adolescents may not have decreased at all. According to the 2019 Pew data, about one in four teens (24%) said that religion was "very important" to them, 27% said they pray daily, 34% said they attend worship services at least weekly, 40% say they believe in God with absolute certainty, and 33% commonly look to religious leaders or religious teachings for ethical guidance. These rates are not all that different from the data collected 16 years earlier.[38] What we can glean from the Pew data is that there are still about one-quarter of teenagers in the United States right now who are intensely religious and probably grew up with religious parents.

Religious Restraint

John and Brittany don't sound like kids raised in the styles of natural growth or concerted cultivation because it turns out that there aren't only two childrearing logics. Lareau's data didn't suggest the presence of a third logic—how religious beliefs passed down by parents help their children navigate the journey of life. I call this childrearing style "religious restraint," and I find that it exists across all social class groups.[39] Lareau argued that social class matters to children's schooling because parents still influence their children even after they exit their house. She was right—parents still influence children even after they enter school. It just so happens that religion does, too.[40]

What does an upbringing of religious restraint look like? An upbringing of religious restraint is consistently and constantly reinforced through children's social environment, starting with the family environment. Intensely religious parents often follow a regimented approach to raising their children. Their homes are marked by a sense of order. Family time is prioritized: family members eat meals together as much as possible, and harmonious relationships among them are emphasized. And, of course, they share a common commitment to their faith, oftentimes reading scripture and praying together. Kids learn to follow rules, to obey their parents, and to be kind. Importantly, intensely religious parents are not alone in implementing this childrearing strategy of religious restraint. They regularly attend church with their children, where their children socialize with other adults. Adults in religious communities watch over each other's children, reinforcing the values taught at home. Finally, for religious restraint to work, adolescents need to opt in. They need to feel intrinsically motivated to participate—to embrace religion themselves and make it their own in order for it to actually influence their behavior.

As a result of this community endeavor and intrinsic motivation, most children develop intense religious convictions. I refer to adolescents who are intensely religious as "abiders," a term I borrow from Lisa Pearce and

Melinda Denton.[41] These are teens who say they believe *and* belong.[42] Having been socialized into a religious community, abiders learn to orient their entire life around God, see themselves as children of God, and profess a personal relationship with God. These teens espouse conservative Christian commitments, emphasizing the role of faith in their daily lives and their felt closeness to God, and attend religious services and pray on a regular basis. Abiders aspire to help others and raise their own family with the cultural logic of religious restraint. In sum, teens raised with religious restraint live their life to please God, which affects their attitudes and behaviors—both outside of school and while in it.

To understand how an upbringing of religious restraint affects one's education, we need to look at the entirety of the road from secondary school to college. Scholars who have examined the relationship between students' religious backgrounds and their academic outcomes have thus far only looked at either K–12 education or higher education.[43] But these are not isolated systems—students' performance in elementary school paves the way for middle school, which subsequently affects their progression through high school, college, and potentially into graduate school.

When we look at the entirety of the road from secondary school into college, we can decompose teenagers' academic trajectories into "performance effects" and "choice effects." The terminology comes from research about how inequalities in educational opportunity get generated at different transition points along one's educational journey.[44] Performance effects reflect how students perform academically, with grade point average (GPA) being the most common measure of performance. Choice effects reflect the decisions that students make conditioned on their performance.[45] These decisions are most common at educational transition points, such as the transition between grade levels or the transition after high school. Since college is voluntary, students can choose whether to apply to college and which colleges to apply to. It will come as no surprise to hear that a student who has a high GPA in high school has more opportunity with respect to higher education than a student who has a comparatively low GPA.[46]

While the decisions that students make about higher education when faced with an educational transition are shaped by their previous academic performance, the decision is also influenced by other factors because students consider the costs and benefits of the different choices. Depending on how students perform and the choices they make about their education, some students have more opportunities than others.[47] This book tells a story about how religious restraint influences teenagers' academic performance and their educational choices.

~

If religion matters so much to Americans, readers might wonder if the topic of academic trajectories of intensely religious teenagers is one scholars have already examined. The answer is complicated. Religion was once considered a core factor in the socioeconomic stratification process and featured prominently in the writings of early sociologists like Emile Durkheim, Karl Marx, and Max Weber.[48] The specific link between religious upbringing and downstream educational outcomes was first documented by sociologist Gerry Lenski, who initially identified educational gaps between Protestants and Catholics.[49] Lenski's book was published in 1961 at a time when differences between religious traditions profoundly divided Americans.[50] But a decade later, studies began to show that educational gap differences between Protestants and Catholics faded once social origins were taken into account.[51] In other words, Protestants and Catholics achieved different levels of schooling not because of differences in their religious cultures but due to differences in their socioeconomic position. In the 1970s and 1980s, there was waning interest in the topic of religious upbringing and educational attainment, especially as socioeconomic status convergence between Mainline Protestants and Catholics came to dominate the literature.[52] The research also lost momentum as secularization theories—which predicted that religion would lose its authority as societies became modernized—became more prominent.[53] Another contributing factor is the liberal and secular nature of the academy (and especially sociology),[54] which makes scholars reticent to view religion as a serious area of inquiry. All these factors likely combined to create a consensus that religion does not have any explanatory power once social class is accounted for.

The 1990s saw a slight rekindling of interest in religion and education.[55] Two factors contributed to this mild resurgence: the evidence that religion would continue to be an influential institution despite secularization theories and several studies that began to explore whether religious upbringing did indeed predict educational attainment beyond social background factors. After conducting an extensive search, I found that in the 30 years between 1990 and 2019, 42 studies were published about the relationship between religious upbringing and academic outcomes.[56] However, the knowledge about this research is confined to a fairly small group of sociologists and a few economists who study religion, and these studies are published in scholarly journals with a narrow academic readership.

This is not to suggest that interest in educational outcomes has been lacking during these years—quite the contrary. There has been a slew of books and articles (both within academia and in the popular press) about the role of race/ethnicity,[57] social class,[58] and gender[59] in shaping academic outcomes. Nor is it to say there are no books about religion and adolescents— there are several excellent books that have depicted what religion looks like in the lives of teenagers and emerging adults.[60] But most sociologists, education scholars, and the public are unaware of the role religion plays in the economic stratification process, influencing both how many years of education you complete and where you complete that education.[61] But to understand the link between religion and economic stratification, we must first identify how religious upbringing shapes academic trajectories and educational choices.

Many books have been written about the role of social class and academic success, and there is no doubt that social class plays a central role in shaping young people's academic performance and their educational choices. But as sociologist Melissa Wilde has argued, religion does not operate on its own—it is intertwined with social structures like social class.[62] To understand why one's religious background and their educational pathways are related, we need to consider how religion is part of the social reproduction process.[63] Following this approach, I illustrate how religious restraint creates differences for teenagers who grow up in different social class groups as well as within the *same* social class group. This helps illuminate the unique effects of religious restraint.

My central argument is that an upbringing of religious restraint affects the quantity and quality of education. Nonaffluent teens who are intensely religious complete more years of education than nonaffluent teenagers who are less religious. Affluent teenagers who are intensely religious complete *similar years* of education as less religious affluent teenagers, but those who are intensely religious attend *less selective* colleges. Put simply, an intensely religious upbringing helps kids complete more years of schooling, but often at lower quality institutions. This is the paradox of religious restraint.

Why does religious restraint affect the quantity and quality of education differently based on social class group? The answer lies in how religious restraint routes kids on the road to college. Recall that college is a steep and bumpy climb for nonaffluent kids because they lack the social and financial resources. Here is where an intensely religious upbringing becomes valuable: it offers resources to nonaffluent kids that their more affluent peers already get from their neighborhoods, parents, and social networks. Nonaffluent abiders get these forms of social capital from an intensely religious upbringing. In other words, religious restraint compensates for a lack of class-based social capital and boosts the academic performance of nonaffluent kids enough that the road to college becomes flatter and smoother.

For affluent kids, the road to college is already smooth, so religious restraint doesn't make it much smoother. They tend to get good grades and therefore have a greater range of choices when it comes to college destinations. And yet they end up at unexpected destinations. Here is where an intensely religious upbringing also impacts their academic trajectory: religious restraint recalibrates their academic ambitions after graduation, causing them to rarely consider attending selective colleges despite their excellent academic performance in high school.

A God-Centered Existence

John was one of several working-class kids who benefited from religious restraint. Living for God helped John stay on the narrow path to academic success.[64] It's as if God had erected guardrails that kept John from getting off the ramp too early in his high school career. Despite saying that peer pressure was the greatest stress problem facing teenagers, he stayed disciplined enough to avoid falling into a pattern of drug and alcohol abuse that proves to be so damaging to academic success. When he is unsure of how to handle a particular situation, he looks to his minister and scripture for answers: "the church really helps me decide what's right and wrong . . . it helps me to [pause] to see this situation that's in the Bible . . . and it kind of helps me to decide how I'm gonna act." For example, according to John, "going out drinking and getting drunk" is wrong, whereas "something right to do is like always be a helping hand to some folks." John suspects that if he weren't part of his weekly church youth group, he would be "doing a lot of things wrong." What is it that he does with his youth group? Some of the time he is participating in social activities like rafting. But much of his youth group functions like a support group. John and his peers gather weekly at the minister's house to do devotionals and discuss things going on in their lives—especially things at school and any troubles they are experiencing. His religious life both at home and at the church gives him a purpose and helps him overcome teenage angst: "[it] helps me in my problems or when I'm down, they help me see my way through that." Without having participated in the group John believes he "wouldn't be the person I am now."

Religious restraint also shaped John's behavior in school. As he worked to please God and do "the right thing," John acted in a way that was both conscientious and cooperative—dispositions that are highly rewarded in school and that are associated with academic achievement. Being conscientious and cooperative may not make you an A+ student, but it could nudge an almost failing student into becoming a middling student. In John's case, religious restraint set him on the path toward college and a successful career.

But religious restraint operated quite differently for Brittany and her professional-class peers. Part of what helps Brittany be a good student is that she is excellent at following the rules, which she attributes to religious teachings like the Ten Commandments. Both Brittany and her parents describe her as having a good temper and not being rebellious—watching R-rated movies like *Blood Bath 2000* with her friends is as far as she goes in terms of bending the rules. Instead, Brittany strives to act in ways that are pleasing to God, which means that she avoids doing things that might hurt other people. She specifically points to her faith to explain her actions: "[Religion] influences the way I treat people—it gives me criteria to look at things through. It colors my worldview." When it comes to interacting with peers and teachers, she tries to be accommodating and respectful. "I don't cause trouble and I'm a good student, so they're willing to help me when I need help . . . there's kind of a mutually friendly relationship [between teachers and myself]." In fact, she sees school as having a negative effect on her faith because it's where she encounters peers who behave differently and are more rebellious than she is. Observing these peers makes her question and sometimes second-guess her own religious commitments:

> School is the main place where you meet opposing values, even if someone isn't saying, "Oh, you can't do that." You get all the options and you see people who are living completely oppositely from you and [they] seem to be okay. That kind of toys around with how I feel about it [religion] . . . it's never audible pressure, but there is a [feeling] that, you know, they look okay and they've been partying since Friday night.

But Brittany remains steadfast in her religious commitments. She follows the rules, maintains self-discipline, respects authority, and is kind to others. Her conscientious and cooperative behavior goes a long way in helping her get good grades.

Yet Brittany was one of several professional-class kids whose religious restraint improved her academic performance yet constrained her educational choices. Brittany's self-concept—which I describe as being God-centered—influences her life purpose, including her educational and career aspirations. As Brittany explains, "[Religion] is important because it gives people a purpose and it gives them hope and it gives them something larger than themselves to belong to." We would expect that Brittany, a well-resourced girl with straight As and multiple AP classes under her belt, would want to attend a selective college. But this is not the case. Despite having a lot of academic potential and the social and cultural capital to make it in college, her aspirations—shaped by religious restraint—were instead tied to serving God.

~

In writing *Home Advantage*, Lareau argued for scholars to pay more attention to the role of social class by examining the linkages between homes and schools. When she considered the interinstitutional linkages between families and schools, she saw that children raised with a strategy of concerted cultivation developed an academic advantage. She succeeded in making her case, and the terms "concerted cultivation" and "the accomplishment of natural growth" are now a regular part of sociologists' vocabulary. I am similarly urging scholars to pay more attention to the interaction of religion and class, and how this interaction seeps into the educational domain. This book reveals that an upbringing of religious restraint improves academic performance yet in some cases limits educational choices.

When it comes to performance, religiously restrained students who live their life for God fare better because they are conscientious and cooperative. This is the case regardless of students' social class upbringing. Working-class abiders have better grades than working-class nonabiders, middle-class abiders have better grades than middle-class nonabiders, and so on. But this story changes when we look at the next stage involving educational choices.

Since religiously restrained students have better academic performance in high school, we would expect them to make more ambitious choices about higher education. This is generally the case, except in one social class group: adolescents from the professional class. When it comes to the transition to college, students from the professional class who live their life for God make less ambitious choices about where to attend college than we would expect given their stellar report cards. God-centered students undermatch in the college selection process because educational decisions are social decisions that highlight the effect of the home environment on norms and values surrounding education. God-centered students make choices that reflect their familial and social ties, rather than making a choice to optimize their social class standing. There are millions of young men and women who do not live to impress college admissions counselors. For them, it is God who matters.

Methods

My data in this book primarily come from survey and interview data from the National Study of Youth and Religion (NSYR). In 2002–2003, the NSYR surveyed 3,290 adolescents between the ages of 13 and 17 and one of their parents. They collected four waves of data and completed the study in 2012–2013. I merged the NSYR with the National Student Clearinghouse (NSC) so that I could track any colleges or universities that NSYR respondents attended and whether they received any type of degree. I supplemented my analyses of the NSYR with data from the National Longitudinal Study of Adolescent to Adult Health (Add Health). In 1994–1995, Add Health surveyed approximately 20,000 students in grades 7–12 and one of their parents and has continued to follow these respondents over the past 25 years.

The NSYR and Add Health each have advantages and disadvantages to studying the role of religion in academic outcomes, and I leverage unique features of each data set. For example, NSYR has extensive data on adolescents' religious commitments but only self-reported data about their grades. In contrast, Add Health has reliable GPA data based on official school records but limited measures of religion. By using different features in each data set, I was able to investigate the relationship between religion and academic outcomes in multiple ways and ensure the validity of my claims. The Add Health data also have a unique sibling component, which allowed me to conduct more rigorous statistical analyses of the relationship between religiosity and academic outcomes than had ever been done before.

Throughout this book, I often describe the relationship between religious upbringing and academic outcomes. Although I do not specify this every time in the text, readers should know that I am holding constant several other factors. In my quantitative models, I control for teens' self-identified race and ethnicity, gender, their religious tradition, the geographic region where they live, whether they attended a public or private school, and their family structure. These controls help me tease out the role of religious upbringing from the various other factors that are associated with academic outcomes.

It's also important for readers to understand how I account for the role of social class. Using the NSYR parental data, I created a composite socioeconomic status (SES) score based on combined parental income, each parent's education level, and the prestige score of each parent's occupation.[65] I then disaggregated the teenagers into quartiles based on their SES score: poor, working class, middle class, and professional class. For example, teens who fall into the bottom 25% of the socioeconomic distribution based on their parents' income, education, and occupation are classified as poor, while teens who fall into the top 25% of the distribution are classified as professional class. In some of my quantitative models, I hold SES constant to avoid conflating the role of social class from the role of religious upbringing. In other models, I conduct subgroup analyses where I compare abiders to nonabiders from the same social class group.

To illuminate the patterns in the survey data, I turned to longitudinal interviews with 216 racially, socioeconomically, and religiously diverse adolescents who were queried repeatedly over a 10-year period beginning in 2002. The bulk of this book features case studies from this set of 216 interviews (details about these teenagers are provided in the Appendix). Some of the details I provide about the teenagers (such as information about their close friends) come from their surveys, whereas most of the information I provide about their parents comes from the parent survey.

More details about my methodological considerations can be found in the Appendix.

Book Overview

The book proceeds as follows. In Chapter 1, I introduce readers to religiously restrained teenagers from different genders, social class backgrounds, racial backgrounds, and religious traditions. These abiders seek to please God, which affects how they perceive themselves, how they carry themselves, and how they imagine their future. In Chapter 2, I argue that schools and churches promote similar ideals—both institutions value kids who abide by the rules and respect authority figures. Abiders are precisely these types of kids—they are deeply conscientious and cooperative. As it turns out, the very dispositions that are meant to please God are also the dispositions that help kids earn good grades—a phenomenon I call the "abider advantage."

In Chapter 3, I explain why academic performance in high school matters for long-term educational attainment. High school GPA is among the strongest predictors of academic success in college, but the extent to which the abider advantage translates into additional years of college varies by social class. Kids from the professional class already have good grades, so the additional abider advantage doesn't translate to more years of education. Poor abiders also don't see much benefit. Despite earning better grades in high school than nonabiders, the economic precariousness saddling poor kids makes the road to college too steep. For whom does the abider advantage matter the most? Working-class and middle-class kids. Earning better grades in high school gives working-class and middle-class abiders a significant educational attainment bump.

In Chapter 4, I dive more deeply into why abiders from working-class and middle-class families go on to complete more years of education than nonabiders. I show that an upbringing of religious restraint gives kids of modest means access to social capital, which helps them stay on the path to college. In Chapter 5, I turn to abiders from the professional class, who do not see an educational attainment bump. Not only do they not benefit from their early abider advantage, but they also "undermatch" by attending less selective colleges than they could probably get into based on their great grades. They see college as important, but don't care about which college they attend because they are not focused on lucrative careers and prefer to stay close to home.

In Chapter 6, I offer an alternative account of how kids come to be academically successful by introducing readers to atheist teenagers who say they don't believe in God and bring home report cards that look just as good as teens who center their entire life around God. Rather than being God-centered, conscientious, and cooperative, these atheist adolescents are autonomously motivated individuals who think critically, are motivated by their own curiosity, and who are open to new experiences—traits that are also highly valued in academic contexts.

In the Conclusion, I examine how religiously restrained kids fare in the long term in terms of their earnings, health, happiness, and attitudes about gender equality. I also consider what the trends among religious Americans' educational outcomes might suggest when it comes to the state of inequality and progress in our country.

1

Living for God

Andrew is a 16-year-old African American teenage boy who lives in a house just off the highway, which his mother and stepfather have owned for the past 5 years. Andrew's biological parents got divorced when he was 9 years old, and his mother remarried 2 years later. It is a difficult time for Andrew's family. His stepfather—to whom Andrew is close—has cancer and in the past month has become so ill that he hasn't been able to work. They have been having a lot of visitors because it's not clear how much time his father has left. On the weekends, his 18-year-old sister comes home; she is a freshman at a public historically Black college about 3 hours away.

Andrew's home is in a tiny town of about 930 residents in North Carolina, just a few miles south of the Virginia border. Walking down the main street to his house, you'd pass only a small hardware store, pharmacy, auto parts store, gas station, and two restaurants—pizza and Chinese food. Andrew describes the area as remote, with the closest McDonald's 30 minutes away, and as not having "a lot of good opportunities." Nonetheless, Andrew's mother feels very safe where they live. She identifies as very conservative politically and is involved in the political and social life of their small town. About 56% of the town is African American, and the remaining 44% are almost all White. The median income for a family living in this town is about $30,000 in 2003, and about one in five residents is living in poverty.

Compared to others in their town, Andrew's family is faring well economically. Andrew's mother has a bachelor's degree from the same college her daughter is attending and works about 30 hours a week as a sixth-grade teacher. His stepdad has a high school diploma and owns a truck company, where he worked for about 60 hours a week until a month ago. Together, his parents earned about $55,000 in 2003, and they report having a lot of savings and assets. Given his parents' income, employment, and the fact that one of them has a college degree, Andrew's family falls squarely into America's middle class.[1]

The Logics of Childrearing

In her seminal book, *Unequal Childhoods: Class, Race, and Family Life*, Annette Lareau argues that families with a similar social position as Andrew's family use a childrearing strategy she calls "natural growth."[2] Although parents make sure to supervise their children so that they stay safe, they are generally uninvolved in their children's activities such that their kids have a lot of free time and can choose what to do. Many children play with friends and with extended kin, and grandparents are quite involved in the childrearing. There are also clear boundaries for behavior, and children do not negotiate these rules.

In some ways, Andrew resembles Lareau's description of Tyrec, one of the Black working-class boys she featured in her book. He also does not have many structured activities, and his weekends are generally spent visiting family. He has several extended family members he is close with, including his grandmother and all of her sisters. His mom also imposes several rules to safeguard his behavior. She monitors his activities very carefully, including what he watches on TV and what he does on the Internet. It is very important for her to know where he is and who he is with at all times and to have a say in who his friends are.

But there are also some key differences between Andrew and Tyrec that suggest Andrew is not being raised in a style of natural growth—differences that emerge when you look at the sources of parental involvement. Andrew describes his parents as being less worldly than some of his friends' parents, born out by their insistence that Andrew not swear. Maybe more telling is the fact that Andrew embraces, instead of accedes to, their conservative outlook. Indeed, Andrew doesn't so much follow their rules as embody them. Unlike many of the rules in natural growth systems, the rules are not designed to enforce respect for Andrew's parents. Their involvement in his life therefore does not resemble surveillance so much as teamwork toward a commonly shared end. How else then to explain his mother's remarkably laissez-faire attitude to Andrew driving to the store, even though he's not old enough to have a license yet. Instead of respect being the guiding value, it seems trust is the ground for Andrew's family.

In contrast with the parenting in working-class and poor families, the middle-class homes Lareau studied appeared faster paced and more structured, with the children feeling more pressure. A key feature of her middle-class homes was that parents organized their lives around the kids' activity calendar. She used the term "concerted cultivation" to describe how these parents attempted to foster the talents of their children by incorporating organized activities into their lives. For example, in one such family she looked at, the parents were constantly shuttling their three boys between soccer and baseball practice. A characteristic of this approach was the role parents played as passive onlookers, resulting in moments like when the father went to get a cup of coffee in the middle of one soccer practice because he was bored and needed a change of scenery. In the family that Lareau described, the constant focus on the kids' activities also meant that they were rarely all together during the week during mealtimes. Those practices stood in stark contrast with the natural growth approach of working-class and poor parents.

But just as Andrew's family didn't exactly fit the pattern of natural growth, it didn't fit Lareau's portrayal of concerted cultivation either. While parents who employ a strategy of concerted cultivation observe their children in structured activities, Andrew describes doing a lot of activities together with his family. They would usually spend their weekends visiting family living in the area or going to the state fair or the beach. They have cookouts and play a lot of card games at their dining room table. Andrew's mother likewise thinks it's very important to spend time doing activities *with* him—she is less interested in spending time watching him doing his own activities. Over the past 6 months, she reports they have gone to a museum or historical site together, gone to a play or concert, visited the library, built or fixed something, and exercised together. Unlike a typical middle-class parent, she doesn't care too much if Andrew plays sports, although she does want him to be involved in extracurricular activities. And Andrew's family usually eats dinner together seven times a week.

In short, Andrew's experience neither fits Lareau's portrayal of natural growth nor concerted cultivation. It turns out that there's a reason why Andrew and his family don't comfortably fit either of Lareau's categories, because it just so happens there is one aspect of their lives that is missing in the description given here—and it turns out to be *the* crucial factor in understanding adolescents like Andrew: They are religious. Deeply religious.

~

While Andrew's upbringing doesn't fit either of Lareau's models, it is quite typical of a third parenting logic—what I call "religious restraint." Andrew's mother says her religious faith is extremely important in providing guidance for her day-to-day living and how she raises her children. Andrew's parents are of the same faith, and they attend the African Methodist Episcopal church in town at the same frequency. Along with about 70 other members of the church, they attend religious services at least once a week, and usually more often. In addition to joining worship services, each week Andrew's mother can be found at her church at a Bible study or a potluck. She has been attending the same church for 5 years and feels that her church has been very supportive and helpful to her in raising Andrew.

Her faith has taken root in Andrew as well because in his words he was "raised in the church." What that means to him is something far more profound than simply going to church on Sundays: "I was raised to be a pretty good person. I was raised on the Bible." Andrew gives a lot of credit to how he turned out to his parents, and he contrasts them with those of some of his friends who are a little more "worldly" and who "go to clubs" and drink and smoke. Andrew's parents do not do any of these things, and they are raising Andrew to act the same way.[3]

But it's not just Andrew and his family who are intensely religious and act accordingly. All five of his closest friends share his religious beliefs and are members of the same church. He and his friends are also sincerely devout in their beliefs—the kind of kids who organize contests to see who knows the most Bible verses. As Andrew explains, "Like I'll say a Bible verse and my friends will be like 'Man, that ain't right,' . . . And then we'll try to get a little contest to see who knows the most." Like Andrew, two of his five closest friends are involved in a religious youth group, and Andrew feels comfortable talking about religious matters with all five of them. None of Andrew's closest friends drink alcohol or do drugs, and none of them have gotten in trouble for cheating, fighting, or skipping school. Andrew is also part of a social network with closure, where the children and adults all know each other. Three of his friends' parents know Andrew's parents, and only one of his friend's parents doesn't know Andrew by name.

The Ties That Bind

Teasing apart the elements of religious restraint is important for understanding its different dimensions, and nowhere is religious restraint more evident than in the connection between parents and children. An upbringing of religious restraint is consistently and constantly reinforced through children's social environment, starting with the family environment. The religious fervor of religiously restrained kids reflects those of their parents, who have the strongest amount of influence on their children's religious lives. Several studies consistently find that families and faith are deeply entwined. In the largest-ever study of religion and family across generations, sociologist Vern Bengston[4] and his colleagues followed more than 350 families composed of more than 3,500 individuals whose lives span more than a century—the oldest was born in 1881, the youngest in 1988. Bengston and his colleagues found that despite enormous changes in American society, a child born into a religious family is more likely to remain within the fold than leave it. As sociologist Christian Smith and his coauthors[5] described in their 2019 book about how American parents pass their religion on to their children, parents view it as their job to ground their children in religious values that provide resilience, morality, and a sense of purpose. And parents are remarkably effective at transmitting their religious beliefs. According to my analyses of both the survey and interview data, abiders almost always share their parents' religious views. For example, 93% of abiders in the first wave of the National Study of Youth and Religion (NSYR) had parents who said religion was "extremely" important to them, suggesting that children who see religion as central were raised by parents who also saw it as central. The interviews show a similar pattern: abiders almost always find religion to be a source of connection with their parents rather than a source of conflict. Andrew is no exception, describing that he and his parents share the same religious views.

But how does this intergenerational transmission of religious belief and behavior happen? On the surface, we can see that Andrew and his parents share religious views, but what does it look like for children to adopt their parents' religious faith? Do Andrew's parents teach him how to be religious? Or does he learn by watching them? Educational theorist and cultural psychologist Barbara Rogoff suggests it's the latter.[6] Being religious is something children learn by observing and pitching in, not by explicit instruction. It turns out that attitudes are not something that can be actively taught but are instead something intentionally but passively shared by example. Rogoff made this observation after studying indigenous heritage communities in Guatemala and Mexico. She noticed that weaving was one of the central activities of the community. What struck Rogoff was that young girls were already well-versed in how to create complicated patterns. When Rogoff asked the older women who taught the little girls to weave, they said, "We don't teach them—they learn."

From this insight, Rogoff developed a theory that is fairly intuitive yet not widely accepted in Western society: children learn best by observing adults around them and then imitating them. When adults want to transmit beliefs or skills to their children, the best way is to incorporate them into a range of ongoing endeavors within their families and communities. Treating children as regular participants in the community means that there is a community-wide expectation that everyone contributes and providing them just like everyone else with several opportunities to join in according to their interests and skills. In turn, children become eager to contribute because that is how they can belong. Other people who are present, such as grandparents or other community members, may guide or support the children's contributions. The goal of learning is to help the child—or any learner for that matter—shift away from being a passive participant to being an active contributor to the community. But instead of trying to acquire skills and knowledge just for the sake of it (or just to please the parents), the child is trying to acquire skills and knowledge so they can be an active and valued member of the community.

Now recall Andrew's family and how the church is an integral part of his family's life. Not only does his mother attend services, but she also participates in the social life of the community. Andrew has ample opportunity to observe not only how his parents but all the adults in the church behave—how they greet and treat each other, reference scripture in their speech, and give God credit for things going well in their life. Wanting to belong to the community, he starts to internalize their speech patterns and modes of behavior. He sees older people acting godly and follows their lead. At home, he takes initiative to say grace at the dinner table, and he even takes on roles at his church such as singing in the choir. Because of the nature of Andrew's environment, Andrew inevitably learns religious restraint.

~

But religious restraint in families is not merely for the middle class nor is it just evident among boys. Take, for example, 17-year-old Gina. She is the youngest of three girls, each born 2 years apart to a politically prominent family. Her mother is a superintendent and the former chairman of the school board, while her father is a member of the state house of delegates. Both parents have college degrees, and they are solidly in the professional class.

They are also very religious. Religion and talk of God permeate Gina's life in a way we might not expect if we only considered her family's professional status. Gina's mother identifies as an Evangelical Christian and says religion is extremely important to her. Religious activities are central to the entire family, and Gina thinks being Christian creates harmony at home. When asked to describe the atmosphere in her household, Gina says, "It's great compared to other people, you know. My family, we've never hit each other or anything. Other people are like 'Our family will yell at each other.' Well, we don't do any of that. We're such a Christian-based family, so it makes it a lot more livable and we're happy." Because of her parents' careers, they travel a lot, but they pray together before and during their trips. Gina says this makes them feel closer. Gina is also very close with her grandmother, who "disciples" her. They talk at least twice a week: "She [my grandmother] says a lot of scripture, and we talk a lot about what's going on in my life. And we pray, and my grandpa, too . . . we usually have like a lot of devotions together, all three of us, and they end up praying over me. We pray for each other. It's just a really fun experience."

Gina's positive relationship with her parents and grandparents is not unique among abiders. The interview and survey data suggest that deeply religious families are closer and more cohesive. This is one by-product of shared faith among family members. Importantly, this works both ways: it's not just that religion keeps families together—it's also that families are more likely to stay religious if the parents stay married because churches are more welcoming to traditional family structures. But regardless of which way the influence flows, it is still the case that parents and children feel closer to each other when they are religious—especially if they are both equally religious.

One way we can observe this cohesiveness is by looking at parents' and children's perceptions about their relationship with one another. In the first wave of the NSYR surveys, parents were asked how close they felt to their child. Among parents of abiders, 60% said they felt "extremely" close to their child, compared with 50% of parents whose children were nonabiders. And parents of abiders don't just feel close to their children; they think it's more important to spend time with them. Among parents of abiders, 51% think it's extremely important to spend time with their teen, compared with just 38% of parents of nonabiders.

Gina's mother feels very close to her and says Gina's dad also feels very close to her, too. The closeness that parents feel is not a figment of their imagination. Abiders also report feeling very close to their parents—much closer than nonabiders feel to their parents. In the first wave of the NSYR surveys, adolescents were asked eight questions about their relationships with their mother and another eight with their father. Compared to their nonreligious peers, abiders feel closer to their parents, get along better with their parents, are more willing to talk to their parents about personal subjects, and have more fun hanging out with their parents. The last point should not be taken lightly, as adolescence is not a time when children generally enjoy spending time with their parents. Gina has a very similar view toward her parents, especially her mother: "It doesn't matter what goes on, I talk to my mom about it." In fact, she says her mother is one of her heroes.

Abiders are also more likely to feel close to their father. This close relationship between children and their fathers is especially important from the perspective of religious transmission. In their study, Bengston and his colleagues found that a crucial factor in whether a child keeps their faith is the presence of a strong fatherly bond. Abiders are also more likely to report that their parents—both their mother and father—hug them, praise and encourage them, and tell their children they love them. It should thus not come as much of a surprise that, compared to their nonreligious peers, abiders are also more likely to feel cared for and accepted, and less likely to feel that life is meaningless. Abiders' strong sense of self-worth and self-esteem is a direct result of their relationship with their parents.

The case of Tyah illustrates what happens when you take away one set of key authority figures out of the equation: the parents. Tyah was a 14-year-old African American girl growing up right outside of Washington, DC. Her father is not around and her mother suffers from a cocaine addiction, which casts a long shadow on Tyah's life. At one point, she and her mom lost their house and Tyah was constantly on the move, shuttling between group homes and family members.

Throughout her adolescence, Tyah maintains a strong belief in God: "I feel like God is everything. God is my every day. He created us. God controls everything, He controls my future, everything. So God just always has to be in there." Tyah finds comfort in God and asks Him regularly to watch over her mother, who is involved in a lot of risky behavior. "If I'm ever feeling scared about my mother, if something's just on my mind, something might happen to her tonight or she could be with this guy in this alley, just anything . . . I ask God to protect her, surround her, be with her at all times . . . That just makes me feel so much better, and able to relax."

But Tyah struggles to abide by religious teachings. For example, she knows she shouldn't lie "because God said so," but she admits that she doesn't "really follow the Bible too much, because I do sin on a daily basis." When she does behave in a way that is inconsistent with religious teachings, she feels like a hypocrite: "A lot of times I would sit in church and I'd be thinking, wow, last night I was just sitting . . . smoking weed, drinking, just sitting around cussing, breaking every rule in the Bible, breaking every rule. And now, the next day, I'm sitting here in church. It was a guilty feeling, so I didn't participate [in the service]." What Tyah is referring to by "breaking every rule" is repeated instances by her of criminal activity and reckless behavior. By age 16, she had robbed a house, gotten pregnant, dropped out of high school (after ninth grade), and was headed to prison.

Abiders do so well in school because they live profoundly structured lives. This structure is put in place by parents and religious institutions, which mutually reinforce each other. Abiders know that not just God but their parents and adults from church are watching them, and they want to please these authority figures. This is especially important for children who live in poor communities that tend to have high rates of substance abuse and crime. This isn't because poor people are naturally more deviant. It's because poverty creates a feeling of despair that reverberates through entire communities. When people live in despair, they turn to substance abuse, which often leads to other nonsocial behavior.

Despite being God-centered, Tyah is conscious of the fact that she completely lacks structure—in fact, she openly yearns for it. In reflecting on her life and all the struggles she has endured, she is quick to observe how easy it was for her to veer off course: "From starting off from when I was little. No stability, no discipline, nobody kept me into one thing. I was able to venture off to wherever I wanted." She has God, but she doesn't have a stable parental figure to reinforce the religious teachings that might keep her on the straight and narrow. In prison, Tyah continues to look to religion for stability. She doesn't "go a day without praying" and reads the Bible regularly, noting how it served as a moral touchstone for her:

> I was stable when I was reading the Bible. It's like I knew exactly right from wrong. Everything was laid out. If somebody came at me with this, I already knew. I'm not doing that, because that's wrong. I'm on this side, trying to do the right thing in my life, not the wrong thing. So everything was just there, reading the Bible. When I'm not reading it, it's like I don't have that reminder always. Sometimes I'll slip up and do what I want to do.

At 18, Tyah has her first child and is adamant about wanting to raise her with religion because she felt she had a "much brighter future" when church was a part of her life. The only thing standing between her and church attendance is a car: "I'm gonna go. Once I get my car, definitely. I'm not missing a Sunday, because my daughter needs to be in a church. I was raised in the church from a young age, and I was much better when I was little. I had a much brighter future. I just want to keep her in the church."

Extended Family

The role of adults in the lives of abiders doesn't end with parents. Consider Alex, a White Baptist who is on the cusp of turning 15 during the spring of his eighth-grade year. He lives in a suburb of about 9,000 people 15 miles away from Greensboro, North Carolina. He and his friends, who live in his neighborhood, like to play sports and video games and listen to music, especially Blink 182, Sum 41, Linkin Park, Queen, and even AC/DC. His mother, who is very organized and cooperative, has a bachelor's degree and works at home typing transcriptions. His dad has an associate degree and works as a property surveyor determining property boundaries and preparing sites for construction. During his summers, Alex accompanies his dad to work and earns $4/hour to hold markers and plot stakes. Their combined income in 2003 is about $55,000. Based on his parents' education levels and income, Alex's family also falls on the middle-class spectrum.

Alex is also an abider. His idea of leading a "good life" is entirely bound up with religion: "serving God, respecting your family and others, trying to bring people to Christianity, and keeping yourself morally straight." He sees religion as central to his life: "Religion: I would say that is the most important thing in life." Because he views religion as so integral, his self-concept is shaped by his yearning to please God. Religion is interwoven into his daily life: "It shapes how I live, it guides me," he explains. In an interview 2 years later when he's 17, Alex reveals that his self-concept continues to be driven by his faith: "[Religion is] part of who I am" and "part of everything I do." What this means is that Alex continually strives to emulate God by behaving well. As Alex says, "God is a role model, what I should be doing in life. . . . You want to do the right thing." He reiterates this by saying that believing in Jesus "means you try to act as much as possible like Him and try to be and believe that He is the ticket to heaven . . . it has everything to do with getting to heaven, and how we live now. He [Jesus] set the overall morals in how someone is supposed to act."

One might wonder if any parent acting alone could inculcate such a mindset in a child, but the strategy of religious restraint doesn't rely solely on the influence of the parents. Indeed, the strategy of religious restraint relies on children living in communities where they see other religious kids and adults. Alex is embedded in a network of other religious peers and adults who role-model fervent faith. For example, Alex says that his good friend, Jack, who lives down the street and goes around "witnessing" (i.e., sharing his faith with other people) inspires him to be more engaged with his church: "I was already serious [about my faith, but after] hanging around [Jack], I wanted to go to church more often." Similarly, Gina's religious beliefs are not just reinforced by interactions with family members but also by her closest friends, most of whom are from her church. For fun, she and her friends do "fasting challenges," where they give up something like TV and devote that time to God by reading the Bible or working by cutting grass, pulling weeds, and dog sitting in their neighborhood to raise money for missionaries and other charities. The survey data confirm that the closest friends of abiders are likely to share their religious beliefs: 58% said that at least four of their five closest friends share their religious beliefs.

When asked if he has any positive or negative relationships with adults other than his parents, Alex mentioned Brian, a church youth leader who he finds more relatable than other adults. Brian is available to both talk about problems but also to have fun and play basketball: "If we're having trouble in school, he'll [Brian] tell you how to handle it, he'll give you good advice if you're having problems." Sociologists refer to Alex's relationship with adults like Brian as evidence of the social and organizational ties that religious institutions facilitate. Through them, abiders like Alex develop relationships with adults that create crucial webs of support.

American religious institutions happen to be one of the few major American social institutions that are not rigidly stratified by age and emphasize personal interactions over time, with most central congregational functions such as worship services and fellowship gatherings mixing participants of all ages. As a result, youth socialize with adults and can develop relationships that cross age boundaries. And those ties generate the potential for relationships with congregants, affording adolescents access to otherwise less available sources of opportunities, resources, and information—creating what sociologists refer to as social capital. The more adult ties youth have in their congregations, the more likely they are through them to land a good summer job, be recommended for acceptance into a competitive program, know someone who can and will help them fix a broken computer or car, and so on.

Alex also benefits from his relationship with Brian because Brian provides additional oversight and influence over Alex beyond his own parents. Sociologists refer to this as network closure.[7] American religious congregations provide relatively dense networks of relational ties within which youth are embedded, involving people who pay attention to the lives of youth, and who can provide oversight of and information about youth to their parents and other people well-positioned to discourage negative and encourage positive life practices. In religious congregations, adolescents can develop relationships with youth ministers, Sunday school teachers, choir directors, rabbis, parents of friends, and other adult acquaintances who can relationally tie back to their parents. These ties can operate as extrafamilial sources reinforcing parental influence and oversight. Because of the social nature of religious congregations, parents can build relationships over time with their children's friends and the parents or kin of their children's friends. Moreover, these relationships are likely to exist among people who share similar cultural moral orders, facilitating higher levels of agreement and cooperation in collective oversight and social control. Thus, network closure creates conditions of increased support for and supervision of youth, encouraging positive and discouraging negative behaviors among youth.

The NSYR wave 1 survey confirmed that abiders have more social capital and network closure. They report knowing many more adults to whom they can turn for help than nonabiders. For example, aside from their parents, there is a 59% probability that abiders have more than four adults in their lives whom they could turn to for support and advice, compared with 41% of nonabiders. This pattern persists even after accounting for adolescents' socioeconomic status, gender, race and ethnicity, geographic region, and age.

Abiders don't just know more adults—they also report being more comfortable talking with adults aside from their parents. Of those interviewed, 61% report being very or fairly comfortable talking with adults, compared with only 49% of nonabiders. While it's true that more privileged children learn to articulate themselves and are comfortable speaking to authority figures,[8] even after controlling for background characteristics, abiders still feel more at ease conversing with adults. It is likely that constant exposure to and interaction with adults in their religious institutions help them overcome feelings of awkwardness that many adolescents experience when talking with adults.

One of the ways we can discern if abiders have closer networks is by looking at whether adolescents' parents know both their friends and their parents. The NSYR survey asked adolescents to name their five closest friends and then asked a series of questions about these five closest friends to reveal the closeness of their social network. Abiders appear to have tighter networks than nonabiders by several measures. More than half of abiders (54%) say that their parents know the parents of at least three of their closest friends, with the rate among nonabiders only 41%. Abiders are also more likely to have friends whose parents know them by name. If Alex's parents are worried about his whereabouts, it is likely that they can call his friends' parents to find out where he is. In other words, it really does take a village to raise an abider.

Look Who's Talking

Of course, religious behavior is not just a matter of saying a prayer—it is a way of life and a way of seeing the world. This is what Andrew means when he says he was "raised in the church." Over time, Andrew has come to feel a sense of belonging in the church. In some ways, church even supersedes school: "I'm so young, I got a lot of other things that I want to do, but that [religion and church] is about the one and only thing that I should be doing other than going to school." In fact, Andrew says that if there was a school party during the time he goes to church, he would prioritize church. It is not that Andrew doesn't care about school—he most certainly does—but academic achievement is not in and of itself the ultimate goal as it is for many middle-class children, and especially upper middle-class children raised by parents under the rubric of concerted cultivation.

If school is not Andrew's primary goal, what is? As he puts it, "The most important thing is you have your faith in God, and you give your heart to Him. And you try to live right, day to day." Andrew organizes his life around God: "God is the only true living God, so if you don't have religion, what do you have?" In fact, he wishes he could be even more involved in his church youth group because "it would be pleasing to God . . . I want something to show him that I trust Him." Unfortunately, Andrew can't be more involved at the moment because he has to help take care of his sick father. But that doesn't stop him from acting in a way that is pleasing to God: "Before we do anything, we should think about what would Jesus do." Andrew doesn't just believe in God—he has an active and reciprocal relationship with Him: "I feel like I can talk to Him, you know whenever I want, I feel close to Him."

Andrew is not alone in feeling like he has a reciprocal relationship with God. When Alex talks with God, God talks back. Alex describes his relationship with God in personal terms: "I pray every night and I feel safe with myself [because] I trust in Him when I'm afraid." When asked for an example, Alex says he is nervous about a potential war with North Korea and has been hearing people (this is in 2003) talk about nuclear weapons. But Alex has a way of dealing with anxiety: "I pray about it and usually I just forget about the fear." Two years later his resolute faith even makes him less anxious about the idea of death, which he sees as a common concern among his friends who are worried about getting drafted (at this point in time, 2,000 service members had died in the Iraq war and the war in Afghanistan is still raging): "If I die, well, [laughs] I'm kinda okay with it . . . because of my religion, [because] I would expect to go to heaven." For adolescents like Alex, religious restraint is a safe haven, not a straitjacket.

As anthropologist Tanya Luhrmann describes in her book *When God Talks Back*,[9] people like Andrew and Alex want to experience God intimately, personally, and interactively. They want to reach out and touch the divine here on earth. For them, God is mighty, but He is also a person among people. Especially in Evangelical and Charismatic churches like Andrew's, pastors encourage their congregants to hang out with God—to go for a walk with God or even share a cup of coffee with him.[10] Religiously restrained adolescents have learned to speak with God and recognize God's voice like they recognize their mother's voice on the phone. As Luhrmann explains, people who yearn to develop a relationship with God come to think of their mind not as a place where they generate their own ideas and thoughts, but rather as a place where they meet God. They come to realize that some of the thoughts they think are their own are actually God's thoughts being given to them. They learn to discern God's voice from their own and use their inner senses to imagine themselves next to God on a picnic bench with His arm around their shoulder. Luhrmann describes this process as developing a "participatory" theory of mind in which those who seek to hear God have to learn to view the "mind–world barrier as porous."[11]

As Luhrmann argues, this cultivation of the inner senses is a skill—hearing God talk back is something people learn to do over time.[12] Belief is not something people have, but rather something people acquire slowly as they begin to pay attention to their world and their mind. And as people practice this skill, their image of God and the sound of God's voice become more vivid. Over time, God becomes more real and talks back. In a society full of religious skeptics, these practices make God more relevant. God shifts from being a 45-minute engagement on Sunday morning to something you are doing throughout the week, making God more alive. Understandably, this type of religious experience resonates at churches where the intensity of one's relationship with God is primary.

~

It is no surprise to discover that adolescents who grow up with nonreligious parents are often not engaged in any religious practices and therefore don't see religion as important in shaping their life. Although they still believe in God, the God they envision is much less personal; God doesn't talk back to them because they're not shown how to talk to God in the first place. As a result, these nonabiders are very unlikely to integrate religion into their life. When faced with difficult decisions about right and wrong, they do not think of what will please God; instead, they try to do what makes them happy.

Take, for example, James, a 16-year-old White male living in Seattle. James's parents divorced when he was in eighth grade and he lives with his mom, who thinks religion is not important. James calls himself a Christian but says he doesn't have any particular religious beliefs: "I believe in God and stuff, but I don't really live my life like that." Instead, James's purpose in life is based on going outside of his comfort zone and seeking personal fulfillment. While James is not ready to reject the idea of religion altogether, it is not the polestar upon which he navigates his life's journey. In fact, he is open to the beliefs of many religions and argues that "there may be truth to all of them." Religion just does not have a foundational role in his own life. He summarizes his religious beliefs by saying, "I believe in God and I believe there are religions, but I just don't choose to go down that path." Without having been raised in a culture of religious restraint, there is not much likelihood that an adolescent like James will choose such a worldview.

But when an adolescent is immersed in such a world, then God suffuses every aspect of their life. Consider what life is like for Gina. She describes God as "a father, a friend, someone who places challenges in your life or helps you get through challenges—always there, something great." God is always talking to her. In her words, "If you know the truth and He [God] is the truth, then I think you're set." For her, God is personal, demanding, loving, caring, and awesome. As is the case for most abiders, Gina's relationship is active and reciprocal. Gina is one of the millions of Americans who have learned to hear God's voice. She talks to Him, and He talks back:

> He has weird ways of talking to people . . . like I know I'm being called to be a missionary when I graduate high school . . . I'm scared to leave people behind but oh well . . . He demands [a lot] out of me, but it doesn't matter, you know, He's still loving, He's so caring, you know. He's awesome.

Gina's gushing over God is not empty rhetoric or extrinsically motivated by some reward or pressure from her parents. She is driven by internal rewards and by her own self-satisfaction. We can see evidence of it in the struggles Gina describes about her faith. She readily admits a period around eighth grade when she was feeling depressed and stopped believing in God. Looking back on it as a 17-year-old, she attributes that point in her life to a test that helped her solidify her faith: "I did stop believing, but I think everyone goes through that so it didn't bother me. It's just one of those tests in your life that you gotta overcome." Since then, Gina's faith has been resolute. Now she regularly looks to guidance from scripture to help her: "It's just amazing to know, 'cause even if you're having hard times, you can [see what scripture] says." In describing a difficult time when her dad was badly injured, she says it was God who helped her get through it: "I mean God brings you to it [the struggle and pain] and He'll get you through it, so my faith is everything." In fact, she attributes her energy and enthusiasm for life to God. When people jokingly ask her what pill she is on that makes her so energetic, she says, "I'm on the God pill [laughs] . . . It [my energy] comes from, I guess God. I've prayed a lot about being happy and here I am, always smiling." As James Wellman and his colleagues describe in their 2020 book,[13] Gina is "high on God" and can't wait for her next spiritual "hit," as the religious ecstasy she experiences is a full-body experience.

"I'm All in": Abiders and Authentic Commitments

Are abiders sincere about their religious commitments? It would seem so, but some might question whether their responses were just intended to please the interviewer. Scholars have long been concerned that when it comes to certain topics, people choose responses they believe are more socially desirable or acceptable rather than choosing responses that are reflective of their true thoughts or feelings—a phenomenon called social desirability bias.[14] It's one of the reasons that political polling isn't entirely accurate—people sometimes lie about whom they will vote for if they feel self-conscious about how the pollster will perceive them. Social desirability bias is also commonly seen in polling about religion. People try to look pious, especially in front of an interviewer, and will exaggerate their religious convictions.

But it does not seem as if abiders are falling into the trap of social desirability bias. One reason is that adolescents like Andrew don't hold back in their critiques of aspects of their religious experience. Andrew, in particular, expresses frustration with the clergy in his church, noting that it's inappropriate for his ministers to constantly comment on congregants' behavior, like condemning female congregants for wearing short skirts. He thinks his minister should be more focused on interpreting the Bible: "When I go to church, I want the preacher to pick a Bible verse, and the whole time he's preaching, I just want him just to tell me what that Bible verse is saying." In fact, at times Andrew gets so annoyed with his own church that he considers exploring other churches. But his belief in God is resolute: "I still believe in God. I'm gonna always believe in God."

This is an important fact about abiders—they are not forced to believe but intentionally embrace religious restraint. An intrinsic commitment on the part of abiders is critical, and adolescents who grow up with religious parents but don't share their parents' enthusiasm for religion wind up not leading lives oriented around pleasing God. Sixteen-year-old Quinn is one example of this. She lives in a small town in Virginia and alternates living one week with her mother and then one with her father. Quinn's mom is an Evangelical Christian who says faith is extremely important to her, but Quinn says it's only somewhat important to her. Quinn attends church every Sunday not because she finds personal growth by hearing God's word but to please her mother. Unlike abiders like Andrew, Gina, and Alex, who are intrinsically motivated to go to church and talk with God on their own, Quinn appears extrinsically motivated. She sees religion as something she needs to do because it's what her parents want—not something she gets a personal reward from. And unlike religiously restrained adolescents, who describe church as a warm and welcoming place, Quinn is nervous about going to church because she doesn't want others to see that she isn't well-versed in religious theology. Needless to say, Quinn reports that she doesn't follow the path an abider does when faced with a decision: "I'm not reading the Bible and not doing my daily prayers and living for Him . . . I'm more along the lines of trying to figure it out myself, trying to do it myself and not asking for Him to help."

Now contrast Quinn's story with that of Anthony. Both of his parents have a bachelor's degree and in 2003 together earned approximately $75,000, which puts Anthony solidly into the middle class. Religion was a major part of Anthony's childhood as his parents belonged to the Church of Jesus Christ of Latter-day Saints; however, he didn't really "buy into" his parents' faith. But around the time he turned 15, he had a revelation where he realized that the Book of Mormon was true:

> The more I read the Book of Mormon and then I prayed about it and then I was kind of told it was true [by the spirit] . . . [the spirit] was a feeling which I had never felt before and I never felt after . . . now I care a lot more [about my faith]. It's my whole life.

Since having his transformational experience, Anthony says his faith "dictates" what he "chooses to do" and he relies on his faith "for all kinds of things." In his words, "I believe in my whole religion where you try to be good and if you're not good then you should just try to get better."

Quinn and Anthony's stories illustrate that it's not enough for parents to share their religious beliefs with their children. Religious restraint requires adolescents to "opt into" religion. In fact, when Anthony is asked why he goes to church and whether his parents have any influence on his church attendance, he says, "They have no influence if I go or not. They just let me choose and I choose to go." Interestingly, when he wasn't interested in attending church, they did not say anything about it or pressure him. Perhaps they understood that while children learn to be religious by observing and pitching in, for religious restraint to work, adolescents need to feel intrinsically motivated to participate. They have to embrace religion themselves and make it their own in order for it to actually influence their behavior.

~

The converse is true as well: if parents do not embrace their faith and stick with a childrearing strategy of religious restraint, teenagers are unlikely to continue to "opt in" to religion as well. The example of Luca is a case in point. Luca was raised a Catholic but says his parents only did so because they thought religion could serve as a positive influence on him: "At the time they thought that if I had some religious structure in my life, I would be better off." But as Luca got older, his parents invested less and less in his religious up-bringing: "As I got older and was able to think on my own, they decided that it would be best if they just let me pick my own religion and my own belief system." By age 16, religion was not central for him, with his father rejecting organized religion and his mother saying that religion was only "fairly" im-portant to her.

Luca's parents thought he would be fine if they removed the guardrails and let Luca find his own way. Luca was perfectly happy with this—he believed in Christ but not in the Catholic Church nor in organized religion, so the change to opt out of going to church and sleeping in on Sundays was a wel-come development. But unlike teens raised with religious restraint, he hadn't developed a strong relationship with God and certainly did not see himself living a life for God. As he moved away from the structure that religious re-straint provided him both at home and at church, religious teachings were no longer the driving force behind his actions. When he thought about what to do in difficult situations, he did not ask himself what Jesus would do. He in-stead did what he thought helped him get ahead.

An upbringing of religious restraint is therefore a two-way street; adults modeling what it is to be religious and children absorbing their behavior while actively embracing a God-centered life. Religious restraint creates adolescents who see themselves as living a life for God and constantly seeking to better their relationship with him. Andrew's interest in scripture versus the hemlines of skirts reflects his intense desire to keep God's will at the fore-front of his consciousness. Only by hearing God's words can the faithful act accordingly. Indeed, abiders regularly turn to scripture to guide behavior. Gina is so devout that she brings her Bible to work and studies it during her breaks because its lessons are so integral to her life.

The NSYR wave 1 survey asked adolescents how they decide what to do if they are unsure of what is right or wrong in a particular situation. Do they do what makes them feel happy, do what helps them get ahead, follow the advice of an adult, or follow what God or scripture says is right? The rates of abiders and nonabiders who follow the advice of adults are fairly similar. But those who don't have a very different approach to deciding what to do. Abiders look to God or scripture (48%), while nonabiders do what makes them happy (32%) or what helps them get ahead (14%).

Alex is a case in point. He sees the Bible as providing the guidelines for society and the primary source for deciding what is wrong and right in life.

He applies the moral directives to all aspects of his life. For example, the Bible teaches him that you are "supposed to love everyone and if you love some-body you're not just going to let 'em sit out and be hurt." He believes that using the Bible to inform decision-making helps people be kind and positive. And when Alex has questions about his faith, it is scripture and his parents who help him find the answers. He recalls that in seventh grade, some of what he was learning in science didn't align with his beliefs. So he turned to the Bible and then to his parents: "I was kind of questioning 'cause we were going through some science stuff . . . I went home and I read the Bible and talked to them [his parents] about it and kind of came up with solutions."

The kind of faith that stems from reading the Bible and growing up with religious restraint has the power to fundamentally alter one's behavior. Andrew says that living a life for God means being "a good person"—day in and day out. God, Andrew explains, "judges us on what we do day by day to get us ahead" and "if you don't give your life to God, He will send you to hell." Believing that he might actually end up in hell most certainly motivates Andrew to do what he thinks God would want, and pleasing God drives much of Andrew's behavior. It motivates him to read the Bible, to repent, and to act better: "I want to live my life right. Most of the time, as soon as I finish reading the Bible, I repent. I ask God forgiveness of my sins." Andrew also prays: he prays for forgiveness, for knowledge, and for help. This is what it means to be brought up in the style of religious restraint. It means always doing what you think will please God. As Andrew admits, it may not make him "worldly," but it does make him "a good person."

The idea of the afterlife plays a big role in driving good behavior among many abiders. Alex also does whatever is possible to make it to heaven, which for Alex means doing good deeds and bringing as many people as possible to Christ. The way to bring people closer to Christ is to model the kind of behavior that it takes to be a good Christian. That alone won't get you into heaven, according to Alex, but "if you're a Christian, you realize that you're supposed to try to act as much as possible and believe in the Bible and read it and follow its teachings . . . you're trying to set an example as a Christian so other people will follow you [and] want to be like you." His faith shapes his views on morals, how he treats people, and how he behaves. Alex believes that if he emulates God and sets a good example as a Christian, others will want to be like him. The cycle of "good" behavior thus gets perpetuated.

Andrew is even more motivated to behave well because he wants to con-form to social expectations in his religious community. Affect control theory[15] and social facilitation theory[16] tell us that when we are around other people—an informal audience if you will—we tend to be extra mindful of how we behave. When there is a standard behavior in place, we are much more likely to conform to this standard—especially if we want to fit in. An audience makes us especially cognizant of our behavior because we want to make a good impression on others. As sociologists Steven Hitlin and Sarah Harkness put it, "Through interaction, people strive to have their identities confirmed by their behavior and the reactions of others to achieve a degree of consistency between their fundamental ideas about their identity and the feedback they receive from others."[17]

Abiders like Andrew first learn religious behavior by observing others. He sees how people at his church carry themselves, how they talk to each other, and how they talk about God. He notices that people don't swear and that they even give God credit when telling others about good things happening in their life. Andrew becomes so aware of how others behave that even when he moves away from that immediate audience, he maintains his behavior. And since God is always watching, his good behavior has even more sticking power. Since Andrew has learned not to swear in church, he continues this behavior by not swearing at school.

When Andrew experiences a benefit from reading scripture, he is likely to maintain this behavior. Eventually, there is a self-reinforcing feedback loop in which Andrew finds himself repeating and maybe even increasing his religious behavior. Psychologists refer to this as a positive feedback loop, where people receive affirmation for some endeavor and feel more motivated to continue.[18] This is why exercise can be addicting—as people start running, they feel better and then want to continue the behavior. The same goes for religious behavior. Recall Anthony, the Church of Jesus Christ of Latter-day Saints convert; he reported that he didn't pray much when he was younger since he didn't believe in God, but now that he does, he doesn't feel depressed. The feeling that faith improves his emotional well-being further reinforces his belief in God.

Who Am I?

All of this behavior feeds an important fact about abiders like Andrew: his religious identity is very salient for him. According to identity theorists, there are various identities that constitute the self. These identities exist in a hierarchy of importance. Identities that are ranked highest are most likely to be invoked in situations that involve different aspects of the self.[19] Andrew's religious identity is so central to who he is as a person that even if he finds himself at school around kids who do curse, he is unlikely to follow suit. That is to say that while Andrew's views certainly originated in and have been influenced by church and by his parents, by the time he has become a teenager, they are his own. Children like Andrew who are raised in a style of religious restraint become intrinsically motivated to stay religious.[20] As they get older, it becomes a volitional choice rather than forced upon them. As Andrew says, "I see that for myself . . . I read the Bible for myself and I know what He asks of us." All of this feeds a final observation about kids like Andrew: religiously restrained adolescents believe in God so deeply that it alters their sense of self. I refer to this as having a God-centered self-concept.

Self-concept is an overarching idea we have about who we are—in the words of the psychologist Carl Rogers, "the organized, consistent set of perceptions and beliefs about oneself."[21] Self-concept is learned and not inherent. It is something we form and regulate as we grow, based on the knowledge we have about ourselves. Self-concept develops through childhood and early adulthood, but most profoundly between ages 12 and 18—during the years associated with adolescence. This is the stage in which individuals play with their sense of self, including a time when they experiment with their identity, compare themselves with others, and develop the basis of a self-concept that may stay with them the rest of their life.

Two primary sources that influence our self-concept are childhood experiences and evaluation by others. We want to feel, experience, and behave in ways which are consistent with our self-image and which reflect what we would like to be like: our ideal-self. The closer our self-image and ideal-self match, the more congruent we are and the higher our sense of self-worth. Congruence occurs when adolescents develop a vision of their ideal and future self that comports with the norms of others in their social and cultural milieu. But Andrew doesn't just alter his behaviors based on how he wants to be evaluated by others. He adjusts his behavior because he is being evaluated by an even more important force: God. Pleasing God is of the utmost importance for Andrew, and it fundamentally shapes his self-concept—how he perceives himself, how he carries himself, and how he imagines his future self.

The role God plays in shaping Andrew's self-concept is very different from the role he plays in shaping the self-concepts of teenagers who were not raised with religious restraint. Take Simon, a professional-class White Catholic 16-year-old from Hartford, Wisconsin. His mother sees faith as "fairly" important, and the family attends church every Sunday. On top of this, Simon attends Confraternity of Christian Doctrine (CCD) religious education classes once a week. But unlike Andrew, Simon and his family do not make faith central in their daily lives. As Simon says, "I definitely believe that there is a God and that, you know, He's there. I'm just not sure how completely I believe it. I mean, it's definitely a good thing to have faith, but . . . you know, [I'm] still trying to figure stuff out and what I believe in, feel, and think." Unlike religiously restrained adolescents, who feel like they have a strong and personal relationship with God and are committed to pleasing Him, Simon sees God as more of a supporting actor in the story of his life. He describes God as just "looking over" him and trying to help guide him through trials and tribulations, but God is not constantly talking back or answering his prayers. Simon hasn't experienced any "divine revelations" or "massive spiritual happenings" despite the fact that he tries to pray nightly and attends church every Sunday.

Lacking a clear model of religious faith at home, Simon instead looks to other sources for guidance. One place where he explicitly doesn't look is scripture. In fact, he reflects quite a bit about issues that can't be reconciled with the Bible. In his words, "I have faith that there's, you know, like God out there, and I always just try to lead a moral, righteous life, [but] there are some things that I'm not sure about." As an example, he points to the big bang theory: "I don't quite believe that Adam and Eve like that, in 7 days, He just put them there . . . it just makes you wonder, it's one of those questions that we can't answer as humans, or I can't answer personally . . . so it's like, where does that come from and that's where faith comes in?" While Simon thinks religion is valuable because it teaches him to treat people with respect, it doesn't drive all his decisions. At age 18, Simon explicitly acknowledges that religion helps him "consider your choices and have a conscience," but it is not what he centers his life around: "[religion] is not my one sole purpose for living my life."

Although one might think that Simon's attitude is typical of adolescents, Andrew's upbringing of religious restraint and his God-centered self-concept are far from unique. About 1 in 4 adolescents I interviewed had a God-centered self-concept. These adolescent abiders center faith in their daily life, have an active and reciprocal relationship with God, look to scripture for guidance, and are intrinsically motivated to stay faithful. Living to please God completely shapes how they see themselves and how they behave.

What's fascinating to note about abiders is that they aren't clustered in any one particular demographic. They are Black, White, and Hispanic; male and female; poor, working class, middle class, and professional class; and Catholics, Protestants, and members of the Church of Jesus Christ of Latter-day Saints (they are, however, less likely to reside in coastal areas or in big cities). What matters is the God-centered self-concept that guides their every action. Consider, for example, the life story of one final abider. Nadia is a 14-year-old Hispanic working-class girl who was raised Christian but didn't find faith until adolescence. Nadia's mother has some college education and works as a motorcycle parts manager and mechanic in Bakersfield, California, earning about $25,000. Nadia's parents divorced when Nadia was 9 years old. Her mother has been battling drug addiction, so despite Nadia's desire to be with her mother, she must spend most of the time living with her father. Her mother says religion is extremely important to her, but Nadia didn't become intrinsically motivated to be religious until recently.

What motivated Nadia to become religious was an experience she had when she went to church when her dad was getting remarried. For Nadia, being religious means that "you have God on your side . . . you know you're doing good in your life when you know you have God on your side." Once Nadia became religious, she started attending church on her own. Interacting with members of the church reinforces Nadia's faith commitments because it is an overwhelmingly positive experience. Although she wished the sermons were a little more exciting, she describes church as welcoming and warm because everyone greets her with a smile and a hug and refers to her "family." As social psychologists argue,[22] the sense of belonging she describes is an important element in cultivating intrinsic motivation.

Attending her church youth group has also helped her religious journey, where she learned about God's word and spent time with her friends: "I wouldn't have been as religious as I am right now [without youth group]." Church was an especially important source of social support for Nadia when her mother went to jail for drug possession. One of the people she is closest to is the pastor's wife, Sandra, who even threw Nadia a birthday party at her house when her mother was incarcerated.

All of this social reinforcement led Nadia to develop a God-centered self-concept. She describes God as a father figure who is loving, forgiving, and actively involved in her life. In her words, "[God is] like a counselor. He can help you with your problems . . . He can help you with things that you want, maybe, like if you really want something really, really bad and then it comes true, you know God helped to make that come true." Religion helps her get through a bad day, and when she has a question, God will sometimes come to her in her dreams and provide answers.

Nadia feels close to God. She prays every night by talking with God, which to her is a gift versus a chore: "I don't look at it as a job. It doesn't matter how tired I am, I always pray. I haven't missed a night for like 3 years." In her conversations with God, Nadia asks Him to take care of her family members, which she believes He has done: "It's worked so far, they've been fine." And like other abiders, Nadia believes that her future rests in God's hands: "I believe that God makes everything that is here today and what's gonna come and He's like your future, He plans out your future."

As the stories in this chapter illustrate, what abiders have in common is not simply that they score high on typical survey measures of religious beliefs and behaviors. These religious beliefs and practices don't tell us much about why abiders get good report cards. While people do commonly pray before a test, it is unlikely that this is why religiously restrained adolescents do so well. What is underlying this behavior? As I will lay out in subsequent chapters, this God-centered self-concept fundamentally alters their educational pathways. It does so by shaping adolescents' attitudes toward education and behaviors in schools as well as their life aspirations. All of this leads to different and surprising academic outcomes in secondary school and college.

2

Remarkable Report Cards

In the last chapter, we met several teenagers whom I call abiders. They were from different genders, social class backgrounds, racial backgrounds, and religious traditions, but all of them were raised with religious restraint—a childrearing style that led them to center their lives on God. Pleasing God was of the utmost importance for these teenagers, and it fundamentally shaped their self-concept—how they perceived themselves, how they carried themselves, and how they imagined their future.

In this chapter, I make the case that abiders have an academic advantage in secondary school. This advantage stems from a synergy between schooling and religion: both institutions strive to maintain social order. Because religion and schooling promote the same ideals, the types of children who thrive in one institution are also likely to thrive in the other. Abiders like Andrew, Gina, and Alex are precisely these types of children. Their God-centered self-concept leads them to be deeply cooperative and conscientious. They do what is asked of them, they are kind to their peers, and they are self-disciplined. In return, they reap tangible academic rewards: they earn better grades. I refer to this as the "abider advantage."

What Are Schools for?

To understand why abiders have an academic advantage, we first need to consider what schooling is all about. What role do schools play in our society? What is the purpose of schooling? What do schools reward? After all, we might not expect abiders to fare better across all settings. There's no reason to think that they have an advantage on the tennis court or the debate team. Nor would it seem that they would intrinsically have an advantage in terms of popularity. So why would abiders have an advantage when it comes to their academics? If the classroom is like a Velcro toss and catch game, it is intuitively understandable that good readers or writers will "catch on" and get good grades. But what makes religion "sticky" in the classroom as well? In other words, if students with a God-centered self-concept earn better grades, what does that say about the cultural context and reward structure in schools?

The story Americans tell themselves about public education goes something like this. Schools exist to teach people valuable skills that will pay off in the future.[1] They are meritocratic because they evaluate and reward students based on talent and hard work. In short, schools are the path to the American dream, and anyone who tries hard enough can succeed. Unsurprisingly, this idea of schooling closely aligns with the meritocratic ideology that occupies American life.[2]

Schools are so ubiquitous that we rarely question their purpose, but we should not assume that the rhetoric about schools aligns with reality. Unfortunately, the reality is that schools are not an engine of social mobility. As sociologist Lisa Nunn puts it, "the myth of the American dream is a powerful ideology in US culture"—but is still a myth.[3] If schools were engines of social mobility, it would be fairly common to see children who are poor and work hard in school end up in a higher social class group in adulthood. But this is far from the truth. For example, Americans born to families in the bottom quintile of the income bracket have only a 10% chance of making it into the top quintile of the income bracket.[4] Instead of social mobility, we see social reproduction, with children generally remaining in a similar socioeconomic position as their parents. Children's incomes follow the same patterns as their parents, and the cycle continues generation after generation. Nor are schools teaching students technical knowledge that will be valuable for future employment.[5] Whatever it is that students are learning in school, it doesn't provide enough leverage such that the future careers of those students at the bottom of the income scale can leapfrog to the top with enough effort and hard work.[6]

What then do schools teach? It turns out that they are very good at helping maintain social order by teaching children the "rules" of larger society.[7] Rather than rewarding students based on merit, schools tend to reward students based on their ability to demonstrate certain values, dispositions, and tastes that characterize the middle and professional class. This creates a situation in which people at the top tend to stay at the top, and people at the bottom tend to stay at the bottom. Some sociologists even argue that schools don't just reproduce a professional-class culture—they reproduce a White Protestant status culture.[8] Our school system was founded mainly by White Anglo-Saxon Protestant (WASP) elites with the purpose of teaching respect for Protestant and middle-class standards of cultural and religious propriety.[9]

How did a White Protestant culture come to dominate our public schools? Let's rewind the clock by about 250 years to the very earliest days of the colonial schooling system in America to examine its roots in religious ideals.[10] As education historians like David Labaree and James Fraser have documented, commitment to Protestant religion was a major factor that promoted schooling at this time. The belief that worshippers had a direct connection to God was at the core of the Protestant faith. But that connection stemmed from their ability to read the Bible. As a result, the faithful could not afford to be left illiterate because then they would be dependent on the clergy to interpret and transmit biblical teachings (a common Protestant charge against Catholicism). Thus, at the heart of the push for schooling in colonial America was a mission to preserve piety and maintain the Protestant faith.[11]

A less overt religious mission continued to infuse schools even after the separation of church and state in the early 1800s. At that point, a key goal of public schooling (then called the common school) was to ameliorate the social turbulence that took place after the American Revolution and the formation of the United States. Common schools offered a school-based civic religion that could unite a diverse (albeit mostly Protestant) citizenry.[12] As James Fraser argues, religion and the public schools had a similar mission: "To foster a homogenous society united in faith, morals, and forms of government."[13] Thus, common schools became a "new kind of national church, commissioned to create and carry the common culture of morality of the nation."[14] In fact, researchers have shown that the growth of the public education system tracked closely with the spread of religiously motivated social movements.[15] Although churches as institutions were kept out of education, common schools still provided a general type of religious education. Students were even expected to read from the Protestant version of the King James Bible and pray up until the 1960s.[16]

The religio-moral ideology was not only a great motivator of the leaders of the American mass education movement but also led thousands of young female teachers to establish new schools.[17] These teachers felt religiously moved to bring both academic and moral enlightenment to the masses. The Protestant ethos also shaped the view that teachers were imbued with authority: teachers had special knowledge, and their task was to pass it on to students.[18] As education scholar David Cohen explained, "The idea that quiet attention, obedience to teachers, and recalling and repeating material were evidence of learning seems to have been powerfully reinforced by early Protestantism."[19]

In many parts of the United States, overt religious practices have left the public school arena. However, there are plenty of public schools in which students and teachers pray or engage in other religious expressions. Even subtle forms of Protestantism (like asking students to recite the pledge of allegiance with its "one Nation under God") convey that there is a particular religious ethos to the school. The Protestant ideals of common schools left a strong imprint on modern-day public schooling, and it is not difficult to imagine how the values of Protestantism continue to infuse the mission and form of public schooling even today. As David Labaree writes, "Some 200 years later, the common school movement, along with its goal of socializing students to be obedient to moral standards, is still with us."[20]

The Hidden Curriculum and Moral Directives: A Match Made in Heaven

To be effective agents of socialization, schools must rely heavily on authority structures. Schools teach young people the rules of larger society by providing a common moral code, with discipline serving as the instrument of morality. The obligations that students shoulder are key to this moral code. A student's job is to do their homework, not disrupt class, and attend regularly. As Emile Durkheim explained, "It is through the practice of discipline that we can inculcate the spirit of discipline in the child."[21]

For Durkheim, the point of discipline is not to generate a superficial peace and order in the classroom. Kids should not be regulated simply to make it easier for the teacher to induce conformity. Rather, school rules serve a larger purpose: they teach kids to respect rules in general and develop the habit of self-control necessary for adulthood. Since there are so many children in a class, the teacher needs to develop the necessary authority so that the class does not devolve into disorder. For Durkheim, the main duty of students is to follow school rules and develop self-restraint: "When children no longer feel restrained, they are in a state of ferment that makes them impatient of all curbs, and their behavior shows it—even outside the classroom."[22]

Multiple scholars have documented the myriad ways in which schools prioritize children's obedience and respect for authority.[23] As education scholar Philip Jackson wrote in 1968:

One of the earliest lessons a child must learn is how to comply with the wishes of others. Soon after he becomes aware of the world he is in, the newborn infant becomes conscious of one of the main features of that world: adult authority. As he moves from home to school the authority of parents is gradually supplemented by control from teachers, the second most important set of adults in his life.[24]

The emphasis on obedience and respect for authority can be seen in both how schools are organized and what they reward. This is often referred to as the "hidden curriculum" of school, which entails the unofficial "three Rs"—rules, routines, and regulations.[25] These three Rs have to be learned by students to survive and thrive in classrooms. The hidden curriculum is the "implicit demands (as opposed to the explicit obligations of the visible curriculum) that are found in every learning institution and which students have to find out and respond to in order to survive within it."[26]

The hidden curriculum is well illustrated in Harry Gracey's 1975 description of a day in the life of a kindergarten class at the Wright School, where lessons about punctuality, obedience, and respect govern the informal goals of the school. In kindergarten, kids learn the role of "student" as they are shown what type of behavior and attitudes is appropriate for school. The learning of classroom routines is the most fundamental part of this. The hidden curriculum entails teaching kids to fit in with a social system, follow rules and order, respect authority, obey, compete, and achieve success within the boundaries of the system:

> The children at the [Wright School] learned to go through routines and to follow orders with unquestionable obedience, even when these make no sense to them. They have been disciplined to do as they are told by an authoritative person without significant protest . . . children who submit to school-imposed discipline and come to identify with it, so that being a "good student" comes to be an important part of their developing identities, become the good students by the school's definitions.[27]

Although Gracey wrote this in 1975, it doesn't sound all that different from my own child's experience in kindergarten, where she spent much of the first few months learning the rules of school. Most importantly, she witnessed firsthand the value of conformity in helping society function. During a volunteer shift, I sat on the floor while the teacher read a book to the students.

Most of the 17 children sat quietly in a "crisscross applesauce" position, but two high-energy kids were very fidgety and unintentionally disruptive. They were not trying to cause trouble—they just weren't able to be still. These two students were constantly singled out because the teacher (whom I admired and respected tremendously) could not focus on the other 15 children when the others were interrupting. As the teacher constantly reminded them to sit and focus on the task, I could see that my 6-year-old was not just getting a lesson in literacy, but a lesson in the value of self-discipline and the rules that maintain society. She and her peers were constantly learning the hidden curriculum of school: how must I act to help the teacher maintain social order?

Schools can carry out their work most smoothly when students have internalized school rules and cooperate with teachers' requests. As sociologist Richard Arum points out, students are much more likely to internalize school rules when they see school personnel as being moral authorities.[28] Thus, a successful school does not need to enforce rules and dole out heavy punishment because students have internalized the rules and do not challenge authority in the first place: "What lends authority to the rule in school is the feeling that the children have for it, the way in which they view it as a sacred and inviolable thing quite beyond their control."[29]

~

At this point in our story, we have seen that rules, routines, and regulations are the basis of our K–12 school system. Now let's think about the children in it. Which ones are most likely to thrive in an environment where they are expected to sit still, repeat after the teacher, and diligently follow the routine? Probably a child who grew up with these norms and has practiced these skills. And what kind of child already has had a great deal of practice with these skills? Abiders.

It's not hard to guess why this is the case. A central principle of Christianity is a commitment to authority, with God as the ultimate authority.[30] One does not have to search hard to find biblical references invoking the importance of submission to authority. Consider Romans 13:1: "Let every person be subject to the governing authorities. For there is no authority except from God, and those that exist have been instituted by God."

Conservative Protestants—those who constitute about half of the abiders in this book—are thought to be especially "authority minded," believing and socializing their children into a worldview in which there is an ultimate authority accessible to human beings. According to this view, individual and social well-being are only possible when life in all its dimensions is lived in obedience to that authority.[31] In a survey of pastors in 125 congregations in four upstate New York communities, sociologist Penny Edgell[32] found that 93% of Conservative Protestant pastors agreed with the statement "[W]e teach kids to trust, obey parents, teachers, and the pastor [sic]," while not a single one agreed with the statement "We teach kids to think for themselves." Social psychologist Jonathan Haidt found a similar emphasis on authority using different methods. His team analyzed church sermons. They found that preachers in Southern Baptist churches tend to invoke themes of authority, loyalty, and sanctity compared to preachers in Unitarian churches.[33]

Religious groups outside of Conservative Protestantism also put great faith in authority structures and the value of teaching children to be obedient. Moderate Protestants espouse similar beliefs to Conservative Protestants but to a lesser extreme: in Edgell's survey of pastors, just over half (56%) agreed that they "teach kids to trust, obey parents, teachers, and the pastor [sic]," with 43% of Catholic pastors agreeing as well. The Church of Jesus Christ of Latter-day Saints is another faith that is ordered through clearly delineated "lines of authority."[34]

Perhaps the most compelling data on the role of obedience come from a 2020 Pew Study of 1,811 parents and their teenage children.[35] These data are not only the most current but also allow us to look at attitudes based on parents' religious intensity versus their religious tradition. As part of the survey, parents were asked to assess how important it is for their teen to exhibit certain traits, such as being independent, creative, or persistent, and reach certain goals, such as going to college or being financially successful. Pew found widespread consensus among parents with various religious commitments that their teens must be hardworking, independent, persistent, creative, and financially successful. Most parents also say it's very important that their teen go to college. But there was one trait about which parents profoundly disagreed: obedience. Among parents for whom religion was very important, almost three-quarters (72%) wanted teens to be obedient. Among those who were religiously affiliated but not as intensely religious, less than one-half (40%) wanted teens to be obedient. And among religiously unaffiliated parents, only one-third (30%) wanted their teens to be obedient.

Religious views that value authority see children's role in the world as one of respect, and these views are quite conducive to promoting order in schools. Recall Durkheim's observation about how important it is for children to feel that rules are "sacred and inviolable." Adolescents whose parents and church communities teach them to follow rules transition more easily into school environments that promote the same ideas. They already know how to comply with authority figures. And the extent to which adolescents are willing to follow the rules matters, because as we shall see, getting good grades in school is largely about following the rules. Thus, students who are used to following the rules have an academic advantage, and these students tend to be abiders.

But before we examine how obedience to authority leads to better grades, we need to first answer the question of how exactly children learn the rules on which American schools are founded. The short answer is through the moral directives of their religious teachings. According to sociologist Christian Smith,[36] moral directives can be broadly defined (particularly in Christianity) as religious texts and teachings that promote values of self-control and personal virtue. One well-known example of this is the golden rule, which fosters ethical behavior.[37] Moral directives are grounded in the authority of long historical traditions and narratives into which new members are inducted. According to Smith's theory, youth internalize these moral orders and use them to guide their life choices and ethical commitments. Children who have been given moral grounding of this sort are thought to be able to access commands and guidance like "Thou shall not lie" and then utilize them in decision-making when confronting both moral dilemmas and ordinary day-to-day choices. Moral directives are legitimated and reinforced by both spiritual experiences (e.g., feeling that one's prayers were answered or witnessing a miracle) and role models who exemplify life practices shaped by religious moral orders and who reinforce adolescents' ideas of how to have a normatively approved life.

The key takeaway is profound: although we think of religion and public schools as fundamentally distinct institutions, especially given the separation of church and state, religion and public schooling actually promote the same ideals.[38] As education historian James Fraser puts it, "the relationship between religion and public education is simple: for religion and the public schools are meant to foster the same thing. Anything else would undermine the goal of a homogenous society united in faith, morals, and forms of government."[39] Sociologist David Baker makes a similar point, arguing that the institution of religion and the institution of education "have been, and continue to be, more compatible and even surprisingly symbiotic than is often assumed."[40]

Abiders: Conscientious and Cooperative

Moral directives can manifest themselves specifically in what social psychologists refer to as "conscientiousness" and "agreeableness."[41] Conscientiousness is related to self-control,[42] the need for order,[43] the reduction of uncertainty,[44] and the organization of one's life through meaning and goals.[45] You can think of conscientiousness as the propensity to follow socially prescribed norms for impulse control, to be goal-directed, and to plan—in short, to be able to delay gratification and follow norms and rules.[46] Conscientious students are predisposed to be organized, disciplined, diligent, dependable, methodical, and purposeful.[47] Agreeableness is related to the concern for others' welfare and social harmony, "including reciprocal relations with others,[48] rich exchanges in coalitions,[49] and love and protection in close relationships."[50] In general, agreeable students are characterized as selfless, good-natured, gentle, cooperative, flexible, tolerant, generous, sympathetic, and courteous; they also strive for a common understanding and maintain social affiliations.[51]

Research suggests that religiosity is closely linked with conscientiousness and cooperation. One study identified three types of prosocial behaviors:[52] (1) compliant prosocial behaviors, such as helping when asked; (2) altruistic prosocial behaviors, such as helping out of concern for others rather than anticipation of reward; and (3) anonymous prosocial behaviors, such as helping in anonymous situations rather than when others are watching.[53] Education psychologist William Tirre showed that students with high levels of biblical literacy were more conscientious, which meant they were more orderly, responsible, and considerate.

But conscientiousness and agreeableness are not just behavioral traits often seen in abiders. They have also been shown to be closely linked to academic success.[54] According to sociologist George Farkas,[55] these noncognitive habits tend to be "the ones most desired and rewarded by teachers, parents, and employers." It may be especially beneficial when students are willing to work hard *and* cooperate with others.[56] Furthermore, conscientiousness and cognitive ability each *uniquely* explained variance in high school grades.[57]

I argue that abiders' advantage stems from their conscientious and cooperative disposition. It is not just that abiders are less likely to abuse alcohol and drugs, and more likely to volunteer, participate in afterschool activities, take on leadership roles, and have nonparental adults to help them. All of these factors help explain why abiders get better grades, but they alone do not explain the full magnitude of the abider advantage in my statistical models. To understand the abider advantage, we need to look at how abiders narrate their lives. Interviews with abiders exude kindness and compliance, which is hard to capture through survey data. Their God-centered self-concept derived from an upbringing of religious restraint compels them to behave in exceptionally conscientious and cooperative ways. But abiders do not confine this behavior to their church and their family—conscientiousness and cooperation are not like a pair of rainboots and an umbrella that you consciously put on and take off. Rather, abiders learn these dispositions to the point that they embody them, weaving these dispositions into the fabric of their very being. Being conscientious and cooperative comes to define who they are— their self-concept. And because these are highly valuable traits in the K–12 environment, abiders are awarded higher grades.

~

To illustrate how abiders' God-centered self-concept compels them to behave in exceptionally conscientious and cooperative ways, I turn to interviews with abiders during their middle and high school years. In the last chapter, I introduced readers to Alex (Baptist, middle class, White) who sees religion as central to his life: "It shapes how I live, it guides me," he explains. Abiders like Alex who look to religious teachings to guide their lives believe that doing so helps them to be more self-disciplined. For example, according to Alex, being religious is precisely what helps him have the self-discipline to avoid bad behaviors and concentrate in school. For him, being a "good Christian at school" meant avoiding the wrong crowd (who he described as being the kids who did drugs and cursed). Alex believes that his actions in this life will affect him in the afterlife: "You want to do the right thing and realize that Jesus Christ died to save you from your sins," he explained. When asked how he might be different if he were not religious, Alex laughed and replied, "I'd be a troublemaker. I like to have fun, and I'd get out of hand."

But Alex is religious—highly so—and as a result Alex is also highly conscientious. He thinks it is wrong to steal, litter, and lie to his parents. Perhaps not surprisingly, he thinks it is wrong to cheat. In fact, his problem is that people generally want to cheat off him. When asked what he does in that situation, he says, "I tell them no, but sometimes, some people will just grab it off your desk and you can't really yell it out in class, cause you'd get in trouble for it." But what makes him feel most guilty is "cussing." He recalls that in sixth grade, his friends were all "cussing" and he felt like he should do it, too, to impress them. However, his guilt led him to curb the habit; he was pleased to reveal that in the 2 years since he hasn't cursed once.

Alex's self-control is perhaps most visible as a high school student when it comes to alcohol and other drugs because he refrains from smoking and drinking alcohol. Nor is it likely that he is lying or just saying this to impress the interviewer—recall that Alex thinks it is wrong to lie. Indeed, Alex admits to trying marijuana once, but afterward he decided to stop hanging out with this particular group of friends, and he stays away from kids who "do drugs and like to cuss a lot." When one of Alex's friends drinks beer while Alex is at his house, Alex doesn't feel tempted—but he does make sure that his friend doesn't drive after. He knows that getting alcohol and drugs in his town would be quite easy if he wanted it—all you have to do is head into the woods where kids either get drunk or get high. But Alex is not interested, because that's not what a conscientious and cooperative kid would do.

Regular alcohol and drug usage is a significant problem in the United States and a key hindrance to adolescents' academic success. In the National Study of Youth and Religion (NSYR) data, 44% of nonabider boys reported some level of drinking, ranging from "almost every day" to "a few times a year." When it comes to smoking marijuana, 16% report "occasional" or "regular" usage. But among abider males, the rates of usage fall by over half. When it comes to alcohol, 21% of abider males report some level of drinking, and only 7% report "occasional" or "regular" pot usage. Beyond refraining from drinking alcohol, Alex's conscientious and self-disciplined behavior also helps him avoid drugs. Case in point: when Alex was in sixth grade, he was playing football with a group of high school kids when they started smoking pot. Feeling uncomfortable, Alex decided to leave: "I was scared they were gonna get really high and start fighting cause they're really big . . . I never came back . . . I avoided them [and] I told my parents [what happened]."

This story is also one of many that shows how much Alex respects his parents, who supervise him closely. He says they are "very controlling" and that he doesn't have much freedom, yet he doesn't seem to mind. For example, when he comes home from school, his mom (who works from home) makes sure he does all his homework before he can leave to see a friend. And when he goes to his friends' houses, she calls their parents to check up on him: "It doesn't bother me a bit," he tells the interviewer when asked how that feels. Alex's parents also set the controls on the TV such that when he was

14, he could only watch movies that were rated PG and under. But Alex does not complain. He says his parents want to keep a close eye on him because they worry about him—they want him to get good grades, hang out with good people, and behave well. And Alex does not rebel. He is honest with them about what he does, even coming to them after he tried pot. During a 2-hour confidential interview that his parents will never know about, he doesn't complain about his parents at all. He trusts them—and the Bible—completely. At age 16, Alex has a girlfriend, but he firmly believes that he will not have sex until he is married. After all, this is what Christianity teaches him. As the interviewer probes him about this, Alex admits that he has never actually seen the evidence against premarital sex in the Bible, but his parents told him and he believed them: "My parents have always told me it's the way the Bible teaches. So I trust them."

As is probably clear by now, Alex is the very embodiment of a conscientious and cooperative kid. That kind of demeanor goes a long way in school, especially since Alex is not very intrinsically motivated to do well academically.[58] He thinks school is boring and doesn't think grades are all that important in the long run. However, he puts in some effort because his parents have high expectations. When he doesn't get good grades, he gets grounded and loses access to electronics. By high school, Alex seems more self-driven to earn good grades and feels a sense of satisfaction for doing well. At both 14 and 16, he typically earns As and Bs. At one point, however, an F showed up on his progress report, and his father became livid and grounded Alex for a full year—no TV or Play Station 2. Many 16-year-olds would be appalled by this treatment, or at least find it unreasonable. But not Alex. When asked whether he thought his parents' reaction was appropriate, Alex says it was completely understandable and does not take the opportunity to criticize his parents:

> I'm okay with it. I guess they're just worried. I think it was appropriate because I wasn't doing my homework when they were telling me to and so they finally found out because they called the teacher . . . I'd probably do the same thing if my son came home with an F after I told him not to do it again.

Despite not working very hard, Alex does better academically than your average adolescent male. His conscientious and cooperative nature helps him overcome some of this apathy. The teachers probably appreciate his respectful nature and willingness to do what they ask, and in return, they are likely to assign him better grades.

~

When we compare Alex to your average American teenage boy, his behavior is unusual. But when we compare him to other abider boys in the NSYR, his behavior is actually quite common and unremarkable. Some readers might wonder if Alex's behavior is a function of his upbringing as a Baptist, which is a type of Conservative Protestant. But Catholic abiders sound and act in very similar ways to Conservative Protestants. Take, for example, Jacob, who is Catholic. His God-centered self-concept is linked with his conscientious and cooperative behavior in and outside of school. Jacob sees God as an "all-knowing, all-person being" who influenced everything in his life, and Jacob looks to the Bible to inform his behaviors, including his views of right and wrong: "[Morality comes] from the Bible actually, like what Jesus did. I mean how can you argue with God?" Jacob looks to Christian teachings to guide his day-to-day decisions: "There's not a day that goes by when I don't think of God or thank him . . . you've got to make decisions about what God would like you to be, of course." For Jacob this is not empty rhetoric. God wants you to act the right way, and Jacob has internalized that thinking deeply:

> I hate litter bugs. I really hate that. Because I'm a really big hunter and all that. And fisherman and trapper so seeing trash in the outdoors, I frickin hate it. That really bugs me. . . . There's a garbage can 10 feet away from you so get off your lazy butt and throw it in the garbage can instead of dropping it on the ground.

His God-centered self-concept undoubtedly governs his behaviors and attitudes.

Jacob sees peer pressure to do "immoral things" like drugs and alcohol as the biggest problem facing teens, noting that both were readily available to him. However, Jacob rarely drinks (he estimates five instances over the past year) and has never used drugs, which he admits is a decision informed by his religious beliefs: "You don't do drugs. They're sins and they hurt your body." He doesn't "party" nearly as much as his friends because he knows that partying will negatively affect his future and because getting drunk and doing drugs will harm your body. What is most striking about Jacob is not the fact that he doesn't use alcohol and other drugs, but his incredibly strong impulse control and calculated decision-making. Jacob is a football player, which means that his friends are mostly high school athletes who party regularly: "I could get drunk every day of my life. That's how easy it is to get beer and to get weed," he explains.

In addition to easy access, Jacob experiences a fair amount of peer pressure and occasional ridicule for not partying more. His friends try to entice him by saying he isn't enjoying life. But Jacob doesn't just resist peer pressure; he un-self-consciously reasserts his moral values in the face of such pressure:

JACOB: I'm not a big partier at all. I'll go out and party with my friends but I'm not one of those kids that are like every day and every night, every week or whatever. Even every week. I'm not a big beer drinker or anything at all. But some of my friends I'm like wow, I'll be impressed if you make it out of high school, man. I'll just tell them straight out, you shouldn't be doing that, you know?

INTERVIEWER: You tell them if they're doing something wrong?

JACOB: Oh yeah, I'll tell them, like I said I wouldn't be doing that, and they're like, oh it's not your life, and I said whatever, I'm just telling you.

INTERVIEWER: Have they ever opposed you?

JACOB: Not really, they pretty much told me, well, you're not enjoying high school. And I said whatever, I mean it doesn't bother me. Like I always think, I've been called worse by better people and I mean what are you going to say?

This is not to say that Jacob isn't tempted to party sometimes. When asked for an example of a time when he had to make a hard moral decision, he shared the following story:

One time I was at this party and these kids started like making some alcohol cause they thought it would be fun . . . they acted like "Oh, you know, don't be a wuss or something," and I had to make a decision because you know it's wrong deep down inside. But then temptation starts coming like, maybe it's not wrong, you know it is legal, but not legal for you, but it is legal in real life and like, who's gonna know about it and stuff like that . . . [But] I made the right decision.

If Jacob is conscientious with his peers, he is also exceptionally cooperative with adults, willing to do whatever it takes to please them. When asked how adults view him, Jacob said he thought adults hold him in high regard because he always obliged their requests: "[They perceive me as] hopefully good. I can't say no to things . . . I always get asked to play violin for church, for weddings, for organizations, and sometimes I just get overpacked and it's hard to say no." Part of being cooperative also means being considerate, which Jacob certainly is because he takes his cues from the Bible: "Of course, you always think of what the Bible says," he explains. He says he has never lied to his parents and condemns lying and cheating: "I hate liars. Liars and cheaters. I hate them. That's my biggest pet peeve. I hate people who lie."

Jacob's conscientious and cooperative behavior stems from his God-centered self-concept where he tries to be a good Catholic by doing "what Jesus would do pretty much, be a good person." But that self-concept doesn't stop at the schoolhouse door for Jacob, but instead translates into effort, perseverance, and an orientation toward achievement in the classroom. In middle school, Jacob earns all As, and in high school, mostly As. Occasionally he'll get a B or a C, but it's rare and drives him crazy:

> I hate to do bad in class, period. I figure if I'm going to sit through class for 8 hours I might as well make the best of it, so. Like last year, I was seventh in the class. This year was frickin' hell on earth, classes were horrible, but I just don't like accepting that C or that B. I just try to get that A as hard as I can. I mean I accept them [Bs and Cs], but I don't enjoy them, that's for sure.

It's worth pausing to dig deeper into some of the specific behaviors of abiders that give them an academic advantage. Many abiders like Sean, a White Catholic 14-year-old, look to religion to inform their behaviors, particularly the notion of emulating Jesus. He regulates his emotions by imagining that Jesus was sitting close by him: "[Doing so] has an effect on me, if I'm like, if I get really mad or something, I want to restrain myself." In fact, Sean believes that praying to God is an "essential part" of his success. It encourages him to be conscientious and cooperative, which sets him on the right path for academic success. In Sean's view:

> Religion is all the difference. Without religion I would probably be just like them [referring to peers]. I wouldn't really know any better—I'd probably be conceited. But I'm trying to be nice to everybody, trying my best . . . I think religion helps me get good grades and achieve things that I want. I think it's

essential . . . I pray to God to set my feet in the right path where I truly want to go, so I think He's doing that.

Like other abiders, Sean believes it is important to not make his teachers mad, and he describes himself as polite and deferential. "I think they [adults] think I try to be polite and everybody thinks I'm really well disciplined in my school . . . and I don't talk in class very much. Once I'm out of school, I talk a lot, but in school I don't talk that much."

Teens from the Church of Jesus Christ of Latter-day Saints like Anthony also try to emulate Jesus: "This is gonna sound stupid, but we're supposed to try to be like Jesus and I try to do that . . . he was a good guy. Like really good." When asked what qualities of Jesus he wants to emulate, Anthony explains, "I try to really not get angry and to be peaceful and try to help other people." Anthony admires Jesus's agreeable nature and looks to harness that within himself. But Jesus also serves as a moral compass for teens like Anthony when faced with antisocial behaviors. When asked whether he had ever opposed his friends who he thought were doing something wrong, Anthony shared a story about going to a fast-food restaurant where his friends asked for water cups but filled them with soda instead: "I said, well that's kind of stealing. They said no it's not and then I said fine, whatever. Then I stopped going with them, so I wouldn't have to be around that stuff." This story was one of many that demonstrated his desire for planned rather than spontaneous behavior, his propensity to act dutifully, and his self-discipline—a disposition that seems to align with the way religion orders his life.

Those dispositions are precisely what Anthony and other abiders like him bring to the classroom. Adolescents who follow the rules transition more easily into school environments that promote the same ideas. Anthony certainly believes that enacting his faith means following the rules—rules that are not just compatible with those found at school but even more binding:

INTERVIEWER: What do you think it means to be a good Mormon at school? Does it require doing anything in particular or not doing anything in particular?

ANTHONY: Just to do what the rules say to do, I guess.

INTERVIEWER: Like what rules?

ANTHONY: Well, there's all kinds of rules.

INTERVIEWER: You mean, like school rules or . . . ?

ANTHONY: Religion's rules. I don't care about the school rules. I just care about my religion's rules.

INTERVIEWER: What are the rules that come to mind?

ANTHONY: Well, I don't swear, and I try to be nice to people.

For Anthony, being a member of the Church of Jesus Christ of Latter-day Saints meant being kind, respectful, and disciplined, which coincidentally lies at the core of enacting the hidden curriculum.

~

Underlying the hidden curriculum is a fundamental belief in the value of delayed gratification. In many respects, schooling is a ladder that youth have to climb in order to achieve more important desires. But children raised in a culture of religious restraint have the distinct advantage of being provided a rationale for putting off immediate short-term satisfactions in favor of long-term gratification—not unlike what schools ask teens to do so they can graduate with good grades and go on to college.[59]

Given the central role of God in the lives of abiders like AJ, a 14-year-old who lives about 10 miles outside of Wilmington, Delaware, it is perhaps unsurprising to hear that his purpose in life is to "live for God as much as you can." What is striking is how his next sentence carries over into all dimensions of his life: "You'll be rewarded for what you do in the end." Behave well now and you will be rewarded in the afterlife is certainly a religious tenet of his faith, but delayed gratification is also a disposition that is deeply ingrained in the lives of abiders raised in a culture of religious restraint. AJ knows that school success has downstream effects and acts accordingly: "I just want to do well in school so I can do well in life," he says. And AJ does well, earning As and being initiated as a member of the National Honors Society. That's in no small part because AJ is exceptionally attuned to following rules. Like all the abiders we've met in this book, AJ is always thinking about how his actions will be judged by others, including God. AJ sees God as a fatherly figure who has strict rules with consequences: "[He's] authoritative, powerful, all the aspects that a father should be. These are my rules, obey them, if not there's going to be consequences." In Chapter 1 I drew on the work of psychologists to explain how abiders modify their behavior because they want to look good in the eyes of other people and in the eyes of God. AJ imagines himself representing other Christians and tries to act accordingly, knowing that God is watching:[60] "I try to be the best person I can be to do the right thing all the time and show that I'm Christian." But in doing so AJ is not just making himself worthy of going to heaven; he's also reaping the rewards of the hidden curriculum of schools in this life. This is precisely what constitutes the abider advantage.

While the NSYR did not ask extensive questions about school, it is not difficult to imagine how the conscientiousness and cooperation that abiders exude can help them be organized, get along with their teachers and peers, and work on group projects. Abiders may be at a particular advantage because research points to a potential interaction effect between conscientiousness and agreeableness which results from students being willing to work hard and cooperate with others. This type of compliance and kindness likely goes a long way in school environments where students are constantly told to work hard and be nice.

Given the relatively limited range of examples presented here, some may wonder if the abider advantage is limited to White males. If one in four teens is raised in a culture of religious restraint, we would expect to see its academic benefits manifest themselves in girls as well—and that is exactly what we find. Gina, a 17-year-old White Conservative Protestant, is the textbook definition of agreeableness—concerned for others' welfare and social harmony, including reciprocal relations with others, and love and protection in close relationships. Her social network consists primarily of church friends, and she especially loves mentoring younger teens in her youth group: "I'm just a generally happy person, and when I go to church, I usually trust everyone. I always give someone a chance, and they always prove themselves to be so loyal and there for people. They are great people overall." When asked what kinds of people she likes to stay away from, she says those who create a lot of drama. She always looks out for others, and the week before her interview she called the cops on her ninth-grade neighbor because she could see he was physically assaulting his girlfriend.

Gina also goes out of her way to be cooperative and helpful. She describes working at a water theme park and being the only person who proactively volunteers to do the trash run:

> If you knew the trash run at the theme park, it's not very good. But I smiled and sang the whole time and, um, someone came up to me, one of the vice presidents of the park was like you're the only person I've seen happy to do the trash, and I was like, you know, it's great.

She said her face lights up so much from being able to be helpful that even when the water park asks her to clean the bathrooms, she is happy to pitch in. She attributes this outlook on life to her relationship with God.

Gina certainly respects authority. She adores her parents and thinks they help her through tough times, and she credits them for her success and says they keep her safe. If they have a fight, she will apologize even if she hasn't done anything wrong. And like Alex, who described his parents as having a controlling nature, Gina is not bothered by rules like having a curfew. She thinks that if her parents were less strict, she would be out getting in trouble like her peers:

> Usually high school kids say things like "Let's get piercings and do our hair," but no, not me. I guess I just had really good parents that cared. Other people are like "We don't have a curfew, our parents don't care." I'm like, well, I do, but it's okay because most of them are getting drunk and stuff, and I don't really want to be around that anyways.

Although Gina is not particularly academically motivated and doesn't feel like she is very competent, Gina enjoys school because it's another realm where she can exercise her sunny disposition. She gets almost all As and Bs, something that she believes going to church has taught her: "Church doesn't want you to fail; they want you to make good grades and stuff, but they also encourage you not getting into the wrong crowd at school." For Gina her religious and academic worlds are one seamless whole—so much so that she often skips lunch at school to study the Bible.

Nor is conscientious and cooperative behavior just for White kids or girls. Consider Michael, an African American boy living in a city outside of Houston, Texas. Michael was raised in a Baptist church, which he joined when he was about 6 years old. He was baptized and immediately began to sing in the choir. He is on the mime team, which is a church-based dance squad. Michael is also part of the brotherhood, which he describes in the following way: "We come in and like we have a deacon who's teaching us a sermon, just like preaches a sermon and things like that and we go and he talks to us. And we have a brotherhood choir and the brothers sing."[61] Michael is also a Junior Deacon, which means that once a month he participates in a devotion and sits in the front of the church when the pastor is preaching. Recently he also participated in vacation Bible school and in a "youth explosion," which he describes as other churches coming to fellowship with his church.

As should be obvious, Michael enjoys all the activities he does with his church. In his eyes it gives him a chance to do something safe with people his age. He thinks that if he didn't have church his life might look different: "I'm there to keep my mind off bad things and doing wrong. And if I wasn't there and I wasn't raised up in that type of environment, I'd probably be out somewhere or I could be locked up somewhere." He appreciates that the church works to help teens "keep our head on straight so that we don't go off and do the things that everyone thinks teenagers are doing."

At age 15, Michael bases everything he does "on Christ and God" because "that's the way I was raised." As a result, Michael is conscientious and cooperative: "My religious beliefs, they help me see what's right and what's wrong. So everything I do, I try to do the right thing by what my religion says." For example, his preacher recently was preaching about the bad influence that inappropriate music can have on people. Taking this advice seriously, Michael decided to minimize the amount of rap he listens to, intentionally choosing to listen to gospel music instead. Michael's general approach to life is to look to God to guide him: "If I put my faith in God and I'm thinking about the things that I'm supposed to be doing and right from wrong, then I'll become what I want to become."

~

It is noteworthy that Michael's responses appear less informative than the replies offered by Gina, Jacob, and Alex. In fact, his interviewer (also a Black male) noted that it was one of his quickest interviews, and that the "respondent was honest but didn't elaborate on answers much unless probed. [He] didn't have much to say in response to many of the questions and didn't seem to want to get too deep or reveal too much information/feelings." He would answer the interviewer's question but rarely elaborate.

Michael's brevity is likely a reflection of social class. He is among the poorest kids interviewed in the sample. Neither of his parents continued their education beyond high school, and his mom is a school secretary earning about $35,000 while his father is an unemployed electrician. Interviews with Michael and other poor kids reveal a profound difference in communication patterns. Poor kids are terser in their interviews, often giving short answers like "yes" or "I don't know" or "I haven't really thought about that." These clipped replies likely reflect how speech patterns develop among the working class. Sociolinguist Basil Bernstein describes working-class speech as comprising a "restricted code," characterized by relatively simple grammatical constructions, concreteness, and a paucity of counterfactual or conditional statements.[62] By contrast, middle- and professional-class speakers not only possess the restricted code but also employ what he calls the "elaborated code"—a form of speech that is more abstract, is less tied to context, uses more subjunctives, and is syntactically more complex.

In addition to using restricted code, speakers who are poor are placed at a disadvantage when confronting middle-class (or upper-class) speakers in situations that require them to engage in cross-class communication about abstract or unfamiliar topics. They do not have the elaborated code to engage with the interviewer. This might make the speaker feel uncomfortable and reticent to answer questions because they don't want to give the wrong answer.[63] Many of the NSYR interview questions, especially those about religious topics, required abstract-level thinking and elaborated code: "When you think about God, what kind of picture do you get?," "What if anything do you think is valuable or important in religion?," and "What does it mean to you to be religious or to be a spiritual person?" were a few of the questions asked. All are quite abstract and contain nuanced qualifications in their syntactical construction.

The settings in which the NSYR interviews took place may have also disadvantaged poor adolescents and made them less comfortable sharing their views. Here is why: the interviews usually occurred in public places such as libraries, which working-class kids are less familiar with than their more privileged peers.[64] Poor kids are likely to feel uncomfortable when they are removed from their accustomed bounded spatial contexts. Finally, the types of questions asked in the interviews were likely better-suited for middle- and upper-class kids because they were asked about individualistic orientations and values. Poor kids are more likely to feel comfortable in interactions oriented toward collective values and goals, which is not what these interviews stressed.[65]

In Figure 2.1, I compare an excerpt from Michael's interview to excerpts from an interview with Mia, a Black female who, like Michael, is also a Black Protestant. In contrast to Michael's brief answers, Mia provides elaborate answers, even clarifying some of the questions before answering. Readers might wonder if the difference in their speech pattern reflects gender differences—perhaps Mia elaborates more because she is a girl. But judging from interviews with Anthony and Jacob, boys are not reluctant to provide elaborate answers, often giving even more involved answers than girls. The key difference between Mia and Michael is that she grew up in a

Michael (Poor, Black)	Mia (Professional Class, Black)
I: Do you think of yourself as a religious or spiritual person?	*I: Do you think of yourself as a religious or spiritual person?*
R: Yes.	R: Yeah.
I: In what ways?	*I: In what ways?*
R: Well everything that I do I base it on Christ and on God, because that's the way I was raised.	R: Um, I've been brought up to believe that, to believe in God and to believe in Jesus Christ and so yeah, I, I feel that you know my beliefs are an important part of my life.
I: Okay. When you think about God, what do you think of? Who or what is God to you?	*I: Okay. And ah, when you think about God, what do you think of?*
R: God is everything to me	R: Mm, I, I think of a good friend that may not, you may not be able to see him but you know he's there, he's always there to listen. You know.
I: Do you tend to think of God as personal or impersonal?	
R: Personal.	
I: Do you think God is active or removed from human life?	*I: How often, how involved or active would you say you are in religiously, or in spirituality?*
R: He's active.	R: Um, by active, do you mean how many times do I go to church or, active you mean how?
I: Okay do you think of God as more loving and forgiving or demanding and judging or something else?	*I: Um, it can mean that, it could also mean, other people, there are very formal ways in which people are religiously active but there are also kind of informal ways that aren't so rigid, so you know*
R: Loving and forgiving.	
I. Have your religious beliefs changed over time?	R: I, religion is a big, like is, is, like I say my prayers every night you know and I, we bless the table before we eat, you know, so. It, it affects my life every day in some where, in one way or another, you know, so it, it's always there.
R: No.	
I: Okay. How involved or active would you say you are in religion?	
R: Very active.	*I: Okay. Do you ever um, well what, if anything, do you think is valuable or important in religion?*
I: How important or central do you think your religion is in your life?	
R: Very important.	

Figure 2.1 Comparing language patterns by socioeconomic status.

professional-class family in Maryland. Her mother has completed some graduate school and works as a healthcare consultant at a clerical shipping company. Her father has a master's degree and works as a regional manager for a small hi-tech company, where he sells equipment for genetic research laboratories. Together they earn over $100K, and as a result, Mia was raised in relative affluence. This is reflected in her speech patterns and is especially evident when compared to Michael.

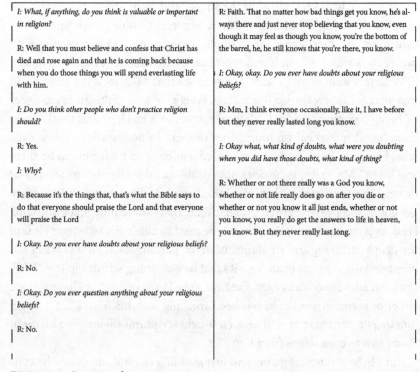

I: What, if anything, do you think is valuable or important in religion?

R: Well that you must believe and confess that Christ has died and rose again and that he is coming back because when you do those things you will spend everlasting life with him.

I: Do you think other people who don't practice religion should?

R: Yes.

I: Why?

R: Because it's the things that, that's what the Bible says to do that everyone should praise the Lord and that everyone will praise the Lord

I: Okay. Do you ever have doubts about your religious beliefs?

R: No.

I: Okay. Do you ever question anything about your religious beliefs?

R: No.

R: Faith. That no matter how bad things get you know, he's always there and just never stop believing that you know, even though it may feel as though you know, you're the bottom of the barrel, he, he still knows that you're there, you know.

I: Okay, okay. Do you ever have doubts about your religious beliefs?

R: Mm, I think everyone occasionally, like it, I have before but they never really lasted long you know.

I: Okay what, what kind of doubts, what were you doubting when you did have those doubts, what kind of thing?

R: Whether or not there really was a God you know, whether or not life really does go on after you die or whether or not you know it all just ends, whether or not you know, you really do get the answers to life in heaven, you know. But they never really last long.

Figure 2.1 Continued

But do Michael's terse responses mean that he is not living a God-centered life? It does not appear that way. Michael's view of God may not be notably elaborate, but his point is loud and clear: "God is everything to me . . . Everything I have [is] because of Him." He credits God with keeping his grandmother on this earth for 80 years, and God wakes him up every morning. He talks with God regularly, asking God to help him find his way and do the right thing.

Michael thinks adults would describe him as a good kid: "They can trust me and I'm responsible and I do my best to be the best," he explains. Michael is very cooperative, regularly helping out at home and church: "When I'm asked to do something like that, I never turn it down . . . it makes me think that God has specifically wanted me to do that [what is asked]," he says. He is also respectful of authority. His mother's approval is of the utmost importance to him, and he repeatedly brings her up throughout his interview. The idea of lying to his parents makes him feel guilty, a feeling that he says comes from "my heart." He also really admires the pastor of his church and his wife because they help keep kids "off the street" and from "doing things that we shouldn't be doing." The kinds of things he gets in trouble for are fairly minor compared to other teens: for example, recently he was out playing with firecrackers with his friends and came home late without having left a note.

With this kind of attitude, it is easy to see that Michael is the kind of kid that teachers appreciate having in class. He is a kid who makes their job easier by being compliant. Indeed, Michael respects his teachers and thinks most are a "good influence" on him: "They're there to do their job to teach me what I need to know and give me an education, and it's for me to be there and listen." Michael says he does not cheat—nor does he use any alcohol or drugs: "That's something that I was raised around [that alcohol and drugs are not good] and I've never used stuff like that. That's something that I won't do." He does go to parties but doesn't feel the need to take risks and steers clear of the people drinking and smoking out in the parking lot. It's not that he's not presented with the opportunity—it's that he has strong self-discipline: "Well, I've been asked to do drugs and I've been asked to have sex, but I haven't done either of them." Recently, he has been working with his friend to try to get him to quit smoking pot, and he even sought scriptural advice from his mom about how to counsel his friend.

But Michael's choices go beyond just avoiding alcohol and drugs; he consciously chooses whom he associates with, knowing that they could have an impact on his academics. "One of my cousins kind of slacked off and that was kind of one of my role models and stuff. 'Cause we was in the same grade, we was real close, a basketball player, and we played and stuff, we was close, and with him stopping [high school] and stuff we kind of slacked off. I kind of moved away from him because I didn't want to get involved with that."

Michael received Bs and Cs as a 15-year-old but then improved to As and Bs by his senior year. Tellingly, during that time span Michael opted in and took ownership of his religiosity. As he explained, "In the past couple of years, [I've become] more religious because I moved to a new church [and] I was able to understand everything better, which has made me more religious. [In my old church], I didn't really understand what was going on; I was just going through my mama's thing." Now it's become his thing, too, and he wants to go to church even more.

How much of an academic advantage did Michael's growing religiosity give him? Quite a bit: "I'm the first male on my mother's side to graduate. Out of like 30 men, uncles and cousins and things like that, I'm the first one. I'll be the first to attend college on my mother's side also and so that's a big thing in my life that

I'm happy about." Despite the various obstacles that Michael had to overcome, he achieved his academic goals—goals that prove elusive for many African American teens like him in similar circumstances who lack the abider advantage.

The Abider Advantage

In sum, abiders have a remarkably consistent narrative about the strict boundaries of their religion and how they applied those boundaries to their lives outside of church. How does all of this translate into higher grade point averages (GPAs)? It's not that God intervenes and answers their prayers before taking a test—in fact, scholars have found little evidence that religiosity is linked with higher test scores.[66] With one in four teens being abiders, it also is not the case that somehow abiders are on average more intelligent. The truth of the matter goes back to the hidden curriculum. It turns out that grades are not simply based on ability and performance on tests and assignments, but at least partly dependent on teachers' subjective assessment of students' demeanor.

Imagine yourself as a teacher of 30 rambunctious high schoolers. In this mix, you happen to have a few kids who demonstrate exceptional self-control. They become quiet when you tell them to, they don't act out, and they are kind. They may not be the most creative or critical thinkers, but they listen, work relatively hard, and don't complain. If like most teachers you are simply trying to get through the day and teach your students, you love these kids because they make it easier for you to do your job. And you reward them—consciously or not—for being good rule followers. You give them better grades because you want to reinforce their good behavior. Abiders do well not because they are smarter or more capable. They get better grades because they are better at following the rules.

Because our public schools were founded with a religious mission, schools (and teachers in them) continue to teach children Protestant and middle-class standards of cultural and religious propriety. They want children to follow the rules, be self-disciplined, and respect authority. This is constantly reinforced through the rules, routines, and regulations of the hidden curriculum. As it turns out, children who regularly attend church, read the Bible, pray, and see God as the ultimate authority—namely abiders raised with religious restraint—come to school with a leg up over other students. They have already learned the rules and moral standards on which schools are founded through the moral directives of their religious teachings. As the interviews show, the God-centered self-concept of abiders leads them to be highly conscientious and cooperative. These traits are not just valued in church—they are also highly valuable for academic success. In short, abiders are likely to have an academic advantage because religion and schools are complementary institutions. Adolescents who thrive in one institution are likely to thrive in the other.

So far, it's a plausible and even persuasive story. But a logical question to ask is if there's anything more than anecdote to back it up. Is there quantitative data to support my claim about the abider advantage? Do abiders in fact earn better grades than nonabiders?

To figure this out, I analyzed adolescents' high school grades using NSYR survey data. Specifically, I compared the probability of abiders and nonabiders reporting top grades—"all" or "mostly" As. On average, I found that abiders had about a 10% advantage, which statistically is quite substantial. To put it in concrete terms, imagine that you had a class of 100 high schoolers. If they were all nonabiders, 14 of them would earn As. But if they were all abiders, 24 of them would earn As. This means that 10 additional students were now bringing home good report cards to their parents.[67] But we all know that earning all As is difficult, so I also investigated what would happen if you expanded the criteria for top grades to include all As, mostly As, and As and Bs. Abiders were still more likely to earn these good grades. Imagine the same class of 100 nonabiders—now 45 of them would earn As or As/Bs. But in a class of 100 abiders, 57 of them would earn As or As/Bs.

If the thought of abiders having a 10% advantage doesn't seem significant, consider this: the probability of a socioeconomically highly privileged student earning As is 22%, compared to 10% for an underprivileged student. Thus, abiders have about the same amount of academic advantage over nonabiders as students in the top 25% of the socioeconomic distribution have over students in the bottom 25%. Thinking back to the beginning of this chapter, you might even be tempted to go so far as to describe the abider advantage as a form of "academic" mobility.

How does this new insight about abiders improve our understanding about who does well in school? First, research shows that girls earn higher GPAs than boys,[68] and my data reflect this trend as well. Girls' academic advantage is often attributed to gender socialization, which means that girls are raised to follow rules set by adults and more likely to want to please others. Our societal expectations for girls are very similar to the expectations of abiders raised with religious restraint. Since girls are already being taught to follow rules and seek approval, then deeply religious girls are hearing this message twice as loudly—and their level of conscientiousness and cooperation skyrockets. Academically, you would expect abider girls to be at the top of the heap—and this is exactly what the data bear out. Abider boys also fare better than nonabider boys because religion is encouraging them to be conscientious and cooperative.

Second, research shows that White children earn better grades than Black and Hispanic students, and my data reflect this trend as well. This has to do with several factors, including the accumulation of multiple decades of past economic, political, and educational neglect.[69] Racial and ethnic minority students regularly confront discrimination and marginalization in schools that depress their academic success.[70] Layering on the abider advantage, we see that abiders across all racial groups fare better than nonabiders.

Third and most important is what happens when we layer the abider advantage onto the story of social class. We already know that children from more socioeconomically advantaged families earn better grades because they have access to a variety of resources.[71] This is reflected in my data as well. Figure 2.2 shows that the likelihood of earning top grades increases as socioeconomic status increases. Layering on the abider advantage, we see that abiders in all social class groups fare better than nonabiders of similar social origins. The abider advantage is so powerful that it makes working-class and middle-class abiders perform as well as nonabiders from the professional class.

Figure 2.3 depicts this story in a slightly different way. Here I look just at family income rather than grouping people by socioeconomic status. But the

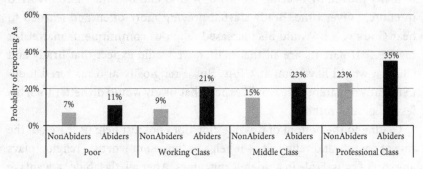

Figure 2.2 Abiders within each social class group are more likely to report earning grades in the A-range.

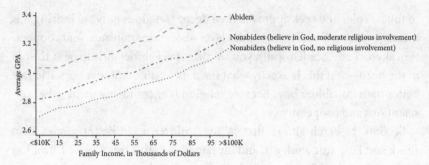

Figure 2.3 Abiders report better grades than nonabiders at all income levels.

story remains the same: grades and family income are positively correlated, and abiders earn better grades than nonabiders at all income levels.

Just a Family Matter?

At this point, readers might wonder how much of the abider advantage is driven by parents. They might find themselves asking, "Are religious kids getting better grades because they have the kinds of parents who sit with them to do their schoolwork or who attend PTA meetings?" After all, I have made a strong case in this book about the outsized role of class-based parenting styles. This should lead us to wonder whether religion plays a role independent of parents. Imagine two brothers—Clayton and Brady—raised by the same biological parents. Their parents were moderately religious, and the family occasionally went to church. Brady felt particularly moved by hearing the word of God and became more involved in church. Over time, Brady started praying more often and learned to hear God's voice. Would his increased religious commitments matter for his GPA? If parents are all that matter, we would expect that Brady and Clayton would have similar GPAs. But if religiosity also mattered independently of parents, we would expect that Brady would do better than his less religious brother.

Getting to the bottom of this question does not just help us tease out the role of parents and religiosity—it helps us figure out whether religion plays any sort of causal role in academic outcomes. After all, the abider advantage could be completely spurious.[72]

Spurious relationships often have the appearance of one variable affecting another, but there is a third variable causing the relationship. This third variable is known as a confounder. In this case, perhaps religious adolescents earned better grades because of some factor at play that can't be captured because it is not measured in the NSYR survey—making it only look like there's an abider advantage. This is a very legitimate concern because there are aspects of adolescents' families and neighborhoods that are especially difficult to measure through surveys.

But studying siblings allows us to overcome this problem. Because siblings have similar family characteristics, it doesn't actually matter whether we can measure all the family characteristics that could lead to academic success.

Let me illustrate with another example. Imagine that we are interested in figuring out how job applicants' personality is related to the number of job offers they get. We could analyze surveys that measure job applicants' personalities and also try to account for all the other things that are related to getting a job, such as their educational history, their physical appearance, and their age. Let's say you found that confident people are more likely to get job offers. But might these confident people come from particularly well-connected families? What you have on your hands is a potentially spurious relationship where confident job applicants happen to be more connected through their parents and can get jobs more easily. But if you analyzed data with siblings and still found that the more confident sibling got more job offers, you wouldn't be so concerned that it was the result of their parents connecting them with their contacts.

Using sibling data is an ideal way to tease out the effect of families versus the effect of religiosity. Would the sibling who was more religious (according to survey measures) fare better in school than the sibling who was less religious? All other external factors being equal, does being an abider actually give students an academic advantage?

It turns out that between two siblings, the more religious one does earn better grades than the less religious one. In a study I conducted with the psychometrician Ben Domingue and sociologist Kathy Mullan Harris (who was the Principal Investigator of Add Health), we found that the effect of religiosity on high school GPA was not driven purely by shared family characteristics.[73] Our findings provide the strongest evidence thus far that the effect of adolescent religiosity has some causal influence on one's high school GPA.[74] (See the Appendix for a more detailed discussion of the methods, data, and findings of this study.)

Of course, even accounting for shared family characteristics does not rule out the possibility that abiders get better grades because of personality differences.[75] In other words, abiders just might be the type of people who are naturally inclined to follow the rules. People who are inclined toward being "risk-averse" or "conformist" may opt into religion because it aligns with their preference for structure and routine. If this is the case, it would mean that abiders don't learn to be rule followers from religious teachings—they are already inclined to follow the rules in the first place. Yet even if this were the case, it does not undermine my central point: regardless of what led them to behave the way they do, abiders earn better GPAs.

In sum, the fact that abiders earn better grades in school says just as much about the power of a God-centered self-concept as it does about the cultural context and reward structure in schools. In the words of sociologists Annette Lareau and Erin Horvat, in schools "not all cultural displays are equally valued."[76] We know that school personnel give unequal weight to students' actions based on their social class, race, and gender. But as this chapter reveals, students who are raised with religious restraint also act in ways that gain the attention of school personnel—and this leads to them reaping an academic advantage. And this advantage persists even after accounting for race, gender, and social class.

3

A Domino Effect

Teenagers across the class and religiosity spectrum are aware how much their academic success in high school matters. It should come as no surprise that teens raised in the professional class make this connection, like 16-year-old Lorraine, who linked her grades with her future life: "If I keep my grades up, then I'll have a pretty promising life." Fifteen-year-old Victoria whose family is professional class also linked high school success to life prospects, saying "I want to go somewhere in life and I know that to get anywhere in life, you have to have a good education." But kids from less privileged families also know that academic success in high school matters. When asked, Hunter, a middle-class 17-year-old, confessed that he cared "a lot about doing well in school 'cause it means so much to my future." On the cusp of graduating high school, a working-class 17-year-old named Paul looked back over his time in school and put it this way: "I really care about [school] 'cause, you know, I think it affects college and everything like that, 'cause I do want to go to college. I think it's pretty important to have good grades." Even poorer kids like 16-year-old Bella who don't necessarily plan to attend college know they need good grades to graduate from high school: "I care [about doing well in school] so I can graduate." Teenagers from across class groups are not oblivious to the role that grades play in setting them up for college and life after college.

But is it actually true? Do better grades in high school translate to better college and life prospects? Does the abider advantage in high school linger in the years that follow graduation?

It turns out that someone's high school grade point average (GPA) is among the strongest predictors of academic success after high school.[1] Unsurprisingly, students who do better academically in high school are more likely to be told by teachers and college counselors that they are "college material." They begin to see themselves as having what it takes to get into college and make going to college part of their future plans. Once enrolled in college, students with higher high school GPAs complete more years of college. This is true despite the very different unwritten curriculum in college—a curriculum quite counter to the messages abiders have been receiving. All in all, there apparently is a domino effect in play: teenagers raised with religious restraint earn high grades in high school, and their higher GPAs mean that they go on to complete more years of college than nonabiders.[2]

College Counts

Before I dive into the details of these findings, I want to spend some time describing the role that college plays in the lives of Americans. Throughout this book, I have used the metaphor of a road to talk about the academic trajectories of American teenagers. The idea of a road emphasizes a very important point: education during the early years of life lays the groundwork for educational trajectories over the course of their lives. Although I focus on the middle and especially the high school years, the road to college begins all the way back at birth. The first 5 years are a crucial time for early skill development, setting children up for success in the K–12 years.[3] Already by kindergarten, many children lack the necessary academic and social skills that they need to succeed in school. By fourth grade, two-thirds of children have fallen behind so far that they are not proficient[4] in math and reading.[5] Students who fail to reach this critical milestone are more likely to falter in the later grades and drop out before earning a high school diploma. The data show that children who do not read proficiently by third grade are four times more likely to leave high school without a diploma than children who are reading proficiently.[6] And those who don't complete high school don't complete college, and as a result they face a lifetime of struggle, including considerably higher chances of incarceration. For example, a 2009 study by researchers at Northeastern University found that high school dropouts were 63 times more likely to be jailed or imprisoned than college graduates.[7]

However, children who are proficient in math and reading are much more likely to do well academically throughout high school. And academic success in high school is hugely important because it positions young people to apply to, enroll in, persist through, and graduate from college. As 14-year-old Chase said upon entering high school, "I think it's important to go to a good college, get a good job, and you need good grades in school to do that." And Chase is right—graduating from college leads to all sorts of beneficial outcomes for students.

Why is college so important?

Americans with a bachelor's degree fare better in several ways. First, they have better labor market prospects and earn more money. As noted in the Introduction, individuals who have a bachelor's degree earn more than twice as much as people who didn't complete college, and of the 16 million new jobs created, only a minuscule fraction could be obtained with only a high school diploma.[8] These differences amount to huge income gaps.

What is it about college that makes it so consequential, especially for the labor market? This question is hotly debated among scholars. The most common explanation is that college builds human capital. Human capital refers to the knowledge, skills, and competencies that a person has that make them more productive. These factors enable people to work and thereby produce economic value.[9] A common argument among economists is that going to college is a worthwhile investment because it increases one's productivity. In other words, people learn things in college that help them in the workplace.

But some scholars are skeptical that college really builds human capital. After all, so many people end up in jobs that have nothing to do with what they learned in college. These scholars argue that a college degree is valuable because of its "signaling" effect. Economist Bryan Caplan makes this point loud and clear in his book, *The Case Against Education: Why the Education System Is a Waste of Time and Money*. The primary function of education, Caplan says, is not to enhance students' skill set. Instead, a college degree "certifies" their intelligence, work ethic, and conformity—in other words, it signals the qualities of a good employee. He points to the fact that decades of growing access to education have not resulted in better jobs for the average worker but instead in runaway credential inflation. We live in a world where employers commonly reward workers for costly schooling they rarely if ever use.

Regardless of the source of the benefits a college degree confers, those benefits do not stop with advantages in the labor market. Americans with college degrees live longer and healthier lives than those who do not. Now it's true that people around the world are living much longer than they used to, and since 1900 the average life expectancy in the United States has jumped dramatically from 49 years to 79 years. With each passing year, a newly born child lives on average about 3 months longer than those born in the prior year. If this continues, it means that by the middle of this century, American life expectancy at birth will be 88 years, and by the end of the century it will reach triple digits.[10]

But life expectancy isn't rising for all groups—it's only rising for individuals with more than 12 years of education, that is, those who continued their education after high school. For those who didn't continue to college, life expectancy has plateaued.[11] Nowadays, a college graduate lives about 9 years longer than someone who did not complete high school.[12] But it's not just that college graduates live longer lives; that would hardly be something to crow about if college graduates lived an extra 10 years bedridden. It's that they live healthier lives as well.[13] There's lots of different ways this happens. For example, by earning more money, more educated Americans gain access to health-improving resources and surroundings. This means they are more likely to live healthy lives. People with higher rates of education are less likely to smoke, be depressed, have heart disease, and have high HDL—all factors that significantly reduce the risk for cardiovascular disease.[14] They also have better access to psychosocial resources and a stronger sense of control and social support, both of which are helpful in dealing with health shocks that come later in life.[15] Individuals with more education are also better prepared to make use of new technologies and to adjust to changing environments, such as a new job or life after retirement.[16] All of these advantages that accrue to college-educated adults translate to longer and healthier lives.

While writing this book, I worked as the Education Fellow at the Stanford Center on Longevity. I was part of a team of scholars from across disciplines—medicine, demography, financial security, environmental science, fitness, and psychology—who were brought together to think about a "new map of life." What would it take to reimagine a society in which many people are living to 90 or even 100? Yet as we were researching how our respective domains fit into this map of life, education kept popping up. The number of years Americans spend in school matters for their health, financial security, and even psychological well-being. After another one of these connections came to light, one of my colleagues turned to me and said, "It looks like all roads lead back to education."

Going and Graduating

It's clear that additional years of schooling matter. Do abiders take advantage of this fact as well?

One way to find out is to return to the Add Health analysis of siblings that I described in Chapter 2. Recall that in this analysis, my coauthors and I were holding constant the role of families to investigate whether children's religiosity yielded better academic outcomes. I intentionally use a more causal term like "yielded" because analyses of siblings that use statistical models with family fixed effects do suggest causal processes. In our study, we examined siblings who had different levels of religious commitment to see if they did better academically. In the fictional example I described in Chapter 2, Brady had become significantly more religious than his brother Clayton and was earning better grades. The question I'm now asking is whether Brady will complete more years of education than Clayton 10 years down the road, or will Brady and Clayton complete similar levels of schooling since they were socialized in the same family environment and shared so many family characteristics?

The answer is that (as was the case with grades) religiosity in adolescence does have an effect independent of family background—it leads to more years of schooling. My analysis of the Add Health data shows that on average abiders like Brady would complete more years of education than their less religious sibling. The sibling study also reveals why more religious students complete more years of education: because they have better GPAs in high school.[17] More religious students are more academically prepared for college—or they can at least signal to college admissions counselors that they are more academically prepared.

~

The importance of these results becomes clearer against the background of college completion generally. Among US adults over age 25, about one-third have earned a bachelor's degree.[18] The National Study of Youth and Religion (NSYR) data are on par with this, with 36% of respondents earning their bachelor's degree (or more) by 2016 (when they were between 26 and 31 years old). But the rates vary drastically by whether or not they were raised with religious restraint. Among nonabiders, 32 of every 100 nonabiders earn a bachelor's degree. But among abiders, the rate was much higher—45 of every 100 earn a BA. That means abiders are about 40% more likely to earn a bachelor's degree.

But that's just for the population taken as a whole. If you subdivide these rates by demographic characteristics, you see a more complicated picture emerge. One factor that often is pointed to in educational attainment is race. In the United States, 44% of Whites have earned a bachelor's degree, which is about twice the rate of Blacks (23%) and Hispanics (21%). The NSYR data are comparable: 42% of Whites, 21% of Blacks, and 20% of Hispanics have earned bachelor's degrees. But does this change when we break it out by abider status? Among Whites, the difference is very large: 53% of White abiders get a bachelor's, compared with 38% of White nonabiders. Among Blacks, there is also a difference, though not as big: 26% of Black abiders get a bachelor's, compared with 19% of Black nonabiders. Hispanic abiders do not see a benefit: both abiders and nonabiders have a bachelor's attainment rate of about 20%. It doesn't seem like race offers a clear explanation for the abider advantage after graduation.

What about gender? In 2016, about 39.5% of 25- to 29-year-old women and 33% of men had completed a bachelor's.[19] In the NSYR, similar proportions held: 38% of women and 33% of men completed college by 2016. There is also a clear abider/nonabider divide: in the NSYR, abiders did better regardless of gender. Among women, 46% of abiders got BAs versus 35% of nonabiders. Among men the difference was even larger: 45% of abiders got BAs versus 30% of nonabiders. My analysis of the interviews suggests that female abiders see slightly less of a bump than male abiders because the dispositions that religious restraint promotes—conscientious and cooperative behavior—are more common among females. In other words, girls already tend to be con-scientious and cooperative even without religious restraint. But like race, gender didn't open any doors with respect to understanding the abider ad-vantage when it came to educational attainment.

But a very different story emerged when socioeconomic class was consid-ered. There I found dramatic differences in bachelor's attainment—though only for certain groups. In the US population, children who grow up in the top quartile of the income distribution are about three to four times more likely to complete a bachelor's degree than those in the bottom quartile.[20] The NSYR data align with this broader national trend: 63% of teens from professional-class families earned a bachelor's, and 15.5% of teens from poor families earned a bachelor's. We saw that breaking out the abiders versus nonabiders for the entire NSYR sample shows a clear difference where abiders are much more likely to earn bachelor's degrees. Yet there is not a large difference between abiders and nonabiders when we look at teens from the professional class: 62% of nonabiders earn a bachelor's, with the percentage only nudging up to 65% for abiders. The takeaway is that among teenagers who come from families belonging to the professional class, abiders don't have much of an educational advantage when it comes to higher education.

To understand why professional-class abiders are not seeing a bump in educational attainment, I analyzed interviews with 77 professional-class youth (36% abiders, 64% nonabiders). Almost all 77 respondents aspired to complete college, and in some cases, even were looking ahead to graduate school. These youth did not make an explicit connection between their social class position and their educational aspirations, but it was clear that almost all of them saw a college degree as a necessity for achieving the type of life they imagined for themselves. In Chapter 5, I will explore some surprising nuances about this by describing what kinds of colleges they imagined themselves attending and how they saw college fitting into their life. But the key takeaway for now is that professional-class teens generally plan to go to college regardless of how religious they are.

On the face of it, this fact should not be that surprising. For these professional-class youth, college is not just a dream. Both abiders and nonabiders have the knowledge and resources it takes to get to get into college. As it turned out, all but four of the 77 adolescents interviewed wound up enrolling in college, and most of them earned a bachelor's degree. Nor is it all that surprising why this group has such high educational attainment rates: they have an added monetary advantage. While their high school grades matter, even those with mediocre grades in high school find a way to get to college.[21] One reason is because universities sometimes accept applicants who are subpar students as long as they can pay full tuition.[22] Although professional-class nonabiders are still less likely to have stellar report cards compared to abiders, it doesn't really hurt their chances of college admission as much as it would for youth who weren't in the professional class. For a teenager from the professional class, the road to college is wide and relatively smooth. Even when teenagers from this group hit bumps in the road, they typically find an on-ramp back onto the path. Consider the case of David, the son of a physician who was expelled from his private school after cursing out a teacher. For kids like him there are second and often third chances—other private schools who are willing to take a "chance" on him as a full-pay student. Even with an expulsion on his record, David still managed to get into a good college and then even went on to law school.

There is one other socioeconomic group of adolescents who also don't see a bump from religiosity when it comes to educational attainment after high school: poor teens. Even when you break out abiders from nonabiders, there's no significant difference from the national average of 15.5%: among abiders, 15% earn bachelor's degrees, compared to 19% of nonabiders.

Why don't poor abiders see an educational attainment bump either? To figure this out, I analyzed interviews with 28 poor youth (29% abiders, 61% nonabiders). Doing so helped me see just how rutted with potholes the road to college for kids from poor families is. Over a quarter (29%) of these poor teenagers didn't even start college. They either struggled too much academically in high school or their lives were so economically precarious that college felt completely out of reach. The guardrails of religion are not strong enough to help these poor teens overcome these life changes.

Daisy is one example of what happens to teenagers relegated to the poverty lane on the road to college. She is a 14-year-old African American girl whose mother earns only $15,000 per year. Daisy struggled in both middle and high school, failing ninth grade twice. Likely one reason why she struggles academically is because she cuts school regularly. Daisy's poor academic performance means that she will not qualify for scholarships, and paying for college is not an option. By 16, Daisy develops a substance abuse problem and smokes cigarettes and marijuana daily. She becomes sexually active and gets pregnant at 17. This motivates her to complete her GED, but her life is too unstable and economically precarious to attend college. She moves between homes while working in the security department of a bus/train terminal. In her early twenties she has another child and is the primary caretaker of her children. Worried about paying her next bill, college is simply not something she can afford to pursue.

Tim's economically precarious life also makes college feel out of reach. A 15-year-old White male, he lives in a small rural town and is constantly moving with his mom from one mobile home park to another. She has a high school diploma and earns about $15,000, while his father has a drinking problem and flits in and out of the picture. His mom homeschools Tim so that he doesn't have to keep moving between schools and because he struggles with dyslexia. Like other kids who grow up in impoverished and unstable households, Tim has trouble thinking past tomorrow. For Tim, the road to college feels inordinately steep. He doesn't even think that college is accessible to people like him: "It's very hard for people who don't get grants and things like loans [to go to college]," he says. During his teen years Tim seemed clueless about the college process, unaware even of the presence of a public university in his hometown. When questions about college came up, he said he never really thought about anything related to it.

But is it not just college that Tim doesn't think about: his entire future is a blank to him. Tim can't imagine his life beyond next week, as evidenced by

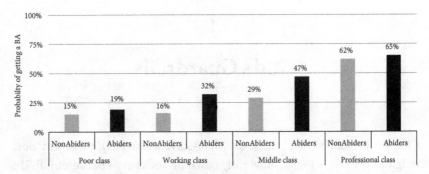

Figure 3.1 Working-class and middle-class abiders see a bigger bump in educational attainment than do abiders who are from poor or professional-class families.

his inability to answer questions about how he might raise his own child one day. In his early twenties, he does become interested in attending the local community college to earn a culinary degree. However, a meeting with a guidance counselor deterred him after learning how hard the courses would be and that going was no guarantee of a job. At age 25, Tim is still moving between mobile home parks with his mother living paycheck to paycheck. He's mainly engaged in brief one-time gigs: "[I'm] sort of doing little odd jobs for people. Or I've worked with my dad a couple of times doing sort of lawn maintenance and putting up fences and things like that."

If abiders from professional-class and poor families do not see an educational attainment bump, then it might appear that the abider advantage ends at graduation. But teens from those groups make up only half the abider population. For the other half of teens from the working and middle class—the middle 50% of the population—abiders experience a huge educational advantage that lasts well past high school. As Figure 3.1 shows, among the middle class, abiders are over one and a half times more likely to earn a bachelor's degree than nonabiders; and the number is double for working-class abiders.

Understanding why that's the case is the focus of the next chapter.

4

God's Guardrails

Chapter 3 ended with a puzzle only half-solved. The puzzle was why does religious restraint operate differently based on social class background? The answer, broadly speaking, is because what religion offers isn't equally helpful to everyone. At the end of Chapter 3, I explain why the academic advantage for additional years of academic attainment after high school isn't strong for professional-class and poor abiders. But in this chapter, I examine why working- and middle-class kids do continue to benefit—and considerably so—from religious restraint. As we will see, religion gives these kids access to social capital, which middle- and especially working-class kids can't access elsewhere. Since boys are especially prone to getting caught up in risky behaviors that derail them from academic success, the social capital of religious communities creates crucial "godly" guardrails that help them stay on the path to college.

~

We met 16-year-old Jacob in Chapter 2. He spends a lot of time at his Catholic Church, where he goes every Sunday with his parents, siblings, and grandparents. Because he was raised with religious restraint, he was guided by his parents' rules, and he readily acquiesces to following them:

JACOB: I figure I live in their house, so I pretty much do what they say. Just to make things smoother so there's not any conflicts. You start to learn you might as well just do it. Like if you're going somewhere, you might as well just tell them where you're going and not lie because if you get caught lying it's twice as much trouble, so you might as well tell them the truth.

INTERVIEWER: Do they always ask where you're going?

JACOB: Oh yeah, all the time, like no matter where I'm going . . . Like who are you going with? The typical questions . . . [Once] mom went down to get her hair done and dad was at work and I was going downtown [but] I didn't leave a note. I was down there all day. And of course, the old man came down there looking for me . . . I should have wrote a note, and [I got] your typical parent speech.

Although Jacob's parents supported his growth in the faith, like other abiders, Jacob doesn't just acquiesce to his parents' views about religion but embraces their faith as his own. He sees religion as a bonding force reaching beyond himself and his immediate family: "I think church and religion does give you like a unity, not even family, but just like unity period." For Jacob his faith doesn't just serve as a moral compass for how he should act but is an integral part of himself. His faith is at the core of his life. When asked why religion is important, Jacob explains that it guides his life: "It gives you everything that you could use, I mean you could learn so much from it."

And learn from it he does. Jacob's religious self-concept follows him everywhere, including when he enters the classroom. It translates into effort, perseverance, and an orientation toward academic achievement. Jacob manages to do well despite going to a pretty mediocre public school where just over half the students are proficient in math and reading. In fact, Jacob gets As in his classes, working exceptionally hard and caring deeply about doing well. As he says: "I just want to do my best in everything that I can." When he got frustrated with his geometry teacher for not caring whether the students understood the material, he didn't just give up by blaming her. Instead, he took it upon himself to learn the content: "I didn't understand anything the whole year, so I had to teach myself." His teacher was stunned when he got the highest grade in the class, but Jacob is not a kid who is okay with being mediocre.

By all accounts Jacob is a clear-cut example of an abider who benefits from his religious upbringing. Like other abiders, his God-centered self-concept is clearly linked with his conscientious and cooperative behavior both in and out of school. But it turns out that what's most remarkable about his academic trajectory and key to solving the rest of the puzzle is Jacob's working-class background.

Social Capital, Network Closure, and the Abider Advantage

Children's academic success in the United States is strongly linked with the socioeconomic status of their parents. Generally speaking, the more affluent you are, the better your children will do in school and the more years of higher education they will complete. One reason why children who grow up in more affluent families do better academically is because they have access to more resources than their less affluent peers. These are not necessarily only physical or monetary resources—kids benefit from familial and communal resources that promote their cognitive or social development. For example, children from more economically advantaged families eat dinner together more frequently and have more frequent and more positive contact with adults than less affluent teenagers. Sociologists refer to these ties between people as "social capital."[1] You can think of social capital as a resource that flows through relationships with people. In relationships abundant with social capital, people trust each other, share information, feel a sense of obligation toward one another, and sanction those who don't adhere to social norms.

Why does social capital matter for academic success? It's not that more affluent teenagers eat better food because they have more meals with their family, despite the clear benefits that proper nutrition has for education. It's because when teenagers interact with adults in their home, they benefit from the knowledge and skills that those adults have. It is often at the dinner table that adults and children discuss school-related matters. Chewing on their broccoli, parents can help their children work out their school-related problem, be it social or academic. It is also at the dinner table that children informally learn from their parents as they talk about what they did at work that day or what happened in the news. Family mealtimes are an indicator of social capital because they suggest the transfer of knowledge that occurs between adults and children. Of course, it is not sufficient for adults to merely be physically present—the adults and children also need to have a good relationship. Trusting relationships lubricate the conversation that happens at the dinner table. A teenager is unlikely to share school problems or ask for advice from an adult he doesn't trust or relate to.

That's certainly the case with Jacob. As noted earlier, he has a very close churchgoing family that raised him according to religious restraint. As a result, he has a stable home life and "great" relationships with his parents. Jacob says his mom "always does what's best for me" and is always going the extra mile:

Um, like [she'll] help me out in everything. Sports, anything I needed, any help, anything. Violin, she used to run me all over for violin . . . pretty much anything that I need, she'll do her best to get it for me.

Jacob has similar praise for his father: "Whatever I need, you know, he'll do his best to get it." Jacob's description of his parents might make them sound like parents who are intentionally trying to foster their child's cognitive, social, and cultural skills—a common sign of middle- and professional-class concerted cultivation. But Jacob comes from a working-class family of farmers, with his mother also employed as a nurse while his father puts in extra hours as a meter reader at an electrical company. They aren't the type of parents who we might imagine shuttling their kids between the soccer field and violin lessons.

Both of Jacob's parents travel to his away games to watch him play, but even more important to Jacob is how his parents invest time doing things with him. This is a hallmark of raising kids with religious restraint and distinguishes his parents from those who pursue a concerted cultivation approach and offer their support from a distance. As a result, Jacob feels close to his parents: he could talk to either of them concerning "just about everything." Jacob is particularly close to his dad. "We always hunt and fish together," Jacob notes, and they also enjoy spending time collecting "shotguns and rifles." He even uses the money he earns to buy his father presents related to their activities—"stuff for trapping, stuff for fishing"—and he fondly reminisces about the day he "bought dad a shotgun for his birthday."

Relationships with adults outside the home are also an important source of network closure and matter for academic success. Consistent with other research, more affluent teenagers in the National Study of Youth and Religion (NSYR) have more adults to turn to for help than less affluent teenagers. When teenagers have trustworthy relationships with adults, they have people to turn to for help. These nonfamilial adults also provide additional oversight and influence—what sociologists refer to as "intergenerational closure"[2]— so information can be gathered and common expectations and norms can be enforced through the use of sanctions and rewards. These connections among individuals serve to strengthen the level of social capital that exists between them—in this case, between generations, that is, adolescents and adults.

This also very much describes the life Jacob enjoys. His grandmother and step-grandfather, with whom he also goes to church, live two doors down from his parents, and Jacob reports that he "works down at the farm with Pat [his grandfather] all the time, so that's pretty much at least four or five times a week with him and I go see Gram a good deal of time." For Jacob his interactions with his grandparents are another key element in his home life; indeed, he calls his grandparent's house "my home away from home." When asked if he would change anything about his relationship with his parents or his family in general, Jacob pauses, as if puzzled by the question. "I don't know . . . I sort of like my family how it is . . . I don't think I would change anything actually."

Of course, many teenagers do not live near close family members, so where might they find adult contact? The simple answer is church.[3] American religious institutions are one of the few major American social institutions that are not rigidly stratified by age and emphasize personal interactions over time. Although some religious programs are age-stratified, most central congregational functions (worship services, fellowship gathering) mix participants of all ages. As a result, youth socialize with adults and can develop relationships that cross age boundaries. And those ties generate the potential for relationships with congregants who may express care for youth. Sociologist Christian Smith, one of the principal investigators for the NYSR, stresses that adolescents' ties to older members of their congregations may also afford them access to otherwise less available sources of opportunities, resources, and information.[4] All this helps foster and reinforce the kinds of constructive life choices and behaviors that can facilitate better academic achievement.

But the benefits of the relationships forged with adults whom they meet at church is not simply a matter of opportunities for internships and the like. What really impacts the lives of these adolescents is the relatively dense networks of relational ties that permeate religious congregations. Youth who are connected to these institutions encounter adults from youth ministers to friends of their parents who notice them—to the point where they function as a surveillance network for their parents, ensuring oversight and even more importantly encouraging teenagers to follow the rules, avoid antisocial behaviors, and stay on the road to college. And just as the parents of their friends can offer support, because of the social connections forged in congregations their parents in turn offer oversight to their friends, creating a web of seemingly inescapable parenting. Because these relationships are among individuals who share a common outlook on life, in effect these adults extend the scope of the social control (in the form of religious restraint) that these adolescents experience as they grow up. Network closure therefore has far-reaching consequences for these abiders as they navigate their way on the road to college.

~

To assess network closure, the NSYR asked respondents to list their five closest friends. They then asked a series of questions about those friends, including the ties between the NSYR respondent and the friends' parents. The data show that more affluent teenagers are more likely to have more friends whose parents know their name (i.e., Jack's friends' parents know Jack by name) and more likely to have friends whose parents know their own parents (i.e., Jack's friends' parents know her parents). This means that if Jack, who is in a closed network, fails a test in school, disrespects a teacher, or gets caught smoking pot in the school parking lot, he will probably disappoint adults aside from his parents. This guilty feeling may deter him from doing something wrong. However, if Jack is in an open network and fails a test in school, disrespects a teacher, or gets caught smoking pot in the school parking lot, he will probably disappoint very few adults. Without that guilty feeling, he may not have much incentive to improve his behavior. Network closure creates conditions of increased support for and supervision of youth while encouraging behaviors that are generally considered as prosocial and positive for youth development. Sociologist Bill Carbonaro aptly titled an article investigating the relationship between intergenerational closure and educational outcomes "A Little Help from My Friend's Parents."

Lots of things can disrupt the connections to adults and flow of social capital, such as frequent moving,[5] family breakup, or the loss of important social institutions where people gather.[6] Less affluent teenagers are much more likely to experience these disruptions. Compared with middle-class teens, working-class teens' parents are more likely to get divorced, to raise children as single parents, and to move around. This forces children to repeatedly sever ties with family members, neighbors, and peers. As Tim Carney argues in *Alienated America: Why Some Places Thrive While Others Collapse*,[7] working-class families are struggling because they do not have an abundant ecosystem of social capital.

The NSYR data demonstrate this point. Overall, most working-class teenagers in the sample do not have strong social relationships with their parents (especially their fathers) or with nonfamilial adults in their communities. Without the protective web of oversight, working-class teenagers, especially boys, get caught up in risky behavior like drinking, doing drugs, and getting in trouble with the law. Without adults in their lives, they wind up falling back solely on their peers and befriend other rebellious teenagers. As a result, they suffer academically.

But there is one group of working-class kids that enjoys an abundance of social capital and network closure: abiders. Unlike their peers, working-class teenagers who live their life for God have stability, close relationships with their parents (including their fathers), and nonfamilial adult mentors. Abiders tend to live in stable home environments where there are few parental reconfigurations and few geographical moves. They also benefit from intergenerational closure, which is evident in the ties between themselves, their friends, and their friends' parents. Through this abundance of social capital, working-class abiders, who are on a fairly steep and bumpy road to college, manage to do significantly better academically than their nonabider peers.

It Takes a Village: Religious Restraint and Working-Class Boys

Let me make this point about social capital, network closure, and working-class males all more concrete by contrasting Jacob's story with that of Luca from Chapter 1. Both are 16 years old, Catholic, and live with their biological mom and dad. Like Jacob's parents, Luca's parents completed some college, but neither has a 4-year college degree. Luca's mom is a seminar coordinator and his dad is a bus operator, and together they earn just a little more than Jacob's parents. And like Jacob, Luca also lives near a university—in his case, the University of Rochester. All this is to say that Jacob and Luca are roughly identical when it comes to socioeconomic measures.

Since neither set of parents has a bachelor's degree, Luca and Jacob's road to college is fairly steep, but both know that a bachelor's degree is their ticket to economic opportunity. As Luca puts it, "I'm definitely gonna go to college, 'cause you can't get a halfway decent job really nowadays without some college education, so I gotta go." Jacob also knows that college is important for being able to get a job. At age 16, he even toys around with the idea of graduate school, musing that maybe he'll become a doctor.

Though they start out in similar life circumstances and possess similar ambitions, Jacob is the one who ends up accomplishing his educational goals. He attends a private liberal arts college close to home, making him the first person in his family to earn a bachelor's degree. He goes on to medical school and becomes a surgeon. Luca's story is quite different. He winds up enrolling in a local community college and earns an associate degree. At that point, he decides to work instead of continuing on to a 4-year college because he thinks that he has what he needs to earn a job:

If I know what I need to know and I can do what I gotta do after that, fuck college. Not that I wouldn't love to eventually, after I make some loot and got some spare time, go back and learn and take some cool classes because there's some dope classes out there, man, there's some really cool stuff you can learn, but right now I don't have time for that. I want money, I want to be able to make my money while I'm young so I have some of my youth left to enjoy pissing it away.

A few years later, Luca realizes how hard it is to secure a job without a bachelor's degree and regrets his decision to not continue. At age 21, he confesses that

> [I had a] realization that I really should have gotten a degree from college . . . the more I work and the longer that I'm, like, trying to start a family and the nice house in the burbs and stuff like that, the more I realize that it's just, it's a real pain in the ass to do that without a degree right now. I mean, if you want to work for someone. And even if you don't, it's impossible to get along without some sort of a business degree, so. It just makes things difficult.

~

How did these two boys start in similar places but end up in such different places? The typical socioeconomic explanations for their different outcomes don't hold water. We know that it's not because of financial resources, since Luca's family earns more money. We know it's not because Jacob's parents were more educated, since neither set of parents has a bachelor's degree. Could it be that Jacob went to a better resourced high school that better prepared him for college? The opposite appears to be true. Luca attended a Catholic private school where most students are proficient in reading and math. Almost all the students from his school go on to attend a 4-year college—indeed, Luca was an outlier in that regard. Meanwhile, Jacob attended his local public high school. Students from his school were much less likely to attend college, and their college readiness is reflected in their test scores: only 58% of the students scored proficient in math and 54% in reading. Based on this information, we can rule out the idea that Jacob had significantly better academic preparation than Luca that set him up for success.

It turns out that almost everywhere sociologists typically look to explain the different outcomes for Luca and Jacob the evidence is lacking—everywhere, that is, except their religious upbringing. My argument is that Jacob's success is partly a function of his upbringing—and in particular the religious restraint he was taught that made him a prototypical abider. His God-centered self-concept made him act in ways that were especially conducive to academic success. As noted in Chapter 2, doing well in school and making it to college is not just a matter of raw intelligence. It is a matter of putting in effort, being well-behaved in class, showing teachers that you respect them, and being disciplined enough to keep the end goal in mind: a college degree. The road to college is long and requires delaying gratification, which is a particular strength of religiously restrained kids like Jacob.

Luca and Jacob's divergent pathways are not an anomaly—male abiders have much higher odds of getting a bachelor's degree than male nonabiders. In the NSYR, male abiders with non-college-educated mothers had a 38% probability of earning a bachelor's degree, compared with only 23% of male nonabiders. A lot of teenagers do not demonstrate great academic potential nor do they particularly like school. But abiders do better academically because their God-centered self-concept makes them conscientious and cooperative. Added to the abider advantage (or perhaps undergirding it) is the social capital and network closure that abiders have in abundance compared to other kids. This turns out to be particularly advantageous for working-class boys like Jacob.

In Chapters 2 and 3, I showed that abiders from working- and middle-class backgrounds were faring much better academically than nonabiders from the same social class position. In fact, about 23% of abiders from working-class and middle-class families were earning great grades—the same as nonabiders from the professional class. How can such socioeconomically disadvantaged abiders be doing so well? And why does religion seem to play a different role based on kids' social class background?

The answer is linked to social capital—a key resource that contributes to children's academic success. Children who have closer ties with adults, both within and outside their own family, fare better academically. And one reason children from the professional class have an academic advantage over their less affluent peers is precisely because of social capital. Parents who constitute the professional class are part of several formal and informal social organizations through which they develop robust social ties with people who also have abundant resources. Americans from the professional class tend to live in neighborhoods populated by other members of the professional class. They tend to work in professional organizations where they interact with other members of the professional class. And they have robust social networks from college where they met—you guessed it—other members of the professional class. All of these social ties—from the neighborhood, the workplace, and the college campus—provide a web of support for professional-class parents. Whenever they need help—advice about a medical problem, advice about a child development issue, help understanding a legal contract—they are likely to have a robust network of colleagues, neighbors, and college-educated friends to turn to.

But working-class and middle-class families do not have an abundance of social capital. This is especially true for working-class families, who have even fewer ties to social institutions than do middle-class families. Over the past several decades, what few social ties they had have disintegrated even more. The workplace used to be a central social institution for working-class families, but the closing of factories and other large companies has pushed the working class into the gig economy. In the gig economy, it is nearly impossible to feel a sense of stability, to have health insurance, or to develop relationships with other colleagues. Marriage, another source of social capital, is also becoming less common in working-class communities, which means children are often being raised by single parents.

The lack of social ties has unraveled the lives of millions of working-class Americans. Since the early 2000s, just as the NSYR respondents were coming of age, an overwhelming number of working-class men started dying from opioids, alcohol poisonings, and suicide. Economists Anne Case and Angus Deaton refer to these as "deaths of despair."[8] But the despair doesn't die: it gets transmitted to the children, especially to boys who look to their fathers as role models. Unfortunately, the struggles of fathers with drugs and alcohol cast a long shadow on the lives of their sons. In the NSYR, most working-class kids looked out in the world and saw despair. They felt it physically, cognitively, and emotionally. Already by adolescence, their narratives were marked by hopelessness, sadness, anger, and risky behavior. What little hope they had for a better future usually disappears by the time they graduate from high school (if they graduate at all). By their mid-twenties, several working-class boys were on track to repeat the cycle of despair.

~

That is unless they are religious. Religion offers social capital, which working-class and middle-class children have little access to otherwise. In the absence of other social institutions, religious institutions fill an important void, serving as the one remaining set of cultural guardrails for these kids. The social ties these "godly guardrails" generate in religious communities serve as buffers that keep abiders out of despair and on track for college. They help these kids academically in creating compliant and respectful individuals who succeed in school.

Working-class kids raised with godly guardrails have an optimistic outlook on life. Instead of despair, their narratives are marked by hope, health, and happiness. They are also unlikely to get caught up in substance abuse and criminal activity. Through church, kids see examples of adults and children who are happy and not struggling with drug addiction. Religious communities also keep families rooted to a place, which helps their kids develop ties to adults who collectively watch over them. As a result of this social capital, they do not exhibit the same signs of emotional, cognitive, or behavioral despair as other working-class kids. This is largely driven by their steadfast belief in God, their desire to please God, their belief that God is watching out for them and has a plan for their lives—as well as their commitment to look good in front of their church community. They are much more hopeful about their future and more resilient because God and their fellow churchgoers are on their side. Growing up with strong religious ties sets working-class abiders on a healthy and hopeful path that helps them succeed in school.

But the benefits of godly guardrails are not distributed evenly, because not everyone's road to college looks the same. Professional-class kids don't benefit from godly guardrails as much because they already have access to social capital through other social institutions. Their road to college is already smooth, and the rails already are installed. The same is true for girls, though for different reasons. Girls are already raised to be conscientious and compliant, and so already are prone toward developing relationships with adults that constitute social capital. But godly guardrails are especially beneficial for working- and middle-class boys, who are more prone to getting caught up in risky behaviors that derail them from academic success. Access to the social capital of a religious community buffers them against this.

The impact of godly guardrails is quite evident in the cases of Jacob and Luca. Reflecting on his own academic success, Jacob himself admits that he wasn't abnormally intelligent, attributing his success instead to hard work and self-discipline:

> I'm living proof that you don't have to be smart to become a doctor. Like you
> have to have some type, but you just have to work hard. And the medical

students that come on our service, I tell them all the time, I'm like, listen. You don't have to be smart. I just want you to work hard. Don't be lazy. There are enough lazy people in this world. Don't be one of them, 'ya know? And I think that's the biggest thing. I think work ethic speaks volumes.

Although Jacob earned good grades, what is more important is how he earned them. Jacob grew up in an environment where he was held accountable by his family and worked almost daily on the family's farm. The benefits of such discipline and conscientiousness are not always immediately apparent. In fact, Luca and Jacob do not have drastically different report cards—in high school, Jacob earned all As while Luca earned As and Bs. Yet there was a profound difference in their behavior and attitude toward school, which had downstream effects. Luca described being on the honor roll, but he was also completely apathetic about academics in general:

> I don't try at all, I really don't, I don't pay attention in class, and I don't study for tests, I just pass things . . . I don't care because I have been lucky enough to be able to achieve that with a lackadaisical attitude. My teachers tell me that I'd be remarkably smart if I applied myself and I found that, for the most part, I pass everything without even trying.

Why does Luca care so little about his academics? In part it's because Luca believes he's "cracked the code" for manipulating adults. He is succeeding at school while still doing what he wants on the side, signifying low respect for authority:

> I got all the teachers in my school under my thumb because I am pretty good at talking with them and stuff and I can make them think that I'm so good just because I get good grades and stay out of trouble in school, so I'm pretty good at making a lot of adults think what I want [them] to think.

While Jacob also passes his courses, his attitude toward school is completely different, rooted in part in his very different approach toward how he treats adults—including his teachers. Teens like Jacob who have a God-centered self-concept prioritize their religious identity and behave in ways that God would approve of. As Jacob says, religious practices "make you a better person . . . You learn stuff and you just don't go out there and do immoral things and bad things." Jacob's attitude toward adults reflects his religious upbringing; rather than manipulating adults, Jacob tries to please them: "If someone is walking in, you hold the door for them, you know, it's just common sense, or they're struggling with groceries or whatever, of course you help them out. You just try to be nice to them." He helps his adult neighbors do yard work, clean their house, and "whatever they need done."

I noted in an earlier chapter that being well-behaved in class and showing teachers that you respect them are key elements to the abider advantage. Jacob, of course, does all this as a matter of course. But what's interesting in his case is to see the impact of social capital. Jacob has many adult mentors from his interactions at church, but because he's so affable and considerate his circle of mentors even includes his homeroom teacher, Mr. Martin, a man in his late twenties who used to coach Little League with Jacob's dad. Now Jacob and Mr. Martin go camping and hunting together several times a year. He also spends time with Mr. Martin's parents, whom Jacob describes as "awesome" and "a big positive." It's no wonder that with adults in his life like this that Jacob wound up a surgeon; nor is it surprising that without adult oversight and investment that Luca wound up on a quite different path.

Religious Restraint and the Friends You Make

Religious restraint is especially powerful for boys because adolescent boys tend to fall into trouble more easily. Working-class teenagers often grow up in tough communities with high rates of alcohol and drug use and crime. Since their parents haven't gone to college, chances are high they won't go to college either. For them to make it to college would be beating the odds. But a childrearing strategy of religious restraint insulates them and keeps them on a straight and narrow path—they benefit disproportionally from such guardrails as it helps pave the way to academic success.

The interviews with teens provide a general sense of who teens hang out with, but I wanted to learn more about their social networks. Do abiders like Jacob really have different social networks than nonabiders? If so, on what dimensions are they different? I turned to the NSYR survey, which asked teens to name their five closest friends and then asked several questions about each friend.

I therefore learned a great deal about Jacob's five closest friends: Tyler, Billy, Molly, Jenny, and Danny. All five attend the same school, all are White (which makes sense given that 93% of his school's student body is White), and all are involved in extracurricular activities. All but Molly share his religious beliefs, and the other four are involved in the same religious group as Jacob. Jacob talks about religious matters with all five of them. Although Tyler, Billy, and Molly use drugs and alcohol, none of Jacob's friends have gotten in trouble for cheating, fighting, or skipping school. In sum, Jacob's friends are almost all religiously involved, and while they are not perfect, none of them is at risk academically.

There are also close ties between his friends illustrating network closure. All of his friends' parents know Jacob by name, and his parents know all his friends' parents. When all those people are religious and involved in similar religious organizations, the same standards of behavior are constantly and consistently reinforced. Recall from Chapter 1 that people tend to modify their behavior to manage others' impressions of them. Since Jacob's friends' parents know his parents, and also attend the same church, it is extra important for him to leave a favorable impression. Religious restraint helps him with this. Like his friends, Jacob isn't averse to drinking now and again, but he largely steers clear of risky teenage behavior and has never tried marijuana. He has also never skipped class.

Living without a system of religious restraint meant that Luca had more room to experiment, but it also meant there was more opportunity to fall off the path to academic success. Recall that the road to college is not very wide for working-class teens, and it is especially narrow for teens whose parents didn't go to college. It doesn't take much to fail a few tests and fall behind in school. Finding another on-ramp is difficult. Often, teens whose parents haven't gone to college are also surrounded by family and friends who have not gone to college. They are more likely to repeat the pattern than to deviate from it. Without guardrails, kids can easily get caught up with peers who have fallen off the path themselves and get caught up in risky teenage behavior.

This is what happened to Luca, who does engage in some risky behavior. He drinks a few times a month, gets drunk every couple of weeks, and has used marijuana. And it's not difficult to understand why when you look at Luca's five closest friends. In some ways, Luca's and Jacob's five friends are similar. Like Jacob's friends, Luca's friend group is also racially homogenous—all of them except one are White, and all are involved in school extracurriculars. But this is where the similarities end. Unlike Jacob's friends, none of Luca's friends are religious or involved in religious youth groups. More importantly, all five friends do drugs and drink alcohol. Two of them have also gotten in trouble for cheating, fighting, and skipping school. Luca's behavior mirrors that of his friends, who are, on the whole, bigger partiers than Jacob's friends. Another difference is that Luca also has a more open network—while all of his friends' parents know Luca by name, none of his friends' parents know his parents. This means that there are no dense ties among adults, which makes it hard to enforce rules and have oversight. Luca doesn't have to work quite as hard to manage people's impressions because there is less overlap in his social worlds, and less strict communal norms of behavior.

It turns out that Jacob and Luca are representative of a larger trend among teenagers: abiders' close friends are much less likely to use alcohol and drugs, and much less likely to get in trouble for cheating, fighting, or skipping school than nonabiders' friends. This holds true even after controlling for gender, race, and parents' education and income. It is also more likely that abiders have more network closure—their friends' parents will know them, and that their parents will know each other.

Aside from the backgrounds of their five closest friends, it's also interesting to compare how Luca narrates his social ties during his interview. He describes hanging out with people with similar interests and people he thinks have gone through the same "trials and tribulations." When he looks around his community, he sees sex, drugs, and crime. One of his acquaintances is already pregnant. He knows that things have changed considerably from his parents' generation:

> It was very uncommon for guns and knives and weapons to be carried to school and for drug deals to go down in school and for kids to get shot and pregnant and get AIDS and stuff . . . society today has become so violent and so different for kids . . . it used to be a big deal for them to go make out somewhere and now people are having sex in sixth grade and stuff.

When Luca looks out at the world, he sees kids falling into trouble; and for teenagers like Luca who weren't raised with religious restraint, they haven't learned how to cultivate the corresponding self-restraint.

And like his friends who got into trouble and engaged in risky activities, Luca soon followed suit. He began selling drugs, beating people up, and double-crossing his friends—engaging in behavior that in his words involved "illegal transactions that ruined people's lives." By contrast, Jacob's religious life structures his friend networks. In his interview, Jacob describes his friends as "jocks" who play the same sports and "hicks" who hunt and fish together. The only group Jacob doesn't like are the "detention dwellers"—kids at school who "don't really care about anything" and who constantly try to start fights with Jacob and his friends. As opposed to Luca, Jacob heeds his wrestling coach's advice: "If you want to be a good person, surround yourself with good people. That's all there is to it. Don't hang out with a bunch of nobodies."

Do the Right Thing: Religious Restraint and Black Men

Although Jacob is White and Catholic, religious restraint helps teenage boys across racial groups. Cameron is a middle-class 15-year-old Black teenage boy living in San Antonio, Texas, with his mother, grandmother, and his 27-year-old male cousin, whose lived with them for the past 4 years since his mother died. His mother earned a bachelor's degree and earns about $35,000 annually working as a nurse. She works close to 80 hours a week and owns her house, but she is just breaking even financially. Given his mother's long workdays, Cameron's grandmother played a big role in raising him. While his mom earns very little, having a bachelor's degree paves the way a bit for Cameron to make it to college himself. It also makes a difference psychologically for children to attain something that their parents accomplished—it doesn't feel quite as far out of reach. This puts Cameron on the path to college, but given his socioeconomic status, there are numerous "off-ramps" tempting him on the way.

One of the biggest challenges boys like Cameron face is the lack of a father. His parents were never married and his father, with whom he has no relationship, lives in South Carolina. It has been hard for Cameron to grow up without a dad: "I just want the love and care that a father would give me," he says. It has also been quite hard because his father never helped his mom financially: "My mom had to raise me alone with only her income. She worked two jobs, she has bad legs, I mean it's just miraculous that my mom's still standing." Money is undoubtedly a struggle for Cameron's family, and he worries about his mom: "I want my mom to live out her life and be okay and I want her to slow down on her job . . . all I need is the basics. You know, food, place to live, and you know, clothes on my back, and that's it."

Cameron attends his local large public school. He plays on the football team, and most of his friends are football players. Like Jacob, he says he is one of the jocks. Compared to Jacob's classmates, Cameron's classmates are faring a little better: 73% are proficient in math, and 55% are proficient in reading. Cameron himself seems to be doing pretty well in school, describing himself as a "high B" student.

He cares a lot about doing well in school because it will put him on the path to college, something he aspires for. His interest in college is partly financially driven—he wants to be "rich" so he can provide nice things like new cars for his family. But going to college isn't just about getting rich—Cameron wants "knowledge" as well: "Knowledge is power, man." He even aspires to attend graduate school because it would help him emulate God's perfection: "I want to go beyond college. I mean nobody is too old to learn and nobody knows everything. I want to be perfect. I can't be perfect—I know God is the only perfect one. [But] I just want to be perfect."

On its own, striving to emulate God will do little to position Cameron for college. College admissions counselors, at least those working in nonsectarian colleges, won't find his faith a very compelling reason to grant him a spot in their next class. But what admissions counselors do find compelling are strong grade point averages that signal an applicant's ability to succeed in a rigorous academic environment. And since Cameron attended a school where only half of the students are proficient in reading, the B+ on his report card suggests that he is doing better than other students in his school, which admissions counselors do look favorably upon. His good report card is the key to unlocking the door to college, especially since his family has limited financial means. In more affluent families, parents can improve their children's chances of getting into college even if their child doesn't have good grades. They can pay for college test prep courses, hire personal college counselors, and enroll their children in extracurriculars that look impressive on college applications.[9] Many colleges even enroll students with subpar academic track records if they are able to pay full tuition. Doing so allows colleges to have funds to offset the cost of tuition for more academically promising students who need partial or full scholarships.

But for Cameron, grades matter a lot because his mom can't afford SAT tutors and college counselors. Nor does Cameron have the ability to pay full tuition, so he is hoping for scholarships. Yet as we've seen, getting good grades isn't just about cognitive ability. It's about showing up and staying out of trouble. It may sound simple, but millions of American children, especially children of color, struggle to attend school consistently. Consistent school attendance begins early in elementary school and gets much worse by high school. The US Department of Education considers a student who misses 15 more days of school a year to be "chronically absent." In the 2015/2016 academic year, one in six students was chronically absent, with rates considerably higher among students of color. Compared to their White peers, Black students were 40% more likely to lose 3 weeks of school or more.[10]

Chronic absenteeism, especially in the earlier grades, is generally not the child's fault. Getting to school regularly is hard for children whose parents work multiple jobs and who may have unreliable transportation. When a child is truant or consistently absent in the early years of their education, he or she is more likely to experience these problems in later years as well. Truancy that begins in kindergarten is correlated with poor academic performance all the way through high school. Children who are chronically absent in preschool, kindergarten, and first grade are much less likely to read at grade level by the third grade.[11] And as noted before, students who cannot read at grade level by the end of third grade are four times more likely than proficient readers to drop out of high school.[12]

Students with the highest truancy rates also experience high rates of school disciplinary actions. In a report titled *Point of Entry: The Preschool-to-Prison Pipeline*, the Center for American Progress explains that suspensions are the most important initial indicator of longer-term life outcomes that include unemployment, adult earnings potential, and even incarceration.[13] Students who experience out-of-school suspensions and expulsions are 10 times more likely to drop out of school than students who do not experience these punishments. And studies show that African American children are disproportionately absent, suspended, and expelled.[14] Black boys get suspended early and often, which then creates academic struggles, leading to many of the other outcomes noted earlier. Often, implicit bias among teachers and school administrators, most of whom are White, leads Black students to face much harsher consequences than White students face, even for the same infraction.[15]

As we've seen, a central aspect of the hidden curriculum is the need to follow school rules. If teachers think of you as a good and responsible kid—a kid who helps them keep order in the class so they can teach—they will probably reward you with good grades. Classroom management is one of the hardest skills for teachers to master, especially in their first few years of teaching. Teachers appreciate students who are conscientious and cooperative because it makes their job considerably easier. Good behavior can be even easier to judge than how much a student has learned. Nor is academic success just tied to grades. Teachers are more likely to help well-behaved students, check in with them, and write them strong recommendation letters for college. It's a lot easier to endorse a well-behaved student who does average on tests than a detention dweller who nails the test. Good behavior pays off, and good behavior is Cameron's strength. Cameron sees his job as a Christian at school to be "kind and nice." As he puts it: "[I] try not to get in trouble a lot. Stay cool, calm, and collected and do the best you can." When asked whether he thinks religion has anything to do with his grades and achievement during high school, Cameron says it steers him toward the good things and away from the bad things that are so easy for teenagers to get caught up in.

~

Cameron developed this attitude by being raised with religious restraint. His mother says religion is extremely important to her. She has been attending the same Charismatic Protestant church for the past 15 years, attending both weekly services and weekday events. Five other family members go there as well as those people in her immediate household. Cameron's cousin is the preacher at the church, as is his uncle. His cousin's mom—his auntie—was also a reverend and a preacher and a huge influence on Cameron while she was alive. And Cameron goes, too. Over time, he has come to see the value of religion for himself. As he explains, God is something his mother introduced him to, but as a teenager, he has to make a volitional choice to stay in a relationship with God: "My mother chooses for me before then. She teaches me so I can do the right thing and choose for myself. After she lets me go, I choose for myself if I want God or I want Satan . . . [I chose to follow God] around age 13." Nowadays being religious is very natural for Cameron. He doesn't feel like he has to work at his religious faith: "It's basically natural. Natural since my mother raised me right. She raised me [how] God told her to raise me. And it's easy. I have no problem with it."

Cameron certainly has a God-centered self-concept, one that he learned from his peers and family members. "I feel the presence of God," Cameron says. "The Holy Spirit is in the church and everything. I feel it making my eyes get watery, and I see people around me and getting their praise on and everything." For Cameron and other teens who have a God-centered self-concept, God is both personal and active: "He gives you a choice to choose evil from good. You choose [God's] side or you choose Satan's side. If you choose Satan's side, you going to be with Him for eternity and he going to torture you . . . God is judging you on how you deal with things." Cameron describes how he learned to see and feel God, which takes time and is very intentional:

> When I was young, I had no understanding of the Bible and everything. I just was sitting there looking at the preacher and everything preach. . . . These years I understand . . . I know why I'm here. You know, I try to do what he says, I can talk to God. Basically just sit on my bed look at the wall and talk to Him. And He'll talk back. And we'll be talking just like we buddies or something. I talk to Him just like He's a friend, He's a father. I talk to him like He's in the flesh sitting right there.

In fact, talking and praying to God—which Cameron treats as synonymous— has become so natural for Cameron that it happens on a subconscious level. As he answers a question about praying, Cameron says, "I'm basically praying right now . . . I could be on a different subject, like gangs or something, I could be praying in my mind without even knowing it . . . sometimes I'll be talking and then I'll catch myself talking in my head praying." He thinks praying is so effective that he wishes it would be brought back into the school: "I feel that it's [prayer] needed everywhere. That's why it needs to be in school. 'Cause after it's out of school, guns came in, a lot of drugs, drinking, after we kicked prayer out of school." For Cameron, there is a clear link between prayer and risky behavior.

Is prayer and a steadfast belief in God alone enough to alter his behavior? Like the research, Cameron knows believing is not enough. Religious attendance and religious practice reenforce his faith and undergird his actions. Attending church helps Cameron "understand why I am here . . . how God has helped me, and what the Bible is practically saying in laymen's terms." That leads him to act in a godly manner: "without prayer, thankfulness, giving, kindness . . . I wouldn't be here . . . I would be lost. Lost in this world just a soulless vessel." But going to church and learning how to be religious has had a considerable impact: "[it] influences me to be kind . . . [To] love and cherish . . . Do what I got to do. Pray, be thankful. Be kind to my fellow man." Cameron firmly believes that God has a plan, and when he has to make a tough decision, he reminds himself that "God said it wasn't going to be easy." Then he looks to God for advice: "I just listen to God, you know, I pray. I'll be like okay, God help me through this." When asked where his views of right and wrong come from, Cameron quickly points to the Bible.

At church, Cameron tries to keep the peace and act appropriately so that adults can do what they need to do. He says he is quiet and listens to the church service, and if someone asks him a question, he answers them. He sees all the members of the church as being additional mothers and fathers—they may not be blood related, but they all have a positive influence on him. His mantra is, stay quiet, treat adults with respect, and teach little kids to stay out of trouble: "I teach the little kids, don't run or anything. Don't be playing in the church, sanctuary, or anything."

Despite her 80-hour-a-week job, Cameron's mom—like other religious parents who embrace religious restraint—monitors his activities very closely. It's extremely important to her to know where he is, who he is with, and what he is watching on TV. If he wants to go to any type of party, his mom must know the parents hosting the party. Cameron feels a little suffocated by this level of strictness—"it's a little too much protection," he says:

> My mother, she has a problem with me going out and chilling with my friends and everything, that's why I have to be at school in order to chill with them. I can't be outside, I have to be at a football game or something and chill with them and everything. I just can't be outside 'cause she's afraid that something might happen. Of if I act bad and mess up some. Or break some, but you know, I'm like well I'm 15 years old going on 16, you know, and I need to you know get out and see the world.

And yet Cameron doesn't rebel or push the limit. He knows better than to cross his mom, and his attitude toward her is not one of grudging acceptance but appreciation: "I thank God that I'm here and I have a mother and family that cares for me and everything . . . they care for me enough to discipline me when I need discipline, teach me when I need teaching."

Cameron's mom takes an active role in Cameron's life, saying that it's very important for her to spend time with her son. She feels very close to him, and Cameron agrees, noting they have a great relationship: "We play around, mess around, you know, we talk, and we just chill around, watch TV, I mean we have a great relationship." He says he talks to her about everything: "There's nothing I wouldn't talk about with my mother . . . girlfriends I've had, conflicts at school, I mean it's great." Cameron says they do argue sometimes—mostly when he forgets to take out the trash or do some of his chores, but he blames these arguments on himself rather than on her: "[I'm a] teen and arrogant, and my mother is supportive [even having] raised me alone." He says he does what he is told and repeatedly says how indebted he is to her for all she has done for him: "I can't be mad at her for nothing. She's done everything for me and I mean, I'm grateful." This kind of humility is rare among teenagers and reflects an impressive sense of personal responsibility and respect for elders. Cameron shows responsibility and respect for authority in other ways, too. He and his cousin take the lead in cooking and cleaning so that when his mom comes home, she can eat before going back to work again. When his friends complain about their parents, Cameron encourages them to be grateful that their parents have found a way to feed them and keep them off the street.

Cameron's profound sense of respect for authority stems from growing up with religious restraint and opting to stay religious throughout adolescence. Cameron has developed a God-centered self-concept that makes him deeply respectful of various authority figures: "I treat them with respect, they're my elders, they're older than me . . . that's [what] they deserve . . . I treat them nice, treat them right. They come over to my house, I serve them food. If we cook something, I'll be like do you all want something to eat? You want something to drink?" He also speaks highly of his teachers—referring to them as additional "mothers"—who care a lot about him and check in with him when his grades start to slip. He can't think of any conflicts with his teachers, whom he respects a lot. He also speaks fondly of his football coach, who is like a father to him.

Cameron describes himself as very religious, having grown up with family members who "kept me in the church." When he was 6 years old, he had a revelation that God was real. Cameron recalls being sick with a 106-degree fever. He was so hot that he was delusional and almost passed out. "I was sweating like a donkey in the high desert," he recalls. He believes that it was only by the grace of God that he survived: "I learned that God exists," he said. Now Cameron feels very close to God: "I feel his presence in everything that I do. I listen to Him. If He speaks to me, I listen to Him, I do what He says." A sense of grateful obedience permeates all his actions: "I'm very religious, I pray, I give thanks to God, I go to church, and I mean everything's been great for me, you know. I'm grateful . . . If I had 10,000 tongues, man, I couldn't thank God enough for what He's done for me."

Cameron believes that religion gives him purpose and direction. "Without my religion, I don't know where I would be. I would be lost." Cameron says religion allows him to learn from the past and develop a sense of direction: "What I think is valuable is the learning. What you've learned. Learn from your mistakes. The bad things you have done and the good things you have done.

Get rid of the bad and bring the good in. Try to develop a good sense of direction." He also says that it motivates his behavior—"I try to be perfect, 'cause it says in scripture, you know, be perfect as your father in heaven is."

Tellingly, Cameron was not always so perfectly behaved. In elementary school he described himself as mean, selfish, and arrogant. He had a bad temper because kids would taunt him. As he recalls, "They would talk about my mama [and] I'd beat them up." His temper was so bad that one of his teachers was afraid of him, and not without good reason: in sixth grade he kicked a kid and broke two of his ribs.

But Cameron cleaned up his act and shed his "bad boy" reputation by middle and high school. To deal with his "anger problem," he became a choir boy: "I've had anger problems. That's why I'm a choir person now. I don't want to mess with anybody. I don't want to gang up on anybody. I try to solve problems the best way that I know how. That's why I'm quietly calm." It is not just the church choir that helped Cameron become calmer. He also joined his church's drill team that performs, which meets every Saturday to practice marching while singing or chanting in a verbal cadence for their monthly Sunday performances. But these drills have another underlying mission: they teach children discipline, obedience, and self-control.[16] The guidelines of one drill team manual I examined provide examples of disciplinary rules that members will be penalized for, including uncooperative behavior, tardiness, bad attitude, disrespect, and failure to follow directions. These are not just dispositions that help Cameron with the drill team—they go a long way to being self-disciplined and well-behaved in school.

Cameron loves the drill team and recognizes its value, saying it keeps him out of trouble. When asked how he thinks his life would be different if he was not part of the drill team, Cameron quickly replies, "I'd probably be doing something bad. Sneaking out." Throughout his interview, Cameron makes several references to the prevalence of drugs, crime, and gangs around him. He works hard to stay away from drugs and alcohol, even though they are widely available—"too available" in Cameron's words. One reason is that he tries to keep himself clean because he sees his body as a "temple": "God says your body is a temple, you have to take good care of it. You don't want to mess it up. God doesn't dwell in a dirty temple."

~

Cameron's solid performance in high school paid off. First, he graduated high school on time, which is not a given. Cameron attends a high school where most students are racial minorities. The odds of graduating from a school with such high rates of minority students are lower than the odds of graduating from a predominantly White school. For example, if Cameron were attending a school where fewer than 5% of students were racial minorities, 95% would graduate. But Cameron attends a school where most students are racial minorities. According to the National Center for Education Statistics, only about 75% of students who attend predominantly non-White public high school will graduate.[17] Cameron's odds of graduating are also lower because many of his classmates are poor. If Cameron were attending a school where less than a quarter of students were poor, about 93% would graduate. But he attends a school where two-thirds of students are poor, which puts the graduation rate at about 84%. If he were at a school where three-quarters of students were poor, the graduation rate would be even lower: 72%.

The difference in graduation rates reflects many different structural problems in the United States. One key problem is that schools with poor students are perennially under-resourced. Public schools are funded through property tax dollars. If you live in an area with expensive homes, property taxes are high, so public schools receive more money to spend on each student. If you live in a poorer area like Cameron, houses are cheaper, property taxes are lower, and there is less to spend on each student. This funding makes a huge difference. Schools need to pay for high-quality teachers, create small classes, hire guidance counselors, and provide classroom materials. Less money means lower quality schools and fewer resources to prepare students for college and to help students who are not on track to graduate.

As a Black male, Cameron faces a particularly difficult educational journey that his upbringing of religious restraint helped him navigate and overcome several obstacles. Compared with White boys and Black girls, Black boys are less likely to complete high school, less likely to start college, and less likely to earn any sort of college degree.[18] But Cameron fared better than the average Black male. He went on to a community college near his home and was able to earn his associate degree. With his associate's degree, Cameron was able to follow in his mother's footsteps and become a registered medical assistant in the pediatrics unit of a hospital. It is not a very well-paying job—he just earns minimum wage, but he finds it meaningful and fulfilling. "He [God] put me on this earth. I'm supposed to help. Not everybody can do it—not everybody can be in the medical field. I'm not here for the money, otherwise I wouldn't be at this little cheap job of mine . . . But I fell in love with these patients, and I see myself kind of trapped because of the fact that I love 'em so much—they like family." To supplement his income, Cameron works a few side jobs earning cash off the books. He also plans to continue his schooling to earn a 4-year degree.

Is Cameron doing better than his mother? Not yet. But he is faring better than his Black male peers who did not grow up with religious restraint and a God-centered self-concept. According to the NSYR survey data, 28% of Black men raised with religious restraint completed at least an associate degree, compared with 13% of Black men raised without religious restraint.

The Wages of Sin: What Happens When Religious Restraint Is Missing

But many working- and middle-class teenagers do not benefit from the kind of social capital and network closure that Jacob and Cameron had as a result of religious restraint. As a result, they are much more prone to fall into despair about their life prospects and feel hopeless. The buffer that godly guardrails provide don't just mean that early exits are avoided—it means that kids with religious restraint have a sense that their lives are headed in a particular direction. But without those buffers, these kids are more likely to suffer from emotional despair when they encounter the structural obstacles in their path.

That was certainly the case with Nicholas, who was subjected to constant moving after his parents divorced when he was 3. The divorce was partly prompted by the fact that his father was abusive and had a drug and alcohol addiction. After the divorce, Nicholas and his family moved to an apartment in a different part of town that he called "the ghetto." Everywhere he looked Nicholas saw substance abuse and described being surrounded by constant peer pressure to participate in criminal activity: "You know, like robberies, and those kind of things."

Nicholas tries as hard as he can to overcome the challenges he is facing and still do well in school, but it proves to be an uphill battle. As a 14-year-old, he cares about doing well, "because the way that you do [education] right now is the way it's going to go in the future [for you]." He explains that the emotional toll of his parents' divorce, constant moving, and economic precarity has hampered his performance:

When I had that emotional thing, my grades kind of went down, but I brought them back up. I've always struggled in math so now it's hard for me to get it back up.... I get okay grades, you know Bs and Cs... the teachers pay more attention to the kids in the higher grades at my school . . . so if I had an A and the teachers had put more responsibility on me, I would work really [hard] . . . I could probably keep the grade up and not drop down.... But I have an F in this class because when my mom split up, I had emotional problems and stuff like that.

The contrast with abiders couldn't be plainer. Abiders likely started receiving positive attention early on in elementary school, which put them into a cycle of positive reinforcement and helped them see themselves as "good students," which is itself self-perpetuating. Abiders also report being much more emotionally stable. One reason is that they always have God on their side, which seems to help them grapple with the struggles they encounter.

Parental breakup also means that new adults enter the picture, which is often even worse for the children. For example, a little while after his parents' divorce, Nicholas's mom found a new boyfriend who introduced her to drugs, which led Nicholas and his family to lose their house, move around between different family and friends, and get evicted from an apartment that was illegally being shared by 12 people. Nicholas eventually moved to Oregon to live with his mother's boyfriend's family. He described life in Oregon as being equally bad, with his mom being so depressed that she would just stay in her room for days: "She was at the point of like suicide." He recollected a particular evening where he stayed with his mom the whole night to keep her from killing herself. Nor is this the first time Nicholas dealt with suicide. Although he is only 14, Nicholas has already counseled several friends through suicide ideation: "All of my friends that I'm usually around end up being suicidal, like my best friend was suicidal in the sixth grade. I usually end up talking them out of it and being there for them."

Nicholas's life at home was so hard that he wanted to get out of the house as much as possible. He remarked that his mom is depressed so often that he is "starting to not like to be around her cause she's feeling down a lot." At 16 he got a job to help support himself and also help his unemployed mom. Reflecting on this time in his life as a 24-year-old, Nicholas describes his adolescence as "probably the most traumatic portion of my life":

There was a lot of events . . . a lot of drugs involved and they [my mom and her boyfriend] were into methamphetamine . . . it got to a point where we had people coming in and out and if the cops were driving down my street, I would think, oh, they're going to my house because usually they were. It was tough . . . I witnessed a lot of things.

Nicholas is envious of his sister, who "got lucky" because she did not have to endure much of the hardship he experienced as a teenager: "her best friend's family took her in and they took care of her until she graduated high school . . . my sister was really starting to go down this really dark path and she was doing a lot of bad things. They were able to straighten her out real quick." The difference in social capital between Nicholas and his sister literally made all the difference, as the stress he experienced early in life now casts a long shadow, whereas she is on the cusp of graduating from college. When he was interviewed at age 24 and asked how much stress he experiences on a daily basis, he remarked, "I'm paranoid Nicholas, that's what my friends call me. I'm always stressing about something."

All this stress took a toll on Nicholas's academics. At age 24, Nicholas is attending a community college off and on, though he aspires to earn a 4-year degree, which he knows will open up more job prospects: "I want to get my degree. I know I'm capable of doing a lot and I know I'm not gonna be able to really do it until I get that degree." However, Nicholas lives paycheck to paycheck and still supports his mother: "I've been able to support myself and I've also been there to take care of her. You know, if she needs something, I will provide it for her. If she needs to buy a new pair of shoes, I will go buy her a new pair of shoes." This is not what Nicholas imagined for himself when he was younger. When professional-class kids have college aspirations in adolescence, they tend to pan out. This isn't the case for many working- and middle-class kids because they encounter many challenges along the way that divert them off the road to college. As Nicholas says: "When I was fourteen, I had the whole world ahead of me and I wanted so much. I thought I'd graduate from college and be in my career and maybe be starting a family. So that's changed." In fact, that Nicholas even graduated high school is quite an accomplishment. But lacking the guardrails of religious restraint meant that Nicholas found himself at 24 feeling like his life lacked direction and purpose.

Nicholas epitomizes the despair that has rolled into working-class communities like a thick fog. Over the past few decades, working-class men have been battling with opioid addiction, alcoholism, drug abuse, and suicide.

Nicholas's father abused drugs, had an alcohol addiction, and was abusive to people. Nicholas severed ties with his father after he turned 7 and didn't see him again till he was in his twenties: "He had some serious addiction problems and alcohol problems and he's not all there at all. And so talking to him is really difficult because one minute he's really happy and the next minute he's bipolar. One minute happy and the next minute he's calling you, cussing you out, yelling." Nor is the damage drugs and alcohol has done to his father limited to just him: his actions have profoundly impacted Nicholas, who claims that in moments of rage his father has declared that "I'm his biggest disappointment." Even as an adult, his father's addiction has continued to cast a shadow on Nicholas's life:

> I talk to him every once in a blue moon, when I catch him on a good day, [but] most of the time I tend to just kind of ignore him, ignore the emails, ignore the phone calls, and it kills me. But I don't really feel like I can deal with that right now, maybe later. But right now I feel like I don't need instability in my life. I just don't need to deal with it.

~

The outline of Nicholas's story is one that is found across the nation. For example, despite living thousands of miles away in Texas, Ethan's life sounds remarkably similar to Nicholas's in California. Both boys are raised without religious restraint and spend their adolescence trying to cope with their parents' struggles. At age 16, Ethan describes his parents as constantly arguing: "I could always hear like yelling and stuff when I was going to sleep and, you know, I was pretty upset about it." Ethan's parents eventually divorced; in fact, many working-class adolescents have experienced family breakups, which are preceded by long periods of arguing and conflict that take a toll on children.

While Ethan was happier to not hear the barrage of yelling, he also missed his dad: "It's kind of disappointing not to see my dad as much," he said. And when fathers disappear, it often leads to them slipping into drug addiction. Like Nicholas, Ethan's father was addicted to painkillers. His father began taking prescription drugs when Ethan was just 3 years old after he got injured in a car accident. At age 16, Ethan observed, "He got to where he would abuse them . . . he had been struggling with an addiction for those for a long, long time." Two years later Ethan's father committed suicide by overdosing on prescription drugs.

All of this took a toll on Ethan, and by 18 he felt hopeless. In his eyes he's failing to be a good student, a good Christian, and a good guy:

> A lot of times, I get kind of hopeless, you know? A lot of times, I just have a tendency to think, you know, why am I even trying to succeed? I know I won't make it. Things like that, I lose confidence in myself. [I lose confidence in myself] 'cause just growing up I don't feel like I, well, I know I didn't meet up to anyone's expectations of me. I was supposed to be a good Christian kid, good grades, my parents just wanted me to be an average good guy, and just you know... I felt like I was being looked down upon a lot for not doing this and not doing that, and I guess, there's still traces of that in my mind.

His interview reveals several signs of behavioral despair. White working-class teens not only use drugs because of peer pressure but also to deal with apathy and sadness. During his interview he recounted a recent experience coming off a trip after eating mushrooms, and he also revealed daily pot smoking, regular cocaine use during his senior year, followed by experimenting with crystal meth. He also gets "drunk drunk" three or more times a week: "I like the alcohol reality." Ethan also admits to driving drunk and having sex without contraception—clear signs of reckless behavior. His attitude is summed up in the anecdote he told about taking a girl back to his place and then realizing that neither she nor he had a condom: "We just did it anyway. And yeah, like I knew that was wrong, I knew that was stupid, but I still did it."

The despair Ethan describes is not an individual problem. Despair can arise in networks and communities when their members are exposed to the same distressing event. In the wake of such shared exposures, average levels of despair may increase markedly in social groups and, in turn, further compound individual-level despair. For many working males, peers and other community members set the "norm," and as a result kids often grow up thinking that graduating high school is an impossible feat. Their friends are in and out of jail, their father is between jobs or not in the picture, and their home life is marked by financial struggles. It's not at all surprising to find that drugs are abused to deal with this level of despair. And kids are left to navigate these issues on their own, lacking role models and support systems to pull them out of the cycle of despair.

Ethan's academic record starts out decent but turns abysmal as he falls deeper into despair. In his initial interview at age 16, Ethan had big dreams about college. What he wanted to accomplish in life was to "make good grades," "definitely go to college," and "wind up with a career that I'm really enthusiastic about and really makes me happy." He was an A/B student and felt it was "pretty important" to do well in school: "It impacts the rest of your life." He was passionate about science and computers and was interested in going to the state's public university. However, by his junior and senior year, his grades had plummeted. In fact, he didn't graduate high school because his grades were so bad: "Junior and senior year, I just slumped really bad . . . it was just laziness I guess, I didn't really have my priorities in check . . . going out and partying all the time . . . it's not like I was stupid or anything, [but] I didn't really want to learn." Eventually, Ethan completed his GED and enrolled in the only community college he could get into. By age 21, he had not progressed very far in his postgraduate education and decided to enlist in the military instead. By age 26 he is back in community college, still hoping to one day transfer to a 4-year college.

The network closure and social capital that religious restraint offers doesn't only provide emotional stability in a life of purpose and meaning. The guardrails it erects have practical consequences as well, keeping adolescents under the watchful eye of God, parents, family, other adults, and peers. Cameron's early violent tendencies were constrained by religious restraint by the time he reached adolescence. But the lack of religious restraint for kids like Ethan and Nicholas leads to markedly different outcomes.

Back on Track: The Redeeming Effect of Religious Restraint

Some readers might wonder if the addition of religion has the power to change the path teenagers find themselves on. After all, one might wonder if Cameron's reformation was a product of him "naturally" being a good kid, and his deeper embrace of religion as an adolescent a product and not the cause of his improved grades, and so on. But a closer look at certain teens suggests that religion is not just a by-product of behavioral reformation but a driver in the process. Consider the changes that took place in Bret's life between 16 and 18.

Bret was a 16-year-old African American boy who lived with his parents and his brother (who has cerebral palsy) in Queens, New York. His other brother and sister are away at college, and another brother is working and living on his own. His parents both have some college education, but no degrees or certificates. They both work at the US Postal Service as distribution clerks, earning a combined middle-class income of $85,000 in 2003, but they live in constant fear that they will lose their house because they can't always make their payments.

Bret was not raised with religious restraint. His mother says religion is extremely important to her and attends a Catholic church regularly, but his father wasn't interested in religion. As a child, Bret would regularly attend church with his mom, but he would usually fall asleep or not pay attention. Despite his mother's best efforts to make religion a part of his life, Bret didn't opt in—he just didn't feel like God ever answered his prayers. "I used to pray a lot when I was younger but after so many years, I'm not seeing any changes. It's just like, why should I [continue]?" For 16-year-old Bret, God was "distant" and "impersonal." He summed up his beliefs this way: "I believe in God . . . but that's about as deep as it goes."

Adolescents like Bret who occasionally attend church but don't have a relationship with God don't see nearly as big of an academic advantage as those who orient their public and private life around their faith. Sociologists of religion have been debating whether it is the public or private dimension of religion that matters for things like education.[19] The public dimension refers to belonging to a religious congregation while the private dimension refers to belief in God, personal prayer, and the extent to which one sees religion as important in their life. Scholars ask is it enough to believe but not belong, or does belonging without believing confer the benefit? My research suggests that both belief and belonging are necessary. Teens who genuinely believe that God is listening to them and are part of a religious congregation that reinforces their belief are the ones who adjust their day-to-day behavior to fit their religious identity. As a result, they are the ones who stand to see the most academic benefit, as Bret himself knows. Despite his lack of faith, Bret is well aware that individuals need both the belief that comes from religious intensity and the practice found in regular churchgoing in order to change their behavior:

Most people get their self going every day just believing in the Lord, [believing that] someone was watching over them . . . Religious people usually are more happy—you get this sense of goodness and joy from them. But people who just attend church [without having belief], they're like everybody else, grumpy in the morning, you know . . . [they're] not really into the faith and believing in the Lord and following the Bible.

But without religious restraint, Bret didn't have the benefit of God's guardrails to keep him on track to college. At 16 he is on a narrow and bumpy road, earning mostly Ds. He used to be on the track team but got kicked off for failing too many classes. Nor is his poor performance attributable to the fact that he is attending a poorly run and under-resourced school. In fact, his school is an above-average public high school in New York City, where nearly all students are proficient in reading (96%) and math (97%).

Bret's bad grades are not because he has low expectations for himself. He wants to become a computer engineer and knows that will probably require him to get a master's degree: "Throughout my lifetime, people were always explaining to me how important school was and . . . that you can't really do much without it . . . I just decided to make sure that I did what I had to do in school." He sees his goal orientation as distinguishing him from his peers: "I'm the main one who knows what they want to do in the future, like I got goals already set." He credits his grandmother, the adult he speaks most highly of, with inspiring him to set these goals for himself. "That's my heart—my grandmother. I love my grandmother . . . she's just like inspiration and she always teaches me to go the right way. If it wasn't for her, I probably wouldn't even have thought about my future too much and setting goals for myself."

Nor are Bret's poor grades a reflection of his parents not caring about or valuing his education. His mom does not take a lackadaisical approach to his schooling. Bret explains that if he is late for school, "she gets real upset with me about it . . . she start giving me speeches, like I'm about to drop out or something." It's "extremely important" to her that he graduate college. Although she "rarely" talks with him about potentially sensitive subjects, such as friendships, dating, or drinking, she still monitors him very carefully. She needs to know where he is and who he is with. Bret's narrative supports this—he also says she supervises him carefully and knows when he is up to trouble. So why then is Bret doing so poorly academically?

Like many teenagers, Bret gets bad grades because he has engaged in reckless behavior that has spilled over into his school life. He gets into trouble both in and out of school, and his teachers would most definitely not describe him as conscientious or cooperative. As Bret says, his parents feel like he is "messing up" and "pulling apart his life." According to his mother, Bret is "rebellious" and has "somewhat of a bad temper." Nor does Bret talk about his parents with the kind of deference that Cameron and Jacob do. He has an especially bad relationship with his father, describing him as someone who wants "to be the ruler of the house" and is annoyed about how much he and his mom nag him about being at school on time. He describes his dad as stubborn and disengaged. Although he used to be close with his mother, Bret stopped confiding in her when she started relaying some of what they talked about to his father. When he is faced with a choice and doesn't know what is wrong or right, he doesn't go to his parents or other adults. Nor does he have a youth minister like Cameron or a teacher or coach like Jacob. He wishes teachers would be more helpful and stay after school to tutor kids or take the time to understand their problems. Instead, some "just put notes on the board, just so that they get their paycheck." Lacking adult mentors, Bret makes decisions based on the consequences of his actions and whether it will help him achieve his ends. If it's going to get him in trouble with the law, that will deter him; but if it's just going to get him in trouble with his parents, he will consider the severity of their consequences and decide if it's worth it.

Gangs, violence, and crime are rampant in Bret's community: "Anytime that something happens [around here], they [people] always go back, get a weapon . . . try to even the score, maybe even kill a person." Bret has been able to avoid the gangs but does fall prey to other risky adolescent behavior. He started sipping alcohol when he was around 10 and became a more active drinker around age 14, following the lead of the other people around him: "I don't know why I started that. I guess I just did it because my friends did it," he admitted. Just a few months earlier on New Year's Eve, he got so drunk that he passed out and his parents had to pick him up and take him to the hospital. Sometimes his excessive drinking ends in violence: "You start thinking like you just a big guy and that you're unstoppable and usually end up with conflict. You could get yourself hurt and mess with the wrong person." Bret recounted a recent incident where he and his friends were out drinking, ended up getting in a street fight, and one friend wound up getting badly beat up.

Bret has also been smoking pot since he was around 12 years old. He claimed doing so helped him cope with the despair he sees in his community. "I kept doing it [pot] cause . . . it lifted stress and made me stop thinking about the stupid things at home . . . sometimes it even helps me like think better on certain situations." Bret is cognizant that using could easily serve as a gateway to other drug use, but he doesn't have the self-discipline to stop. He doesn't mind being high for a few hours and then feeling normal. That's a stark contrast with religious adolescents, who as we have seen get their high from God.

At 16, Bret and his friends engaged in other risky behaviors as well. On the weekends, they gamble, shoot "girls gone wild" videos, and party at dance clubs. Bret says he isn't much of a "party person" but goes because that's what his friends do. He knows that his friends are a bad influence on him: "I've had like had my little realization period [about] what I've been doing wrong in my life, so that's helping me know what I need to have done so I can accomplish my goals . . . Sometimes I can be too easily influenced by my friends." Taking stock of his life at age 16, Bret vividly describes the state of despair he feels:

> I just sit down some days and think about how my lifestyle been and how I don't really like it sometimes, like I just get into deep thought and it just gets me upset . . . and my father [and I] be having problems . . . [and] my house, it's like falling apart, like the ceiling is starting to drop, everything is collapsing. And at the time when all of this was going on, they [bill collectors] was telling me I was gonna lose my house. It just felt like my life was just coming down on me, everywhere, that I wasn't really doing too good in school, I just felt like things was collapsing.

In short, all indications point to a desperate future ahead for Bret.

~

But 2 years later Bret's life looks drastically different. He succeeded in finding an on-ramp back onto the road to college, going from earning Ds to earning Bs. His drinking and drug habit subsided, and he went from cutting class regularly to doing so only rarely. His relationships with his parents and siblings improved, too. Reflecting on how his life changed over the last 2 years, Bret noted the big changes he had experienced:

> A lot of things got better for me. With school, my family, pretty much every aspect. I calmed down, too. I got a little more relaxed and more focused on what I gotta do . . . I don't smoke anymore, I don't like be out late, I don't be doin' wrong [things] . . . I keep up with my school work and, you know, I don't have different kind of female around all the time . . . [I] basically

did a one-eighty . . . I quit a lot of the things that I used to do that was wrong. I haven't sold [or] used any drugs, I haven't did anything incriminating, I haven't even seen a weapon in I don't know how long. I'm doing a lot of more positive things. Things that nobody might have seen happen 5 years ago.

Bret spent an additional year in high school and earned his high school diploma. "I finally got my diploma to brag about," and then—unlike most people he knows—he went on to college at a New York public university for its engineering program. Being a college student brings him tremendous satisfaction:

I'm in college. I feel good every time I tell somebody that. Just that I'm in college, like, in my neighborhood, I don't even know anybody that's been in college except for my brother, and if they have they dropped out so, you know, or they got a GED. I got my diploma, I'm going to college.

What was the cause of such a dramatic turnaround by Bret? These positive changes coincided with a deeper relationship with God. At the end of his second interview at the age of 18, he said, "By me being religious, it kinda helped out a lot of things." His shift in religion was largely prompted by a new girl he met who was very involved in her church. Bret realized that he couldn't connect with her in the way he wanted to because he wasn't regularly going to church. Keen on staying with her, he started attending church, too. He recalls attending a church breakfast where the preacher asked people to think about what had made them happy or something good in their life. "She said God did that for you. I was thinking about stuff, thinking and thinking and thinking. I thought of my family and my home and all that, but then I got to my girl. She embodies all the stuff that I been praying for when I was a kid, so I like broke out into tears." Bret started participating in performances with his girlfriend's church. He admits to not knowing nearly as much as her—after all, she can quote scripture off the top of her head. He doesn't read scripture often, but when he does, it gives him a "burst of energy" as it usually speaks to "things that I can relate to at the time."

Bret went from thinking of God as somewhat distant to being much closer. He realized that God was "good" and "out there," and entered his life at just the right time:

Before, I didn't believe because as a child, I guess I was in depression or something. I used to pray all the time, but it felt like my prayers was never answered. It's been within these last 2 years that I've realized that God is good because I'm healthy, like I've outgrown my asthma, I have no enemies, at least none that like, antagonize me on a regular basis if at all. My girl is like everything that I ever wanted in life and like she's what makes me happy. You know, she came in my life at the right time, when I was finished with all the nonsense I was doing and I was getting focused on school . . . I definitely believe that God is a good guy—He always on time.

Bret also started attending church more regularly. Doing so has helped bring him and his mom closer, and "now we go to church together and everything." She has begun to trust him more and has been more open with him as a result of his change: "Now she feels more confident in me because she's seen me slowly, slowly changing, changing, but now that she sees me going to church and practicing religion with her, it makes her happier . . . I don't want to say she loves me more 'cause I know she loves me deeply but, I guess now she's more open to me with more things. Now she tells me lot more personal things that's on her mind than she did before." His relationship with his father has also improved, and he notes that his dad says he loves him and shows him that he does as well. Bret said this happened after he let go of the anger he held for his father and just accepted him.

Prayer has also improved his mood and state of mind: "I used to think that praying was stupid, but even if there isn't a God and nobody is really hearing me, just me saying it is making me feel better anyway." And even if God doesn't exist, Bret knows that "church is a good place to be" because "the people there who do believe are such good people that why wouldn't you want to be around them—they always looking to help out." He contrasts the difference in behavior and attitude between his religious and nonreligious friends:

My religious friends, they're more positive people, you know, they doing school and they not into involved in a lot of other stuff that they keep themselves busy, they usually never think about using drugs or being getting pregnant and all that as opposed to my friends who's not so religious—they having rough sex and you know what I mean, not using condoms, they using drugs, you know, they drinking, and not to degrade my friends but, sometimes they're just sitting around and all they want to do is get that next blunt.

When asked how much religion is a part of his life, he says, "I guess it's a lot, but it's not that I'm conscious of it because as I started doing more introspecting on who I am as I was trying to become better, I realized that a lot of my point of views are already parallel to the Bible—so it wasn't like I had to change my life to fit being a Christian." He doesn't think religion is the basis for how he lives his life, and he isn't "fine tuning his life" to "live by the Bible." But now when he has a hard decision about what is right or wrong, he no longer does what helps him get ahead. Now he thinks about what God or scripture says, and whether something will cause other people pain.

Religious restraint has a lot to offer working- and middle-class kids who are vulnerable to driving into a ditch on the road to college. It's as if religious restraint erects mysterious "godly guardrails" to keep them on or guide them back to the path to college. But if God works in mysterious ways, then that's particularly true with respect to the rerouting that happens on the road to college in the case of professional-class teens. We turn to their story next in Chapter 5.

5

Unexpected Destinations

In the last chapter, I described why an upbringing of religious restraint enhances the academic performance of working-class and middle-class kids. In this chapter, I show that an upbringing of religious restraint constrains college choices, especially for professional-class kids. It does so by recalibrating their academic ambitions after graduation, leading them to rarely consider a selective college despite their excellent grades in high school.

~

In Chapter 1, we met Gina, the daughter of a school superintendent and politician who is so high on God that she sings and dances while doing the trash run at the water park where she works. With a report card filled mostly with As and Bs and lots of extracurricular activities under her belt, Gina was poised to have lofty college aspirations. Millions of American teenagers spend their high school years dreaming of and working toward college. And when it comes time to apply to college, the common assumption is that teenagers aim to attend the highest quality institution they can get into and afford.

A common measure of institutional quality is school selectivity.[1] The selectivity of one's education is just as important as the quantity because people who attend more selective institutions see more benefits.[2] The first and perhaps most notable benefit is increased earnings.[3] In a comprehensive analysis of the effects of institutional quality, higher education scholar Liang Zhang found that graduating from a selective college provides a roughly 20% earnings advantage relative to graduating from a comparatively nonselective college. These earnings also seem to increase over the early stages of their careers.[4] In addition to the economic benefit, graduates from more selective institutions are more likely to earn graduate degrees,[5] tend to feel better about the social and economic circumstances,[6] and have better mental[7] and physical health.[8]

But Gina is different. One clear difference is that unlike most of her peers, she has no intention of immediately going from high school to college. After graduating from high school, Gina made plans to go overseas to do missionary work. Ever since she was 10 years old, all Gina has wanted was to bring people closer to God—to "spread the gospel" as she describes it: "[When I was 10], I remember passing a note to my grandma in church and it said, 'I'm going to be a missionary in Australia.' I don't know why I wrote that, but I did." And her dream became a reality: while she didn't make it to Australia, Gina did spend the year evangelizing in South America. During this time, she taught English at a Christian bilingual school, led Spanish worship services at the church near her host family, and hosted craft days and Bible school in local pueblos (villages).

Of course, with the growing popularity of a gap year—especially among affluent teens who can afford to take a year off—Gina's hiatus from college does not appear that striking. And when Gina returned to the United States, she did what is generally expected of professional-class kids: she went to college. The fact that Gina went to college is not surprising because she grew up in a highly educated and fairly affluent family. In 2014, professional-class families like Gina's earning more than $116,000 a year fell into the top quartile, and about three in five children who come from this top income quartile complete a bachelor's degree.[9]

But what is surprising is where Gina went to college. We might expect that someone like Gina—the child of a school superintendent no less with a report card filled with As and Bs and lots of volunteer and extracurricular activities under her belt—to be well-positioned to get into a selective college. And it's also the case that selective colleges welcome students like Gina from the professional class. In fact, according to research by economist Raj Chetty, children of the top 1% of earners—those earning more than $512,000 a year—are immensely overrepresented at top universities. Using income-tax and college-enrollment data, Chetty found that at elite private colleges (which he designated the eight Ivy League universities along with the University of Chicago, Stanford, MIT, and Duke), there are more students from the top 1% than the bottom 50%. In fact, the probability of attending an elite private college is 77 times higher for children whose parents earn over $512,000 compared to children whose parents earn less than $25,000.[10]

Over the past few decades, many American parents have become obsessed with positioning their offspring for selective college admission.[11] Families spend tons of time and money hiring SAT coaches and college counselors in hopes of increasing their children's chances of getting into a selective college.

Journalist Paul Tough describes the extraordinary measures some parents will go to especially well in his recent book, *The Inequality Machine*. During his research, Tough spent time with Ned Johnson, a highly sought-after SAT tutor in Washington, DC. Most of the teenagers Ned works with came from wealthy homes, and so many of them seemed consumed by anxiety—about the SAT but also school, their college applications, and their parents' expectations. As Tough puts it, "that's a hard way to spend your adolescence—even if you do make it to a gold-plated college in the end."[12]

But attending a selective college is not what Gina dreams of. Rather than channeling her years in high school preparing to go to college, she intentionally does poorly on the SATs because she wants to minimize her chances of getting into college: "I kind of went into my SAT's—I didn't try because I didn't want any college to accept me." What kind of teenager would intentionally bomb the SAT to lower their chance of getting into college? The kind whose self-concept is centered on God. Gina does not organize her life to please selective college admissions officers. "Life isn't about me," she says. Instead, she organizes her life to please God.

Despite being the daughter of a prominent political family, Gina was more intent on spreading the gospel in Peruvian prisons and Haitian orphanages than hunkering down in the library. When Gina returned from doing missionary work, she didn't obsess over *US News and World Report* rankings of colleges and universities. She applied and was admitted to the local public university that accepted almost all (87%) of its applicants. In college, she didn't care much about her grades but managed to earn a degree in communications. Having checked off the "college degree box" (implicitly signaling her professional-class status), Gina could now resume doing what she loved: evangelizing. She became an international missions coordinator where she leads teams around the world to spread the gospel.

By age 28, Gina had gotten married to a fellow evangelical and returned to the United States. Since she never had clear career aspirations aside from mission work, she pursued jobs that had little to do with her skill set. First, she worked as a bank teller. Then she enrolled in a community college to become certified as a radiation therapist. She thinks about maybe getting a PhD in cancer research but doesn't have a plan to do this. Is she on track to repeat her parents' social class position? It doesn't look like it at the moment, but that doesn't seem to bother her. She isn't hungry to climb any social class ladders and is happy with her God-centered life.

Selecting against Selectivity: Undermatching in the College Admissions Process

Whereas in the last chapter I focused on the impact of religious restraint on working- and even middle-class abiders facing difficult circumstances, in this chapter I want to look more closely at teens from the opposite end of the socioeconomic spectrum. Adolescents from well-off middle- and professional-class families have at least one and usually two college-educated parents; several of them have parents with master's degrees and even a few PhDs. These are teens on a wide and fairly smooth road to college because their parents' social class position gives them access to the social, cultural, and financial capital that makes college not just a dream but a reality. But what makes the teens in this chapter interesting is that they take unexpected exits on the road to college. They do not follow the path we might expect, given their class position and strong academic track record in high school.

Many of the teens I describe in this chapter were raised with religious restraint and live for God. They have good grades in middle and high school because in the process of striving to please God, they behave in exceptionally conscientious, cooperative, and self-disciplined ways. Raised with religious restraint, they are textbook examples of the abider advantage when it comes to their grades. But religious restraint doesn't just restrain them from antisocial behaviors that might knock them off the track to college. It also recalibrates their vision of their future when it comes to choosing a university to attend. Gina is a teen whose life purpose is to spread God's message. This religious goal, along with altruism and parenthood, is the hallmark of a God-centered life. But exploring new experiences and stepping out of one's comfort zone—hallmarks of leaving home for college—are not. The desire to help others, raise children, and bring others closer to God comes up over and over again in the words of religiously restrained adolescents. But what is conspicuously absent is mention of admission to an Ivy League college and the new experiences and discomfort it might bring.

If a God-centered life is what a teen imagines for their future, it's nearly impossible for them to simultaneously envision a prestigious career, too. In fact, a prestigious career may feel directly at odds with living a life devoted to God. The career path often yields financial wealth but involves long hours at the office in order to cultivate the connections needed to get ahead. People who aspire to become doctors or lawyers often have altruistic reasons, but many also appreciate the status and money that comes with such jobs. But teens from the professional class like Brittany from the Introduction have no interest in fame and fortune. On the contrary, Brittany admires people like Billy Graham because he "didn't build up material possessions" but instead "truly touched people's lives." Brittany admits that she doesn't have "a lot of dreams or aspirations" when it comes to college, and tellingly her parents are not pushing her either: they even try (in her words) to get her to "take easier classes." But what Brittany does have is a clear religious and altruistic life purpose: "My purpose is to love other people and to show God's love." If you are a teen like Brittany—a straight-A student in the National Honors Society but without aspirations for a career—what incentive do you have to even consider a selective college? Very little, it turns out.

Good grades in high school are one of the key criteria for getting into selective colleges.[13] This means that we would expect that those with higher grades are more likely to end up at selective institutions. Given her academic record, Brittany could have probably been admitted to a better-ranked university. Scholars use the term "undermatching" to describe what happened to Brittany—when a person attends a college that is less selective than what they could probably get into based on their academic record.

Scholars tend to think of undermatching as a class phenomenon. In Alexandria Walton Radford's study of valedictorians, *Top Student, Top School?*, she finds that many students who are low income do not consider attending selective schools despite their academic prowess. But my research suggests undermatching is also a religious phenomenon that particularly affects professional-class teens.

How common is religiously induced undermatching? Here I turn to the National Study of Youth and Religion (NSYR), which I have linked to the National Student Clearinghouse (NSC). The purpose of linking the data was to overcome a common limitation of longitudinal research. In this instance, I didn't have complete educational outcome data for respondents who dropped out of the study after wave 1 or who graduated from a postsecondary institution after the NSYR ended in 2013. Using the NSC data, I could fill in the missing data and identify all the higher education institutions that an individual ever attended or graduated from. The NSC match occurred in September 2016 when respondents were approximately between 26 and 31 years old. By this age, most people are likely to have completed their bachelor's degree if they intended to do so.[14]

Most importantly for our purposes in this chapter, I was able to link the NSC data with the Integrated Postsecondary Education Data System

(IPEDS) to obtain the mean SAT scores for students admitted to each higher education institution. The SAT score is what I used to assess institutional selectivity. Why SAT scores? Because studies show they are among the most reliable indicators of college selectivity.[15]

My analyses show that, on average, despite receiving higher grades in high school, abiders graduate colleges with lower average SAT scores compared to the colleges that nonabiders graduate from. In other words, abiders graduate from less selective colleges. How can I tell? First, I compared the average SAT scores of the colleges from which high-achieving abiders and nonabiders graduated from. Figure 5.1 shows the average SAT scores of the colleges that NSYR respondents attended. The first thing to notice is that NSYR respondents who earned As and Bs in high school (the left-hand side of the figure) attended colleges with lower SAT scores than did NSYR respondents who earned all or mostly As (the right-hand side of the figure). This is what we would expect—people who bring home better report cards in high school should end up at more selective colleges. But the figure also shows something we wouldn't expect: abiders graduate from less selective colleges than do nonabiders. We see this happening regardless of their grades. Abiders who earned As and Bs in high school graduate from colleges with an average SAT score of 1112, but nonabiders with As and Bs graduate from colleges with an average SAT score of 1134. Although this gap of 22 points may seem small, it is statistically significant. An even bigger gap exists among the highest achieving students. Abiders who earned As in high school graduated from colleges with an average SAT score of 1135, compared with 1176 among nonabiders.[16] This 41-point difference suggests that abiders are again graduating from less selective colleges.

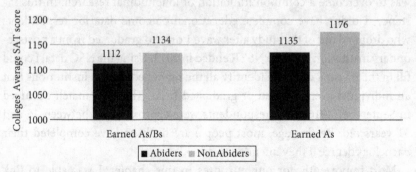

Figure 5.1 Abiders with good grades (As/Bs) and excellent grades (As) in high school attend less selective colleges than do nonabiders with similar grades.

Are abiders undermatching?

Recall that undermatching occurs when a person attends a college that is less selective than the person could probably get into based on their academic record. And recall from earlier chapters that abiders have an academic advantage: they earned higher grades in high school. We would then expect them to attend more selective schools—those with higher SAT scores. But the opposite is happening. This suggests undermatching.

To figure out whether undermatching was truly occurring, I looked at what kinds of colleges high-achieving high school students attended. I found that about one in five (27%) of abiders was at the top of their high school class but then went to colleges where SAT scores were lower than 1300. Among nonabiders, the undermatching rate was much lower—only one in four (19%). When I looked at less selective institutions—those where SAT scores were 1100 or less—I found the same pattern. In those cases, 13% of abiders undermatched. However, among nonabiders, the undermatching rate was more than half that (6%). The point was clear: abiders earn great grades in high school but attend less selective colleges.

But not all abiders undermatch—undermatching is more prevalent among more socioeconomically advantaged students. In Figure 5.2, I show the average SAT scores of abiders and nonabiders who earned As and Bs in high school. Abiders from poor, working-class, and middle-class families attended slightly less selective colleges than nonabiders from the same social class groups. But the most profound difference in selectivity is among the professional class. Abiders graduated from schools where the average SAT score

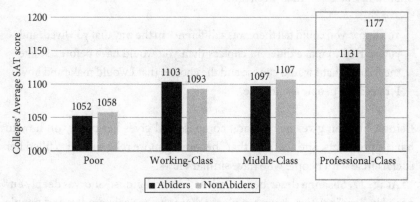

Figure 5.2 The largest selectivity gap is among abiders and nonabiders from professional-class families.

was 46 points lower than colleges that professional-class nonabiders graduated from. Regression analysis, in which I control for high school grades,
race, gender, age, and geographic region confirm this trend: abiders raised in
the professional class attended less selective colleges than nonabiders of the
same class background.

Self-Concept Congruence and Religious Restraint

Susanna is a 17-year-old girl living with both of her parents and 19-year-old
sister in Phoenix, Arizona. She is a huge fan of anything by Jane Austen, especially *Pride and Prejudice*, and steers clear of rap music because some of
the lyrics are too vulgar. Her Evangelical mother, who has some college education, works as a personal trainer, while her Jewish father, who has some
graduate-level education, is a business broker. They earn about $95,000 in
2003—a solidly professional-class family.

Growing up, Susanna learned about both her parents' faith traditions,
but Christianity was a much bigger part of her early life. Her mother took
her to church every Sunday, and Susanna's maternal grandmother, who was
also active in the church, further reinforced Susanna's religious beliefs. At
age 13, Susanna made the intentional choice to follow Christianity and decided to get baptized: "I made the decision to be Christian when I turned 13.
From then on, it [my faith] has become stronger." This decision was not just
rhetorical—it meant she changed how she behaved. "I started living my life
differently," Susanna observed, going on to describe the impact embracing
one's faith makes on their decisions:

> You know, you could tell there was a difference in the way that you lived, and
> you started to make different choices than you would have before . . . like
> the friends that I would choose and the choices that I would make and how
> I treated the people around me.

Being Christian gives her a moral compass and gives her clarity on how to
handle problems. She also says that "becoming more religious" also filled her
social circle with people who have similar views.

At age 17, Susanna described herself as "very religious." She was deeply engaged in her Christian church, a place where she has role models and people
that she can talk to. Talk of her religion permeates her interview. From the

very beginning, when asked about what kind of people she is friends with, Susanna says that four of her closest friends are "very strong in their religious faith." One of her friends has parents who are both ministers. She notes that her friends share the same values and make similar choices. Religious people, she says, "handle problems differently," and "religion changes how you see things." According to Susanna, it's important to have faith "because most of the decisions that you'll make will come from how you view life, in a religious manner, so I think that to make decisions you have to have some kind of basis that you live on."

The way Susanna sees things is not a viewpoint imposed on her by her parents raising her with religious restraint, though certainly that's how she first was exposed to her faith. It's become a worldview that she wholly embraces and that permeates her outlook on everything. She goes to church every Sunday, which she says is not "a habit" but now a "choice":

> When I was younger that was just how I was raised and everything, to always be able to go to church . . . it's not become more of a habit but now a choice, you know, like I choose to go to church.

Now that she makes the choice to attend rather than at her mother's behest, she enjoys the experience even more. As psychologists would say, the shift from being extrinsically motivated (because of an external threat of punishment) to being intrinsically motivated (because of a genuine interest and desire) has made Susanna feel more invested and interested in participating: "[it] definitely changed the whole experience for me 'cause I really want to go. I want to go and learn. I want to have the whole experience of church . . . it's just something I enjoy doing, it's something I look forward to."

Susanna enjoys her high school, where she is a junior and where she appears to be very conscientious and cooperative. Her attitude is "you live the example of [your] religion—you live the way that you would be if you were a true Christian, you know, just the company you keep and the decisions that you make." Susanna is an excellent student, is a member of the National Honors Society, and is involved in several extracurricular activities. She is on the dance line and the track and field team. Yet she is not doing these things because they look good on her transcript but because she is "passionate" about them and thinks they make her a better person. Similar to other abiders, Susanna is intrinsically motivated to participate in school activities and to volunteer: "[I volunteer] because it helps you become a better person; it builds character."

While some of the students we have encountered were not even certain that they would graduate from high school, Susanna has no doubt that she will graduate and go on to college. When asked how she pictures her life as an adult, she takes college as a given: "I know I'll go to college for at least the 4 years and then I guess whatever I'm inspired to do from there."

Susanna's attitude toward college is consistent with the outlooks of other adolescents from professional-class families. If you grow up with college-educated parents who work as professionals, you are immersed in a college-going culture. Yet although Susanna appears to be academically prepared for at least a somewhat selective university, she ends up following in her sister's footpath by choosing a public university that is only 20 minutes from home. The transition to college proves to be difficult for her, partly because she is very family and friend focused. She decides to live at home because it's cheaper but also because she doesn't want the level of independence that comes with living on your own at college:

> I didn't feel as if I was ready to go into the dorm when I could just as easily live, you know, 20, 25 minutes away from there. It just seemed like, you know, forcing yourself to be independent, and I will move out, but just you know when the time is right, when the time feels better.

Susanna is also concerned that living on campus might expose her to things that are "too liberal in the political sense" or "something I wouldn't believe in or went against my own morality." While she acknowledges college as a place that "opens up so many different doors" and offers her a chance to meet new people and learn new things, she is scared of the change it will bring: "It's definitely a different world entirely." Rather than strike out to experience new things and people, Susanna wants to stick to friends who share the same beliefs: "They keep me very focused and they support my beliefs and my morals. I don't tend to hang out with people who have different morals than I do. It just, I think that would be a very difficult situation, but the people that I am friends with, they have the same beliefs, the same morals, so it's, we keep each other in check." Living at home also limits her opportunities for new experiences and leaving her comfort zone, but Susanna doesn't see that as a loss: "The relationship [with my parents] has always been strong so that was the big part of why I stayed at home." After college, she continues to live with her parents until she gets married and moves in with her new husband.

Susanna's life goals throughout the 10 years of study were consistently oriented around altruism and family rather than achieving prestige through a career. At age 17, the main thing she wants to accomplish in life is to make an impact on people, especially family and friends: "I want them to look back on me as a friend who was there for them and who listened to them and that they were able to talk to and everything." At age 20, she has a similar purpose: "Just to help people when I can and to be helped by people in my life." She majors in Family and Human Development because it was something she could use for the rest of her life because it "had to do with marriage and dating and families and relationships." Career-wise, Susanna's journey is unremarkable: her early interest in interior design morphed into working as a wedding planner after leaving college, and at 27 she's a manager at the local DSW store.

Like Gina, Susanna's goals reflect a very clear set of beliefs. Despite her family's professional-class socioeconomic status and her good grades, she does not see college as a stepping-stone to a successful career and, in fact, rejects the allure that selective colleges have for so many teenagers in seemingly similar circumstances. Instead of pursuing new experiences or stepping out of her comfort zone during her college years like so many of her peers, Susanna sticks to the tried and true, and her college years seem to have very little impact on her overall life goals. Her primary ambitions remain the same after college as they were in high school: to start a family, help others, and orientate her life around God. How did Susanna come to develop this worldview?

~

Young people develop aspirations for their future based on their perceptions of what is prized in their social and cultural worlds.[17] Sociologists like Pierre Bourdieu refer to our social worlds as our "habitus." One's habitus is composed of the attitudes, beliefs, and experiences of those inhabiting one's social world. Habitus is the deep-seated set of durable, internalized dispositions, propensities, and predilections to think, feel, judge, and act in certain predetermined ways that we gain from societal conditioning and socialization. Thus, habitus leads individuals to think and act in certain ways.[18] The power one's habitus exudes shapes their inner consciousness and meaning-making activities. In short, habitus is the origin of one's dispositions and the filter for all that one perceives. It is the air we breathe, but not everyone breathes the same air. For those who like sports analogies, habitus is a kind of practical sense for what to do in a given situation—what in sports is called a "feel" for the game.[19]

Central to Bourdieu's theory is the belief that early experiences vary systematically by social class because children in different social class groups develop different mental structures. But as the past chapters have shown, children acquire a habitus that reflects both their social class *and* their religious subculture. In Bourdieu's conception, habitus reflects what is possible for someone in a given social class—one's subjective expectations regarding what constitutes a successful life.[20] But it turns out that one's understanding of their place in the world and the possibilities that lay ahead is also based on what they see as valued by their religious beliefs.[21] And nowhere is that more poignantly illustrated than in the case of abider teenagers from professional-class families.

The habitus that young people inhabit shapes their self-concepts—different ideas of who they are. We saw in Chapter 1 that an individual's self-concept develops through childhood and early adulthood, but most profoundly during adolescence. This is the stage at which individuals take ownership of their sense of self, which includes experimenting with their identity, comparing themselves to others, and developing the basis of a self-concept that often stays with them the rest of their lives. Regardless of what ideal image we adopt, we seek out ways to bring our self-image into alignment with the ideal in order to achieve congruence.[22] Sociologist Neil Gross describes "self-concept congruence" as the process through which people develop a vision of their future self that comports with the norms of their social and cultural milieu:

> People often make decisions and choices without recognizing that by doing so they are making choices out of a social-psychological interest—reinforced by feedback from the people to whom they are closest—in remaining true to understandings they have of who they are and who they would like to become.[23]

Thus, as Gross explains, "what one would like to maximize depends on the kind of person one understands oneself to be . . . these processes usually operate in the background, without much conscious thought."[24] For abiders like Susanna (and for girls like her who share similar socioeconomic circumstances), her self-concept revolves around starting a family, helping others, and orientating her life around God. New and unsettling experiences designed to further one's career aspirations are incongruent with her sense of self. It's therefore not surprising to discover that for female abiders like Susanna, attending a selective higher education institution would not further their pursuit of attaining self-concept congruence.

The Resurgence of Gender Roles

The phenomenon of girls curtailing career aspirations in favor of a life structured around family, service, and God is one I saw over and over again in analyzing the interviews from the NYSR. Take Sally, another high-achieving high school girl who didn't think a selective college was necessary for self-concept congruence. She lives in Salt Lake City with her brother and grandmother; three older siblings are already out of the house. Sally has two college-educated parents who earn about $65,000. Her father owns a store in town, and her mother is a stay-at-home parent.

When asked to describe her friends, Sally said she mostly hangs out with her mom and her brother. Her mom is her "best friend" and she can "tell her anything," even stuff she wouldn't think of telling her friends. She attributes her close family relationships to being religious. Sally grew up in the Church of Jesus Christ of Latter-day Saints, where her dad was a bishop. At age 8, she made the intentional choice to be baptized, thereby signaling her choice to stay in the church. According to Sally, their shared faith is the glue holding her family together: "I think we're a lot closer than we would have been because we have family home evenings and family discussions . . . we would discuss our religion and that would bring out personal things that would bring us even closer." The people she most admires and wishes to be like are her brother and her parents. She especially admires her father, who both works hard and treats her mother really well. Spending time with family is incredibly important to Sally—so much so that she stopped participating in a ballroom dance team because she had to practice so much that it took time away from family and her schoolwork.

Sally feels that God is very active in her life, always encouraging her to do her best:

> I think of God as my heavenly father and I believe that He wants me to do the best I can. I believe that if I do the best I can, and I make the right decisions that I can, um, live for eternity and live with Him . . . I believe that I am important in heavenly father's eyes.

Sally's steadfast commitment to God and desire to do her best translates into a great report card. In her freshman year, Sally had a 4.0 grade point average, and throughout high school Sally earned mostly all As with only the occasional A–. Like many abiders, Sally avoids "people who like to do drugs or listen to hard rock" in part because she "has a temptation to follow the crowd" and doesn't want to engage in behaviors she deems inappropriate. She doesn't do any partying and describes her friend group as both "hardworking" and "fun-loving."

By all accounts, Sally is conscientious, cooperative, and self-disciplined. But her conscientious and self-disciplined demeanor also means she experiences anxiety about trying new things. Sally is nervous to leave her comfort zone—her home and her church. Despite having great grades, Sally only seriously considers attending the nearby public university. Sally did consider BYU, a nearby university associated with the Church of Jesus Christ of Latter-day Saints, but she found it was too competitive for her. By going to the public university, she expects there is a better chance she'll be able to play in the orchestra. The university she chooses is also a comfortable choice—her sister goes there and her music teacher is a member of the faculty. And her good grades in high school result in an added incentive: she's offered a scholarship to attend. Reflecting on her choice, Sally openly admits that "I really didn't think about it too much."

Recall the working-class teenagers we met in the previous chapter—teens who have an economically hard life and who yearn to go to college. Teens like Jacob and Cameron are eager to escape the pathway that their nonabider peers appear to be set upon. They want to improve their class position by gaining a college degree. Something quite different appears to be at work in the case of Sally and her peers. They are content maintaining their class position by attending college close to home and reproducing traditional gender norms. Their life goes something like this: Live for God, behave appropriately, do well in high school, go to a local college while staying close to home and family, find a good marriage partner, have children, and be kind to others. Nor is Sally's vision of motherhood, altruism, and God just a Church of Jesus Christ of Latter-day Saints phenomenon; Protestant and Catholic women who are raised with religious restraint sound very similar.

Sally takes it as a given that she will follow in her parents' footsteps and go to college, but she is not doing it to improve her labor market prospects. Why is she going to college in the first place? It's not to leave her social world to explore what the rest of the world has to offer. Even attending the local public university made her nervous because she expected to encounter viewpoints that didn't align with her religious and social views: "The school is kind of liberal and the classes [were] kind of a fear of mine," she said during her sophomore year of college. It turns out her reason for going to college was to repeat the script: so that one day she can homeschool her own children.

Sally is not opposed to working outside the home, but her vision of that work doesn't amount to what would classically be considered as having a career. Instead, the work she wants to do centers on her commitment to family, children, and God. At 17, she wants to have a piano and art studio so that she can teach children. She takes piano very seriously because when she was 14 years old, she received a patriarchal blessing[25] at her church which told her she would help others through music. But her life purpose is ultimately about living up to God's expectations of her and finding a husband: "I want to become what I'm capable of becoming. I think part of the purpose of life is that we perfect ourselves and that we find someone that we truly love and we make it through all the tough times like in marriage."

Nor did Sally's life purpose and goals change after she got married: they continue to revolve around the domestic and religious realm: "If I could only accomplish one thing in my life, I would say it would be to do my best to be righteous, to be a faithful member of the church, and a loyal wife to my husband, and [a] mother." For her, success in life is not about aspiring to prominence or experiencing new opportunities. It is about permanence and parenthood. In recounting the struggle her brother is having with his career-driven wife, Sally makes it pointedly clear that according to her religion, women should prioritize raising children versus working outside the home:

> My oldest sibling and his wife were married in the Temple and everything, but she kind of has her sights sets on a career, and uh, she doesn't really want to have kids, and they've been married for like 7 or 8 years now, and in our religion, we believe that women should be, yes, well-educated, but that family should come first, and she's decided to put the family thing on hold, and she is an opera singer, and her career is actually growing with that. And so she wants to do that instead.

Sally wants none of that: she instead follows the path laid out for girls in her family. Like Susanna who followed her sister to the local public university, Sally also follows her sister's path by attending the same local public university. She views her sister as an "example" of how her own life should be. Not only do they both attend the same college, but they pursue the same major, play piano, and both get married during college.

Sally appears to be happy doing what is expected, including doing what her church "has outlined in getting married." Sally has no qualms about following traditional gender norms. Her husband's role is to be the "breadwinner," "patriarch of our home," and "the priesthood holder," and he plans on attending medical school. She plans to be a "homemaker" and stay-at-home mom so she can develop a bond with her children—a job she feels shouldn't be outsourced to others. Though she and her husband don't have children yet, they are still "building a family": "I just feel happy and I have a good feeling inside which tells me that I'm doing the right thing."

Career Girls: The Curious Case of Jewish Adolescents

Religious subcultures shape one's goals and aspirations in part by imparting gender ideologies,[26] which are sets of beliefs tied to gender that guide various life choices like education, career, and family.[27] Religious cultures differ in their teachings and norms about gender roles, and specific tenets within religions' doctrines focus on gender relations and women's and men's relative responsibilities for activities like childrearing and maintenance of the home. Since parents play a key role in transmitting religious culture, they help shape children's habitus with regard to gender roles by virtue of both their social class group and their religious group.

The importance abider females from professional-class families attach to self-concept congruence becomes all the more clear when comparing them to another group: girls raised by Jewish parents.[28] The differences in their self-concepts are striking. Girls raised by at least one Jewish parent imagined their futures very differently compared to girls with a non-Jewish upbringing from similar social positions. They were oriented toward achieving prestigious careers as early as middle school and throughout adolescence. Jewish girls saw themselves as making their mark in the world through high-impact, prestigious careers and even becoming prominent figures. For example, at 13, Stacy hoped to become a lawyer, noting that she wanted to be "somebody that people remember in history" and "somebody important." Another Jewish girl, Debbie, also envisioned herself making a lasting impression. When asked at 17 what she wanted to accomplish in life, she said:

> I'd like to make a mark. I'm not the type of person who's okay not being in the limelight . . . I crave attention in that I really want to make a mark that's noticeable . . . like being known in whatever industry I'm in.

In prioritizing prestigious careers, girls with Jewish parents saw motherhood as secondary. They did not disavow having children, but it was not at the forefront of their minds. They wanted to eventually have a family, but during adolescence and emerging adulthood they intentionally worked toward fashioning a career path and assumed they will have kids "down the road." At 19, Emily wanted to eventually have kids but did not imagine getting married until 30: "I have other things I want to do first. I want to get my career and my own thing set before I settle down." Stacy provides a clear example of this "career-first, motherhood-second" mentality when she is asked to describe how she sees her purpose in life:

> I'm career-oriented. I have a lot more friends who are in a relationship, it's very serious, they want to get married, start a family, that kind of thing. I think I'm gonna wanna do that eventually, but I'm 19 now, so I'm just not really focused on that . . . It might be something I get to later.

For Stacy, the idea of becoming a lawyer came from her dad, who thought she would be a good lawyer because she likes to argue, is opinionated, and enjoys discussing politics. The fathers of Jewish girls appear to embrace gender egalitarianism, encouraging their daughters to pursue careers instead of prioritizing having a family as female abiders do.

Girls raised by at least one Jewish parent were also much more supportive of the notion of mothers working outside the home than were girls raised by non-Jewish parents. Sixteen-year-old Amy put it this way:

> I think it sets a great example that they could work and still have a family. Especially if I have daughters, I don't want them to grow up thinking that they're just going to stay at home and cook and clean all day. I would want them to know that they could have a good profession and still have a good family.

While Amy's support for mothers working outside the home was rooted in setting a good example for her children, Leah's support for the idea was focused on personal fulfillment. After saying she was "all for" mothers working outside the home, Leah elaborated: "I think they can be just as good of a parent and I think it's essential for personal happiness . . . I'm just not an idle person." And while girls raised with either one or two Jewish parents were generally supportive of working mothers, those with two Jewish parents were especially enthusiastic about women's careers.

To achieve their career goals, these girls had educational plans that included going to college, and most had plans for graduate school. Even girls as young as 13 years old already had well-articulated visions of their career and educational pathways. Much like the visions of abider girls remained stable, the educational and career aspirations of Jewish girls changed very little even as they got older. Leah's responses to questions about her plans at the beginning of high school at age 14 and then later as a college junior attending the University of Pennsylvania at age 20 exemplify the persistent nature of Jewish girls' self-concept:

Age 14	Age 20
I: *What are your future education plans?* R: I want to go to college and graduate school. I: *What do you want to study?* R: I want to study either business or law, whichever one. Because I want to be in sports management. And some people study business and some people study law because there's both aspects of it. But I don't know which one I want to do yet. I: *And you think you want to do graduate school as well?* R: Yes. I: *What kind of degree do you think?* R: I don't think I want to do business or law in undergrad—I think I want to do it in graduate school. And just do something else in undergrad.	I: *How would you describe yourself when it comes to the question of purpose in your life?* R: Very clear, I've never really felt lost. I think I've always known what I actually wanted to do with my life. I: *And what's that?* R: I want to work in sports and I've known since I was maybe 8 that I loved it. And then I realized it was a career and I was like, Oh!

We can see that even as a freshman in high school, Leah had a sophisticated understanding of different educational paths, even recognizing that she could wait until graduate school to study business or law while choosing a different major for her undergraduate degree.

In addition to having more developed educational plans from an early age, girls with at least one Jewish parent were more likely to focus on being admitted into highly selective colleges. These aspirations developed early in the girls' upbringing. Stacy said she planned to "get into a good college—like an Ivy League kind of college" followed by law school. Another example comes from Jessica, who at 15 also planned to go to "a prestigious school" like an "Ivy League" college. Five years later and now actually attending an Ivy League college, she reflected on how her college planning started as far back as elementary school: "From fifth grade on, your goal is do well so that you can get into Honors classes and then do well in the Honors classes so you can get into AP classes, do well in those so you can get into college." Amy was similarly fixated on attending an Ivy League college and making sure she was on track to get into one: "This is my junior year, I cannot do anything at all that will mess it up . . . I've been working toward college since like the fifth grade, which sounds pathetic, but it's true."

~

It's important to note that the plans these girls made to attend selective universities were neither abstract nor impractical. They took numerous concrete steps during high school to position themselves for reaching their goal. They knew precisely what kinds of accomplishments selective colleges reward in the admissions process and demonstrated sophisticated knowledge of what college-level work entailed. These girls were highly involved in demanding extracurricular activities like Model UN and were more likely to highlight the relevance of these activities for their college applications. For example, in addition to being a stellar student, Debbie prepared for college by being involved in a multitude of extracurricular activities, serving as class president, and winning a prestigious state award for photography. Hannah planned to spend 3 weeks of the summer between her junior and senior year at a camp at Carleton, her first-choice school:

> This is going to be a huge 3 weeks of my life because it's kind of going to determine if I'm going to go to Carleton or not. And if I do go to Carleton, what I'm going to major in. What's that going to mean for the rest of my life?

These sorts of academic and career considerations were markedly different from what abider girls shared as their concerns during high school.

For girls raised by at least one Jewish parent, central to both their plans and self-concept was doing well academically. As Jessica observed, "I'm most proud of my academic successes and that I've proven myself to be good in many different things . . . it makes me feel well rounded and worthy of something." Emily echoed these sentiments, adding, "I care a lot about doing well in school just because it will help my future." She graduated with a 3.9 grade point average (GPA). Stacy's desire to attend a selective college was the primary motivator for her orientation around academics, and by her junior year she was already taking college classes. As she succinctly framed the connection, "I know it's going to be important to what college you get into and your future, so it's pretty important the grades you get." Girls with one Jewish parent repeatedly emphasized the connection between academic success and their future—a future much different from that sought after by abider females, who accordingly attached much less emphasis to their academic performance in high school.

With their focus on selective college admission, it's not surprising to find that one of the most striking contrasts in self-concept between abider females and Jewish girls revolved around being open to new experiences. One's willingness to embrace novel ideas and experiences is important for college because higher education institutions intentionally aim to expose students to new ideas and new people. For many teenage girls, college is likely to be the first time they would live in a completely new environment. For girls raised by at least one Jewish parent, this prospect was exciting rather than fraught with anxiety. Girls with a Jewish parent even cited their faith as encouraging them to question and develop their own beliefs and remain open to new ideas. As Jessica explained, "I appreciate Judaism for being the type of religion [that] allows for questioning all the time, for study, for constant analysis and thought."

Evidence of these girls' openness to new experiences and ideas also came through in how they described the people they admired. Fourteen-year-old Leah sought to surround herself with people who are bold and inquisitive: "I like people who are interested in learning and observing—not people who stay afraid on the surface and hang out there." Debbie respected her English teacher for "speaking his mind." Stacy explained that while she was politically and socially liberal, she wanted to "stay open-minded toward everyone" and that "she wants to live in a place that was diverse and had a lot of people . . . where you can be pretty open and be yourself and be accepted for that." Conversely, girls raised with religious restraint expressed concerns about being around people who had different beliefs and values from them.

At the theoretical level, it would appear that girls raised by at least one Jewish parent acquire a particular habitus shaped by social class and religious subculture. Religious traditions espouse varying views on gender egalitarianism and the kinds of dispositions its members ought to embrace. Consequently, parents from different religious subcultures transmit different habitus to their children. The difference in habitus is evident even when the parents are from similar socioeconomic strata. In turn, girls develop different self-concepts and different conceptions of how higher education can help them attain self-concept congruence. Girls raised by at least one Jewish parent develop a self-concept marked by openness to new experiences and a vision of themselves as prominent careerwomen. They are highly attuned to what these careers take and organize their educational experiences to position themselves for selective colleges so they can realize their professional visions and attain self-concept congruence. Similar girls from comparable social origins but raised by non-Jewish parents have very different visions of their future selves in which higher education at selective colleges is not an ingredient in attaining self-concept congruence.

Do Jewish girls live out their vision of their future—in other words, does having a self-concept marked by ambitious career goals and an eagerness to have new experiences translate to attending more selective colleges? The NYSR survey data bear out this claim: teenage girls (and boys) raised by Jewish parents went to more selective schools than teenagers who were not raised by Jewish parents, even after controlling for differences in socioeconomic status. There was an approximately 100-point difference between the mean SAT scores of colleges that adolescents raised by at least one Jewish parent attend versus those of the colleges that teens attend who were raised by non-Jewish parents (1201 to 1105). This gap is roughly equivalent to the difference in selectivity between an Ivy League university and a prestigious yet still public state university. In other words, while abider girls and Jewish girls are both positioned for admission to selective colleges, their self-concept determines whether they actually pursue the option.

"It's in God's Hands": Undermatching and
Abider Boys

If the advantage of being raised by at least one Jewish parent isn't limited to just girls, it's reasonable to wonder if undermatching by abiders is not just a female phenomenon. Are there reasons apart from the gendered self-concept that female adolescents raised with religious restraint possess that would incline male abiders to also undermatch?

It turns out that the nongendered aspects of the self-concept outlined earlier for abider girls also apply to males. For example, the close ties that abiders have with their families and church communities mean that both male and female adolescents are less inclined to attend selective schools (which typically entails moving a significant distance away from home). Religiously restrained men and women generally have very positive relationships with their parents and aren't trying to break out of their parents' stronghold. Both young adult males and females are perfectly comfortable remaining nearby even if that means going to a less selective school.

And one central aspect of the self-concept of abiders that dictates how both men and women approach the entire process of applying to college—and which stands in sharp contrast with the approach of teenagers who have at least one parent who is Jewish—is that relying on God to shape one's life appears to limit even the effort they put into applying to college. Going to college, even for professional-class kids, requires some agency. Teenagers who live for God may be well-behaved, but they don't see themselves as steering the ship that is their life. Instead, they are more often than not passive actors in God's play, waiting for their next direction. Teenage abiders wait for things to happen to them rather than taking the initiative to make things happen.

This is evident in the case of AJ from Chapter 4, a boy who both wants to stay close to home and who takes a more passive approach to education, knowing that God has "an overarching plan." AJ lives with his parents, little sister, and grandmother, and his family are Evangelical Christians who attend church weekly. His father has a PhD, works as a chemical engineer, and teaches Sunday school at the Presbyterian church on Sundays. His mother has some graduate education and works as a librarian at the Christian school where AJ went to middle school. His love of sports makes AJ sound like another typical teenage boy. At age 14, he dreams of playing in the NBA; if that doesn't work out, he thinks he could become a sports analyst: "I'm a big sports fan. That's really important to me." He has been playing soccer consistently since he was about 5. But sports are his second priority in life. His first priority? God. As AJ says, "God is number one and sports are number two. Those are the two big things in my life."

Like other abiders, AJ isn't averse to delayed gratification—behave well now and you will be rewarded by God in the afterlife. As a result, AJ acquiesces to what God has in store for him, which helps him stay focused:

I feel through God's will and everything that He has a plan for everything, so I feel focused right now. I feel ready and know everything's not gonna go my way, but I'm still gonna try to do my best and hopefully He'll lead me to the right decisions.

What AJ ultimately wants to get out of life is to follow the path that God set for him and help as many people as he can. At the end of his life, he hopes that he can look back on his life and say, "I served my God, my country, and my family well. And I just did the best job I could with the talents that were given to me. And that I made an impact in some people's life and I served my world like God wanted me to serve."

Consistent with other abiders, AJ thinks it's "extremely important" to do well in school. Even after he gets accepted to college, he doesn't want to let his grades drop: "I still want to keep my grades up and remain focused all the way through," he explains. But when it comes time to think about colleges, AJ considers only four schools: two Christian colleges and two public state universities. He winds up attending the local public university, which is about a 15-minute drive from his home. AJ decides to live at home with his parents during college, partly to save money but also to steer clear of what he sees as an intense party scene in the dorms. Reflecting on this decision at age 24, he expresses no regrets, saying that it helped him stay religious. He points to the effect living on campus had on his friends from high school who went to the same college. They started partying and have "gone away from religion":

Some people [from my] Christian high school renounced their faith when they went to [this university] and they just kinda started doing their own thing.... One of the better things that's been about living at home is that I'm still going to church consistently.

After college AJ is still living with his parents and working three part-time jobs that have little to do with his major in sports management. In his interview, he never describes himself as determined or ambitious and describes himself as taking more of a "let's wait and see" approach. His choice to attend the local public college and live at home during his college years reflects this outlook. At 24, AJ continues to believe that God "has an over-arching plan" for his life. God "designs" a "path" for people, and AJ continues to believe that part of living a "good life" means a living life that is "pleasing to God."

This theme of following God's path versus striking out on one's own is very visible in abiders' lives regardless of their denomination or even gender. Kevin, a member of the Church of Jesus Christ of Latter-day Saints, makes this point loud and clear when he describes the world being orchestrated by God:

> We don't see the end from the beginning . . . [but] I do kinda feel like I'm headed the right direction, like I'm going where the Lord wants me to. Where that will eventually lead, I don't really know. I don't feel like I have a very specific calling, but I feel like I'm headed in the right direction.

Even when abiders confront tragedy, they see God as positively directing their lives. Lara had a very difficult childhood. When she was 6 years old, her father, whom she described as a "prominent leader in the community," had a breakdown, packing his bags and leaving the family home to stay with his in-laws. A few days later he committed suicide; Lara and her little sisters found his body lying next to the gun he used. Lara's family had always been very involved in their Fundamentalist church, but in the wake of this tragedy, religion became even more central. Instead of getting her children counseling like some people suggested, Lara's mom put her trust into God, a mindset that Lara also absorbed and came to embrace:

> God used [my father's death] in a great way to shape my mom. [My] mom just really trusted in God and went to the Word . . . we homeschooled for 3 years and we did some really great curriculum. It was just all focused on the Bible . . . you know, God is the father to the fatherless. She really didn't let us become, um, depressed over what had happened and cling on to that. She really kept us going and looking ahead . . . I think it really helped our family.

Even after her family recovered from her father's tragic death and her mother remarried, religion remained a centripetal force for the family, and they attended a Southern Baptist church multiple times per week.

Lara attends a small private Christian high school. Like other abiders, Lara is not tempted to engage in risky behaviors. Her parents' strict rules align with her own biblical convictions and she appears judgmental of those who decide to participate in party and hookup culture. She earns As, serves as Senior Class President, and does a ton of volunteer work. But like other abiders, she is not concerned with having an impressive resume for college and acknowledged that she doesn't love learning. Why, then, does she strive so mightily in high school? Lara does her best "'cause you do everything at your best for the Lord."

Lara's life goals are centered on having a large family raised in the Christian faith, an understanding spouse, and a career working with children. She also expresses Evangelical goals, hoping to spread the word of Jesus and continue growing spiritually throughout her life. Having only attended highly religious schools where the rare non-Christian students faced widespread disapproval, she sought a familiar environment in college. Despite her stellar grades and leadership role as Senior Class President, she limited her search to Christian schools. She considered four and ultimately only applied to the two that were closest to her home in Idaho, winding up at a Christian university in Seattle that is not selective. But in talking to Lara it is clear that she didn't undermatch solely because of social class reasons. She undermatched because of religious reasons: for Lara "everything comes down to God," and because "God has a plan" the choice of where to go to college is relatively unimportant to abiders like her. A future career is the furthest thing from her mind upon entering college; like AJ, the only thing that matters to her is leading a "good life" that is "pleasing to God."

~

The contrast with teenagers who don't wait for God to create a path for them couldn't be sharper. Sage is a 17-year-old African American girl who lives with both of her parents in Queens. Her mother has a master's degree and is a social worker for the federal government, while her father, who has a high school diploma, works as a carpenter. Together, her parents earn about $85,000, own their home, and have some savings and assets, making Sage's family professional class.

Like her mother, Sage identifies as Episcopalian. Her father was raised in a strict Seventh Day Adventist household but no longer actively practices his faith upbringing. Sage believes in God and occasionally goes to church with her parents. However, in stark contrast to abiders, God doesn't play a very important part in her life: "I'm not really affected by God," she says. If it were completely up to her, she would only go to church once every few weeks or when she needs it to "feel better about [herself]." Sage does attend a private Catholic high school, but she doesn't feel a strong connection to the religious aspect of her school.

Sage is one of the few Black girls at her all-girls private Catholic school, where she is a stellar student. Like her Jewish peers we met earlier in the chapter, Sage is highly motivated to do well in school—not because she wants to please God but because she wants to go to a good college. She does her homework and studies hard. She even puts aside dating and getting in-volved in relationships so that she can focus on her schoolwork. She knows her grades matter a great deal for her ability to get into college, and the only time she feels sad or depressed is if her grades slip. It's also important for her to get good grades because all of her friends get good grades. "I try to push myself 'cause my friends push themselves. I wouldn't want to be the only one in the group not doing good. That doesn't make me feel good." In addition to her strong GPA, Sage is also very involved in her school. She's on the student council, is a homeroom class president, and is the incoming president of the African Heritage Club. Sage's narrative sounds fundamentally different from abiders like Gina, Susanna, and Sally—girls who did well academically be-cause they wanted to impress God. Sage wants to impress college admissions counselors.

College is very much top of mind for Sage, and she knows that she wants to get a master's degree to become a nurse: "more power to me," she quips. She thinks about her future a lot, knowing that the decisions she makes now will affect her life in the long term. She does not believe that God has a plan for her; rather, her destiny is in her hands: "I'm the one who decides what I wanna do for the rest of my life." She exudes ambition, determination, and persistence, explaining that "I'm focused on what I want to do with my life." She is grateful for what she has, but she feels as though she has earned every-thing that she has as well: "I'm a driven person," she notes, and does not give God credit for her accomplishments. She views herself as a doer and takes an active role in making her dreams a reality.

Nowhere is that more evident than in her academic journey after gradua-tion. Sage begins college at a public university in New York and then transfers to a highly selective private university near Washington, DC. At age 27, she reports having met her goals from 10 years earlier: she is in a master's pro-gram and working at a job she loves: as an oncology nurse at a cancer center in New York City.

Sage believes that her life purpose is "just to be the best I can with what I have, use whatever talents I have." This phrase may sound familiar—AJ also said, "I hope I did the best job I could with the talents that were given to me." But how they see themselves using those talents is quite different. AJ hopes to use his talents to serve God, his country, and his family. Sage hopes to use her talents to thrive in her chosen career. Sage does not view her career as a selfish decision that only benefits her. She cares deeply about helping others, but it is through her career that she can impact others: "[My profession is about] giving back to people, trying to help people out." While both Sage and AJ want to help others, Sage seeks to help others through her career, while AJ seeks to help others by showing God to them.

And like her Jewish peers, Sage's career-centered self-concept means having children is important, but it can be done simultaneously with having a career. While abider women often think it's better for a mother to stay home with their children, Sage thinks it's good for mothers to work outside the home. Doing so affords them independence, something she really values: "I feel like, for me—I can't speak for all women—but I like being independent. I like making my own money. I can't see myself ever depending on anybody for money."

Comparing Sage to abiders reveals a key difference in terms of their will-ingness to embrace new experiences. Recall how nervous Sally and Lara were about leaving their family and going to college. They yearn for the comfort of the familiar. Sage is just the opposite. She welcomes change with open arms. She "never says never," preferring to stay open to new information and new points of view. In fact, she repeatedly says that some of her least favorite people are those who have an extremely strong personality and refuse to ac-cept that they may be wrong. That is also why she isn't too fond of institu-tional religion—she thinks it indoctrinates people and closes their mind.

That raises an important question: what about kids who reject religion? The final chapter explores the surprising academic outcomes for atheist teens.

6

The Road Less Taken

Up to this point, I have made the case that teenagers who are raised with a childrearing logic of religious restraint develop a God-centered self-concept. They strive to live a life that is pleasing to God, which makes them behave in a way that is conscientious and cooperative. Abiders feel extrinsically motivated to please God and do so by being compliant. These are dispositions that are highly valuable in the school domain, so the religious kids earn better grades in high school and go to college (even if they undermatch).

In this chapter, I suggest that there is another (perhaps more traditional) way teens get good grades and gain admission to college: by being intrinsically motivated to pursue knowledge. In the National Study of Youth and Religion (NSYR) interviews, I found a subset of teenagers who demonstrate exceptional levels of intrinsic motivation to learn and critical thinking,[1] which are also key traits for academic success. These teenagers are also open to new experiences—which turn out to be even more important for academic performance than being conscientious and cooperative.[2] They are autonomously motivated individuals who think critically and are driven by curiosity.[3]

But teens who tend to demonstrate these types of traits aren't motivated to please God.[4] They are teens who reject the idea that God even exists. And it turns out that teens who don't believe in God but engage in self-directed behavior—whom I will refer to as atheists—bring home report cards that look just as good as teens who center their entire life on God. Analyses of the NSYR survey data show that atheists' grades in high school are not statistically different from those of abiders.[5] But because they are not constrained in their college choices by religious restraint, atheists appear to end up at more selective colleges than their abider peers.

~

Janet was one of these unique teenagers who demonstrated exceptional levels of autonomous motivation and self-directed behavior. She had left the traditional public school system in her hometown in Idaho after seventh grade. But Janet didn't leave because she was failing her classes—she left because the classes were too easy. Unwilling to bear the boredom, Janet decided to design her own education. She enrolled in an online high school and by age 15 was taking classes at the local public university. While many 15-year-olds would have been intimidated by the idea of taking college courses and being surrounded by people much older than herself, Janet was not one of them. One of her goals was to complete her associate degree before her eighteenth birthday, so Janet took 20 hours of classes each semester, and then bumped up her hours when she realized she was a bit short on credits as her birthday drew near. And she did all of this while working at the school library. After completing her associate degree in criminal justice, Janet enrolled in the local public university with a full scholarship and majored in communications.

Janet wasn't just an anomaly because she took her education into her own hands. She was an anomaly because she did not believe that God exists. She was an atheist, which made her a member of a tiny yet growing minority in the United States. A 2019 Pew survey shows that 14% of 13- to 17-year-olds said they don't believe in God,[6] up from about 3% in the 2003 NSYR. Janet wasn't raised with religion and did not see it as something she needed. When asked about her religious beliefs at age 15, she shared, "I always sort of thought that religion was just something that people used to just cope with the way things are . . . it's just not something that I really feel that I need . . . [I approach life using] logic."

Although she didn't believe in God, she still wanted to learn more about the religions of the world, particularly how they started. She and her father often engaged in philosophical discussions regarding the origins of religion and how they came to be understood the way they are today. When she was about 20, Janet got sick and was homebound for over 6 months. She slept much of the day, but she also decided that it would be an ideal time to read the Bible—all of it. When the interviewer asked what motivated her to do that, she described being inspired by its pivotal role in society:

> I found this really cool version that, all of the text was color-coded based on what it was talking about. And there was this little, like, laminated thing in the middle, it was like "If it's talking about love, then it's pink, if it's talking about how you should do this, then it's green." . . . This is like the world's greatest piece of literature, you know, it's—it's affected a lot of people in a lot of ways and, you know, the least I could do is read it.

But her thorough reading of the Bible further entrenched her skepticism about the veracity of its contents. As just one example, she described a story in Kings (2:23–24) about young children making fun of a bald man. Janet correctly recounted that two bears then appear out of the woods and proceed to eat 42 of the children. Janet thinks stories like this are absurd and have "cemented" her disbelief in the truth of the Bible and the existence of God.

Yet Janet remained curious about religion even if she herself wasn't religious. After reading the Bible, she continued turning to other religious literature for more insights. One of the books she read was A. J. Jacobs, *The Year of Living Biblically: One Man's Humble Quest to Follow the Bible as Literally as Possible*. As Janet recalled, "He wrote how he tried to live by all the rules of the Bible for a year, and there's a lot of stuff in there that is just plain ludicrous. It may have made sense in that era, but it does not make sense now, [like] you can't wear mixed fabrics and you have to stone people . . . I think that anyone who claims to live their life by the Bible either hasn't read it or is not telling the truth." It's clear that Janet doesn't just thirst for knowledge—she also adapts her perceptions and understandings of the world as she accumulates more of it. She's constantly reflecting on what she has read or seen in her own life to see how it fits or alters her current worldview.

~

Some of the most academically astute adolescents in the National Study of Youth and Religion (NSYR) are the ones who can't reconcile the contents of the Bible with other things they believe to be true. Many like Janet identify these contradictions and disavow their belief in God by adolescence, whereas others come to these viewpoints later in their twenties. In fact, some of the most academically accomplished adolescents were those who grew up with religious restraint but had completely moved from religion by their mid-twenties.[7]

Chase was one of several teenagers who started out deeply religious but lost his faith as he climbed higher and higher up the educational ladder. He was an excellent student in high school, graduated from college, and then went to an extremely selective medical school. In terms of educational attainment, he was one of the teenagers who accomplished the most.

For Chase, the move away from religion involved a lot of internal wrestling with his beliefs and manifested itself over time. At 16, Chase identified as Catholic. He regularly went to church with his parents, though his family were not strict adherents. His parents took an unusually critical stance toward reading the Bible and maintained that people—not God—control their lives. In college (a public university in Ohio), Chase did something surprising, given his questioning of religion during high school: he joined Evangelical campus groups like Campus Crusade and identified himself as a conservative Christian. This lasted about a year before he began to experience "cognitive dissonance"—mental discomfort that results from holding two conflicting attitudes—between the criteria that guided his academic self and the criteria that guided his religious self. He realized that he didn't have sufficient evidence to back up his faith. This led to a rift between him and his friends: "I don't believe in miracles and that's something I've always been at odds with [my friends] about because they all fervently believe in miracles and I believe in science." After immersing himself in the teachings of his church, studying the Bible on his own, taking college classes about religion, and talking with other people, Chase came to an unpopular opinion: none of what the Bible says is "real":

> I [had] considered myself a conservative Christian. I would say [that] I kinda got sucked into it, like the emotional part of it. Even when I was hanging out with this group of really Christian kids, going to church every Sunday, studying the Bible on my own, I still questioned everything. It's just my nature, it's who I am . . . I was a wholehearted believer and I think that's fallen apart since October [when] I was beginning to fall apart about this faith that I thought I had which I don't really think is that real at all. What I've learned at school and just reading things on my own and just talking about things with people [is that] I'm not really sure if I believe this.

By 26, Chase became an atheist, saying he didn't believe in God. But like Janet, he remained curious about religion: "I am very interested in religion from a philosophical, theological, philosophical level. I love to read about it. I'm fascinated by it. But me personally, I don't really have any religious beliefs."

Some readers might wonder about the demographic backgrounds of atheists. Atheists in the United States, as well as in the NSYR, are more likely to have college-educated parents and more likely to be White and male.[8] Chase is a case in point. He is a White male from a highly educated family. Both his parents and his grandparents have advanced degrees from selective colleges. But Janet doesn't fit this stereotypical atheist profile. She is a White female from Boise, Idaho, the daughter of a handyman and childcare provider who together earned only $15,000 in 2003.

Despite growing up in completely different social class backgrounds, Janet and Chase have remarkably similar qualities: they question everything and do not follow the status quo. People like Janet and Chase stand in stark contrast to the way the majority of teens we have met in this book get good grades. But Janet and Chase show that there is another way to get good grades. What distinguishes Janet and Chase from abiders is that they demonstrate exceptional levels of autonomous and self-directed behavior, which leads them to be more open to new experiences and ideas. Their motivation to do well in school is driven by the intrinsic desire to learn, not by the desire to be well-behaved. As a recent study states, "Although it is often assumed that characteristics such as hard work, perseverance and diligence are key to academic success, the current findings point to the importance of other aspects of personality, such as curiosity, enjoyment of learning and self-belief, captured by the super factor of Openness, in fostering academic abilities, and particularly reading skills."[9]

Autonomous Motivation and the Value of Self-Direction

To be clear, disavowing a belief in God is not what causes Janet and Chase to do well academically. Instead, it's a selection effect—the kinds of people who are exceptionally curious and therefore engage in self-directed behavior tend to be the kinds of people who are willing to go against the grain and take an unpopular religious view. There is a strong stigma attached to atheism in the United States,[10] so people willing to disavow the existence of God tend to espouse an uncommon set of dispositions that are evident in other domains of their life.

Sociologists Lisa Pearce and Melinda Denton also noticed that teenagers in the NSYR who didn't believe in God were unique. In their book *A Faith of Their Own*, which draws on the NSYR data, Pearce and Denton found that 44% of atheists felt that it wasn't important to fit in with what other teens think is cool, which is substantially higher than teenagers who believed in God.[11] Youth with a nonconformist identity are more likely to fit a religious profile that requires some level of nonconformity to the mainstream religious ideals of our culture. They conclude that atheists "overwhelmingly stand out from other youth their age in confidence and intellectual ability, and they seem relatively immune from or at least irresponsive to peer pressure."[12]

What distinguishes Janet and Chase from abiders is that they are self-driven, not God-centered. Janet and Chase possess a strong belief in their autonomy, which puts them in the driver's seat with respect to what happens in their life. Chase makes this distinction very clear when at age 14 he compares himself to his best friend who is Evangelical: "His religion is like, God controls everything you do . . . [but] what's the point of living if God controls everything you do?" Janet and Chase believe that they chart their own path, academic and otherwise, as opposed to heeding external authority figures that tell them what to value. By being self-directed, Janet and Chase exude analytical thinking, openness, and curiosity.[13] They are rarely content with the status quo.

Laurence, a 16-year-old atheist, also doesn't put his life in God's hands: "You control the present, you can't control the future. But you can control preparing yourself as best you can for the future, you know, giving yourself the most windows and opportunities through the present." Laurence and other atheists don't wait for God or anyone else to control their destiny. He recognizes that school, along with extracurricular activities and interpersonal relationships, is a means through which he can contribute to the outcome of his own life. Not only does he think critically about what is within his control, but he discerns what he wants so that he can position himself to take advantage of opportunities as they become available. Laurence has seized the reins of his own life; he makes education work for him and not the other way around. And he values education not just to go to college, but for the sake of learning: "I like to have knowledge . . . I like to become smarter."

Recall that abiders attain self-concept congruence by adhering to what they think God expects of them. But since Janet and Chase don't believe that God controls everything, they need to find a way to make all their worldviews align. Thus, they constantly examine and scrutinize their many different beliefs, ensuring that none of them are incompatible. They rarely believe something just because their parents or society tells them to believe it. Here is how Chase puts it:

> I don't believe a lot of the same stuff they [my religious friends] do . . . I have no problem with anyone challenging what I believe because I can't ever know if I'm really right. And I'm always really ready to reexamine my beliefs and try to perfect them and get everything in a logical position that

I possibly can, but I don't share the exact same tunnel vision that they do. . . . some of my friends, they don't really think outside of the box for the most part. . . . And they don't ever question anything ever and like just the way that—I'm the kind of person who questions everything.

People like Chase and Janet analyze various arguments independently, pick out the pieces of those arguments that make sense to them and complement certain aspects of other arguments, and synthesize all of those pieces into one cohesive argument. This type of approach is evident in the views of Vanessa, a 15-year-old atheist who was asked how similar her religious views are to those of her parents:

> I would say the only thing that differs is that maybe I'm a little bit less atheist than my parents in the sense that, logically, I totally don't believe in any organized religion and neither do they. And I would say, I think that some-times things happen for a reason. And if you think things happen for a reason than not, then there are some things that are coincidences, but some things aren't coincidence, then how would that be going on if something wasn't going on? Like logically, I can't say I'm completely anti anything bigger than us because that would be contradictory.

While abiders maintain self-concept congruence by behaving in a way that is pleasing to God, atheists like Vanessa maintain self-concept congruence by taking a different approach. They weigh different viewpoints to see what makes sense to them.

Vanessa's self-directed thinking means she is self-directed in her educa-tion. She grows up with very highly educated parents, but she is adamant that her dedication to school is completely independent of any parental in-fluence. She declares, "I don't really listen to anybody else. I just do what I think I should do." Vanessa says she does not work hard in school to get good grades because of her parents—she works hard because she wants to. She is autonomously motivated to do well in school in large part due to her confidence in her intelligence: "When I get less than an A–, I get really mad. Not because of what my parents think or what other people think, but be-cause I know I could've done better." Atheists like Vanessa generally dem-onstrate a self-directed way of living life that then translates to an intrinsic motivation to learn.

Allan, who was the valedictorian of his high school graduating class, is also intrinsically motivated to learn and complains that the traditional public school education doesn't promote learning. In his interview he repeatedly referenced "the poor quality of the school system." His complaints generally stem from the conflict between what he thinks education should be like and how it actually is. In Allan's view, the curriculum is "too easy, and most of it is irrelevant" to what he considers actual education. This is a stark difference from abiders, for whom the traditional public school education works because it is largely built around compliance and conformity. This very quality of successfully navigating school is what feels so constricting to people like Allan.

Not only are atheists self-directed, but they are also more comfortable instigating action even if it means standing up to authority figures. Compliant is certainly not a word that describes them. In high school, Laurence was a stellar student, but he didn't get good grades just by being well-behaved and cooperative. When he was unhappy with something at school, he didn't sit idly by but instead took action: "If I have a cause, I get people to deal with it." In fact, he took pride in being an activist, once galvanizing 500 kids to show their dismay for how the principal treated a student after he got involved in a school fight. While this provocation might jeopardize his standing as a student, Laurence takes pride in his behavior, claiming that his "ability to get a large group of people to do something [reflects] my leadership characteristics." Laurence seems to emerge from high school without suffering any academic consequences for his authority-challenging behavior. He goes on to attend one of the most selective colleges in the United States and becomes an early employee of the highly successful startup company, Lyft. It's possible that his independence and audacious behavior become an asset to him after high school—the place where he articulated in an interview his vision of what a successful future for him would look like: "I would probably create a mode of transportation that [would help] completely stop the use of dangerous fossil fuels and things of that sort, you know, in combination with a new way of energy and building materials and kind of a new environmentally friendly thing to stop global warming and stop poisoning of the air and water and stuff."

~

When people look to God or their parents for guidance, we would expect to see them stick with what they know, and not venture out very far into unexplored territory. Conversely, when people are exceedingly self-directed, they should theoretically also act in ways that are more open-minded, inquisitive, and adventurous. That is precisely what we see among the atheists. They are highly open to new experiences and new ideas and take charge of their learning. Max, a White 17-year-old atheist, described how his own curiosity and not his parents urging led him to start reading more outside of assigned schoolwork:

> I just started casually reading on my own, you know, and it's something I really like. Learning something that actually does excite me, you know, just the pursuit of knowledge. I really like to absorb all the ideas . . . and to gain a lot of knowledge . . . that's something I really like, just always, always learning.

The autonomy of atheist students often manifests itself through highly independent and unconventional behavior. By the time she is 17, Janet no longer lives with her parents, opting to instead live in an apartment by herself for the sake of living a more independent lifestyle. Aware that she is unlike most of her peers, Janet takes no issue with living her life in an independent manner, driven by her thirst for knowledge and curiosity about that which she has yet to learn. Her desire for intellectual stimulation was a major driving force for her: whether it be through philosophical conversations with her father or discussions about her favorite literature at the library with her coworkers, Janet is happiest when she is interacting with someone who can "keep up" with her intellectually. Although she has friends, Janet does not prioritize establishing a community in which she fits in. When asked why she does not have as many friends as her peers, she responds bluntly: "I don't really have many friends because I don't feel like I have very many equals."

If atheists can be said to be beholden to anything, it is the primacy they place on logical thinking. That certainly describes Kyle, a White 14-year-old boy from Los Angeles, California, who demonstrates remarkable self-direction and intellectual curiosity at an early age. He spends his free time during high school reading the likes of Plato and Nietzsche and idolizes logical thinkers like Richard Dawkins, making him reluctant to believe in something that is not proven by scientific evidence. Kyle's parents did not raise him with religious restraint, and when asked about his religious affiliation, he identifies as nonreligious. While he is open to the idea of there being some higher power at age 14, he does not believe that power is God, and by age 24, he is firmly atheist. He is also very accomplished academically. In high school, Kyle often made the honor roll (3.5 GPA or above), and after graduating went on to study and graduate from a private university in New York City with a degree in economics.

At 14, Kyle demonstrates the type of questioning attitude we have now seen repeatedly in teenagers who don't believe in God. When he states that he doesn't want to believe in something that he doesn't "know is true," he means something that hasn't been proven scientifically. Nor will he "blindly listen to what other people say." Kyle is inquisitive and doesn't take in new information at face value, but rather scrutinizes it before accepting it. Kyle considers many different possible answers to a question or problem before opting to align his thinking with one of them. When asked about how he decides what's morally right and what's morally wrong in a given situation, he asserts that he thinks deeply about it, taking "a bunch of different things into account."

At age 19 he was asked what he would most likely do if he "were unsure of what was right or wrong in a particular situation." Would he decide by listening to God, following the advice of an adult, do what helps him get ahead, or do what makes him happy? Most teens give a straightforward answer to this question, but not Kyle. He decides to combine two of the answers and provide a logical rationale for why:

> I guess do what would help you get ahead and assuming that it would then make you happy . . . because I don't believe in God . . . because I don't like just kind of blindly listening to what other people say you should do because just because they are older does not necessarily mean that they are smarter than or know right and wrong. . . . I say both because they are kind of intertwined in my mind. I mean you can have happy without ahead but you can have ahead without happy.

We can see that Kyle prefers to answer questions by thinking them through "logically." This type of rationale is commonly offered by atheists but not by abiders. Interviews with abiders reveal that they often make their moral decisions based on what they think the Bible says, not what would benefit the greatest number of people or what they perceive to be the most rational decision. But atheists sound very different when talking about their moral judgment processes, with many of them being moral relativists.

Like other teens who are autonomously driven, Kyle is curious and constantly seeking new and exciting experiences. He exudes all components of self-direction: openness, curiosity and questioning, and independence in thought and action. For Kyle, life is all about "trying to see and understand as many things as possible." Attending college in New York City, he thrived on the opportunity to spend 4 years experimenting with new and foreign subjects, reading a lot, and having deep, intellectual conversations with other smart people. Conversely, he would consider himself a failure if he "was comfortable all the time"—he always wants to be "uncomfortable and expanding."

Becoming an Atheist: Parenting and the Role of Place

Given the focus so far on religious restraint, it's fair to wonder what role parents play in the lives of kids who are atheists in adolescence (or who become atheists by emerging adulthood).[14] Like many of the other questions posed in this book, this one has a surprising answer: a role that is surprisingly similar to that played by the parents of abiders.

Ample research has found that parents play a crucial role in transmitting religious beliefs and behaviors to their children by modeling their own religious commitments. But how did atheist teenagers like Janet, Laurence, and Vanessa come to believe that God doesn't exist? From their parents. Teenagers who are atheists commonly grew up with parents who thought critically about the role of God and religion and were often atheists themselves. As Vanessa puts it, "My parents basically raised me atheist." A 2019 survey of 1,811 parents and their teenage children (13 to 17 years old) found that among parents who are religiously unaffiliated, 86% of their teenage children follow suit by identifying as religiously unaffiliated.[15] Among kids raised with religious restraint as well as those who are atheists, there is religious cohesion. In most cases, atheist teens are not rebelling against their parents. They are charting their own life course with the approval and encouragement of their parents.

Do fathers and mothers play different roles in transmitting religion? Scholars have often credited relationships with mothers as being more important than relationships with fathers when it comes to the religious upbringing of adolescents.[16] But my analysis of the NSYR interviews suggests that fathers play a more important role than previously thought. While reading interviews with NSYR teenagers, I noticed that both boys and girls reference their fathers more often as the parent who they talk to about intellectual matters. It doesn't matter whether the topic has to do with religion or not—fathers are the go-to parent for intellectual engagement, while mothers are the go-to parent for emotional support. As Janet said, "My father and I have a lot of just general philosophical discussions, which are quite interesting." Caroline makes an even clearer delineation between how she sees her parents: "I had this idea of my mom [who is] a second-grade teacher who majored in home economics—she was not an intellectual heavyweight by any stretch of the imagination." Caroline goes to her mother to talk about her problems, but it's her father who she sits with at night watching Fox News commentators like Bill O'Reilly and Shepard Smith: "[My father is] never wrong and he's got serious opinions. . . . I can relate to him on an intellectual level and we have the same interests."

Since teens tend to see their fathers as their intellectual thought partners, it is also fathers who serve as thought partners when it comes to religion. Chase's analytical attitude toward religion and his attempts to reconcile religion with science was an approach he learned from his father early on. Chase described his father as someone who took a critical stance to what the Bible said, always trying to reconcile it from a scientific and philosophical perspective. In high school Chase described how he and his father often discussed how to make sense of the Bible, given that some of the events didn't happen as described—like how scientists have disproved that the earth was created in 7 days:

> We talk about views from other religions and then we talk about our view, too. We don't like say, "Oh, that religion's wrong." We just say what we believe and we compare [it] to other religions. And he [dad] talks about what he believes [and] how it's supposed to be interpreted . . . he reads and doesn't believe it word for word, but he [considers] what the real meaning is supposed to be. That's how he looks at it, and he's kind of put that into me.

Chase continues to cite his father often when discussing religion, making it clear that his views are deeply influenced by his father's views: "[My dad and I] talk about the existence of God a lot. And whether or not exists or not. We get into a lot of philosophical arguments."

While Chase doesn't cite his mother as a conversation partner for discussing the intellectual side of religion, she plays an important role in modeling another side of religion: the "emotional side." Chase says that the emotional dimension of religion resonates more for his mother, so he finds himself asking her about the role that "religion plays in people's lives" and why people who are more religious feel more "complete."

~

Relationships with parents also help explain why people who move away from religion do so at different points in their lives.[17] Some people, like Chase, know that rejecting religion will not ruin their relationships with their parents because their parents are the ones who taught them to be critical about religion in the first place. But people who grew up in more fundamentalist homes know that moving away from religion will be detrimental to their relationship with their parents. These people might have doubts about religion early, but they repress those doubts until they are independent and living away from their parents in their twenties.[18]

This was precisely what happened with Caroline, who didn't disavow religion till she was in graduate school. Raised in a fundamentalist Christian home, Caroline led a completely God-centered life throughout her adolescence. In her teens she exuded conscientious and cooperative behavior, noting that being a good Christian meant to "follow the standards and do what's right." Like other abiders, Caroline saw her life purpose as "living for God" and "becoming more like God."

But in many respects Caroline already sounded different from other religiously restrained teens early on. For her, living for God meant following her "calling," which wasn't wrapped up in having children and staying close to her family. Her "calling" was to go to college so she could eventually become a college professor. This is an unusual goal for an abider, but Caroline aspired to become the next CS Lewis, a scholar and writer who taught at Oxford University and became a renowned Christian apologist (perhaps most famous for his Christian allegory *The Chronicles of Narnia*). Unlike other abider females like Susanna, Caroline also wasn't nervous about going to nonreligious colleges far from home. And unlike Sally, she wasn't afraid of being in a secular academic environment because she saw herself as an apologist who would defend her faith through her academic work as a historian.

After attending college at a public university in California, Caroline went on to earn a master's degree in medieval studies at a highly selective university. But by the time she finished her graduate work she no longer considered herself a Christian. For her, studying medieval religious practices in an academic context fundamentally changed her understanding of religion in general. When she was asked how she would describe herself religiously at age 25, Caroline had difficulty coming up with a label. She described the struggle in this way:

> I'm coming in from this evangelical perspective that rejects the Middle Ages . . . I've started realizing how dependent on culture Christianity is and how, when you start looking across religions who make exclusivity claims and you start realizing that they all use the same language, they all are actually doing the same sort of work. So I've simultaneously pulled away from a really explicit understanding of religion. Like the type of thing that you would find a really hard-core Evangelical making claims, I'm just like—you can't say that.

Caroline and Chase's move away from religion counters the common narrative among sociologists that Americans deviate or completely fall off their religious path as they move from adolescence into emerging adulthood. Decline is most evident when it comes to attendance at religious services. There are a couple of reasons why this might occur. First, people might simply lose interest. As sociologist Jeremy Uecker and his colleagues suggest, "emerging adulthood brings with it a host of responsibilities (e.g., work, school) and opportunities (e.g., increased autonomy) that simply and subtly crowd out religious participation."[19] A second explanation might be weak religious socialization. As Uecker and his colleagues suggest, teens who lack the "language" of religion because their parents didn't raise them with religious restraint are more likely to "shed" its strictures once leaving the home and entering higher education.

Yet Caroline's move away from Christianity was anything but an expression of apathy or weak religious socialization. Caroline's conflict was an intellectual one[20]—one in which she couldn't reconcile religious teachings with her intellectual discoveries as a scholar of the medieval era. It might then appear that graduate school is responsible for Caroline's turn away from religion, but even that explanation is too simple. A look at her relationship with her parents, especially her father, helps explain why her shift away from Christianity occurred later in life.

Caroline grew up in a fundamentalist Christian home where her father was exceptionally strict: "My father's version of Evangelical Christianity is basically derived from early twentieth-century theological interpretations . . . he's convinced that they're the only way to be a true Christian." Caroline described her father as "authoritarian" and believed that he had manipulated her into being religious. In sixth grade, Caroline said her father threatened to have her locked up if she didn't become a Christian, which cast a long shadow on her psyche:

> [By late elementary school] I didn't really feel a lot of spiritual connection. If I could get away with it, I wasn't reading my Bible every night before I went to bed [and I] just found the whole thing pointless. [My father] started taking me under his control . . . [he] basically used a massive personal crisis that I had in my life to tell me that if I didn't immediately become a Christian, that I was either going to go to jail or wind up in a padded room . . . so I sort of wound up having to assimilate his version of Christianity in order to have psychological wholeness . . . but it took 10 years to go from trying to force that onto myself versus sort of working through why I didn't think it was working and to recognize that it wasn't working.

Graduate school offered her the place and time in her life where she finally had enough freedom from her father that she could re-evaluate her views and assert her independence without severe consequences.

~

It may also surprise some readers that Jacob from Chapters 2 and 4 also disavowed religion as he climbed the educational ladder. One of the issues that conflicted with his Catholic faith was its stance toward homosexuality:

> Another thing that I don't necessarily agree with [about Catholicism]—the view on homosexuality and that it's a sin, that it's wrong. That's a narrow-minded view. We should be accepting. If you're in love with another guy or a girl or whatever and you know you're a homosexual, that's fine, you know, I'm accepting to that. The Catholic [Church] isn't very accepting to that.

Jacob was one of many NSYR participants to bring up marriage equality and LGBT rights in his interview. (Same-sex marriage didn't become legal in the United States until 2015, and marriage equality was a hot-button issue in the United States during the period which the NSYR was conducted.)[21]

Despite Jacob's disagreement with Catholicism's stance against homo-sexuality at age 21, he continued to attend weekly church services and played the violin with a youth ministry group on his college campus. He also read the Bible even more than he used to. However, by age 26, Jacob's frustration with the Catholic Church's position on LGBTQ + issues came to a head. He was fed up and intentionally distanced himself from the church, stating that he could not in good faith attend religious services when he had such significant disagreements. Reflecting on his change, Jacob said:

In the past 5 years, I would say that religion has kind of changed a lot. I used to go to church [and] Mass all the time. I was born and raised Catholic. . . . I think growing up changed it—having different perspectives. When I went to medical school, I went to Mass up there, the first year and a half, solid. And then, I decided not to go. And I remember why I decided not to go. I was tired of going to church and hearing about politics. And I was tired of going to Mass and hearing about how we can't let the gays get married. There was one moment, well, two moments. One moment—it was this big election up in my state . . . and every sermon at the Catholic church was about how we can't let the gays get married. They can't raise children. God save the kids, ya know . . . I said [to the padre], "For a church that says they're accepting—we pride ourselves on being holier than thou—you guys are pretty discriminatory. And I don't appreciate it. . . . I used to love coming to church, [but] I don't anymore. It's because every time I come here, you tell me who I should be and who can do this and who can do that."

He also viewed the Catholic Church as "corrupt" and felt turned off by them always seemingly asking for money: "Every church I went to, they would ask me for money . . . I finally got up and left mid-sermon one day and I just walked out. And I said, "Ya know what? I'm done. I can't come to church.'" Like Caroline, Jacob does not passively fall away because of apathy or disinterest. He makes an active decision because of what he sees as irrational contradictions within the church. He subsequently said he no longer saw the Bible as the word of God and decided it was written by humans.

What prompted Jacob to evaluate his stance on religion and the Catholic Church? Jacob believes it was the experience of moving away from home to a college campus. He specifically makes a link between going to college and his questioning of Catholicism, and he attributes his openness to the fact that he left his small hometown community and gained new perspectives:

> I think going to a liberal arts college definitely opens you up to different ways of life and different views. I mean, living in the same town for their entire life, they [my parents] sort of have a narrow-minded view just on the world as a whole. I'm not saying they're stupid or they're ignorant in any way, but I've been exposed to so many different things [at college] that have opened my eyes.

Conversations with other students and classes he took fueled his religious doubt. Is God a figment of our imaginations? Is it fair to restrict priests from marriage? Isn't it narrow-minded to view the Genesis story of creation literally? These were some of the big questions that Jacob said he wrestled with in college.

What Jacob experienced is a conflict that scholars have documented—a conflict between the cultural and curricular content of higher education and certain religious beliefs. Higher education leads to greater scientific knowledge, an emphasis on the scientific worldview, and exposure to diverse opinions and cultures.[22] These aspects of higher education can directly conflict with religious beliefs, as demonstrated by debates over Darwinian evolution or the age of the Earth, and more broadly conflict with religious perspectives and a general reliance on faith. Going to college also puts you in contact with new people who hold diverse perspectives, which may also lead to a decline in religiosity.[23] Encountering new people who don't share your beliefs can be especially jarring since religious commitment and worldviews are reinforced through regular interaction with a religious community.

Jacob went to college and engaged in a process of learning and reflection—which is precisely what colleges oftentimes say they are about (particularly liberal arts colleges). As William Deresiewicz, former Yale professor and author of *Excellent Sheep: The Miseducation of the American Elite and the Way to a Meaningful Life*, argues, college is the ideal time for young people to think critically and creatively—to engage in a process of self-discovery.[24] For abiders like Jacob, this process of self-discovery can eventually lead to taking a radically different position on religion. Ironically, his shedding of religion may be the very thing that led atheists like him and Chase to medical school.

Why Belief Is Not Enough: The Perils of Not Practicing

Teenagers who are atheists are seemingly able to chart their own path and are motivated enough to follow it. But the story is different for kids who still retain a belief in God but don't engage in any religious practices. While it might seem that kids who don't believe in God aren't that different than kids who do believe in God but don't go to church—because both appear to be religiously disengaged teenagers—it turns out that there are marked differences.

One way to understand the difference is by comparing their self-concepts. Teenagers who do believe in God yet aren't engaged in any religious practice aren't charting their own course. They subscribe to a normative stance that God exists, but then are not following through with any of the normative behaviors that are supposed to accompany that belief. They are breaking the rules, whereas atheists are making their own rules.

If that's truly the case, then we would expect to see that rule-breaking attitude reflected in their grades. To understand if that is happening, we need to look at how the grades of nonreligious theists are distributed. In Figure 6.1, I show the distribution of grades by three religious categories: abiders, atheists, and nonreligious theists. This figure shows that there is a larger proportion of poor-performing students among nonreligious theists than there is among atheists and abiders. Among nonreligious theists, 37% report their average grades to be Cs, Ds, or Fs. But among atheists and abiders, only about 20% report such low grades. In other words, nonreligious theists are more likely to bring home bad report cards than are abiders or atheists.

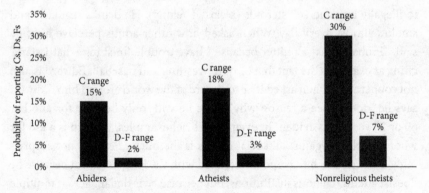

Figure 6.1 Nonreligious theists are more likely to report bad grades than are abiders and atheists.

Given the abider advantage, the fact that nonreligious theists do worse than abiders perhaps comes as no surprise, and in light of what has been said about atheists the fact that nonreligious theists get worse grades would be expected as well. But they also do worse than teens who believe in God and are moderately engaged in religious practice. That's because teenagers who believe in God but aren't at all engaged in religion are much more likely to be experiencing trouble in multiple areas of their lives.

Take, for example, the case of Edward, a 17-year-old White boy who believes God exists but doesn't engage in any form of religious practice. His mother saw faith as very important and Edward occasionally had to attend Catholic church and participate in Confraternity of Christian Doctrine (CCD). But he hated all of it. While he believes there is "definitely a God," he also says that everything in the Bible is "crap." He suspects that Jesus was likely a regular person who was able to convince people to follow him, like a cult leader. He doesn't think there is anything valuable or important about religion, and he didn't believe that "going and telling some guy all your problems is going to wash away all your sins."

Edward's attitude toward his mother's views about religion is reflective of the attitudes of nonreligious theist adolescents, and in this respect stands in contrast to how both atheists and abiders align with their parents' values. Familial divergence in religiosity often creates conflict or manifests existing conflict in the family, and Edward's defiant stance on religion is reflective of his defiant attitude more generally. Edward isn't just pushing back against the institution of religion or his mother's wishes, but against social norms more broadly. For example, Edward has had several run-ins with law enforcement for possession of marijuana. He took $3,000 from his college savings account to illegally buy and sell steroids (a class 1 felony). He drinks regularly and smokes almost every day. When asked how other adults perceive him, he said, "Probably [as] a quitter because I have trouble finishing what I start," citing as examples the fact that he quit wrestling and baseball. Edward is also not cooperative: when asked if he took care of the world around him, Edward says he "doesn't see a reason why" since he will "only be alive for another 60 or 70 years." As evident in even these brief examples, Edward is a kid for whom rebelling against all social norms is the norm. Perhaps not surprisingly, Edward also has a report card filled with Cs. He gets Cs not because he doesn't attend religious institutions, but because he is defiant across multiple domains of life—including school.

Conclusion

In 2016, when I set out to understand how religion shapes young people's academic outcomes, I had no idea how the story would unfold. As a social scientist, my job is to analyze data and present it in as nonbiased of a way as possible. In this book, I have tried to show how an upbringing of religious restraint shapes the academic pathways for teens of different class backgrounds. If you were a teenager who grew up within a system of religious restraint, your life probably looked something like this:

Ever since you could remember, you lived according to a set of principles: be kind, respect authority, follow the rules, and practice self-discipline. These principles were in the air you breathed. They were likely all you ever knew. And if you did anything that wasn't acceptable—maybe you broke a rule or spoke disrespectfully to an adult—you faced consequences. More likely than not you didn't break rules because you didn't want to disappoint the many adults in your life. But you also followed these principles for a bigger reason: to live a life that was pleasing to God.

You were a kid who saw God as a core part of your life. God was such a deep part of you that you couldn't even recognize the effect He had on your thoughts and behaviors. Following religious teachings was just part of who you were. You believed that you were created by God and that you are on this earth to bring glory to Him, through Him, and for Him. You yearned to bring others to know Him. You didn't just believe in God. You talked to Him regularly, and He often talked back.

As a religiously restrained kid, you didn't just believe in God but belonged to a God-infused world. Your needs and desires didn't come first. You were part of a social community, a network of family members, friends, and other adults who had deep religious commitments. As you participated in a religious community, you became entrenched in the flow of social capital. Everyone in your network was connected, which made it hard to escape the notice of others. If you did something wrong, adults you respected would likely find out and you would lose favor in their eyes. It was as if God had put up guardrails around your life to prevent you from taking an off-ramp that would divert you from college. All these influences provided you clear guidelines for how to live your life, creating stability at a period of life when many adolescents experience chaos.

God helped your family connect with each other and with other people. Religion was a source of bonding, not conflict. It meant that your family often ate meals together and spent a lot more time together than the families of your less religious peers. Your parents seemed to get along well and you felt close to them. You went to church and maybe even participated in religious youth group activities. Maybe you played basketball with your youth minister.

And since religion was so important in your life, you parlayed the traits you learned into other domains of your life. You always acted kindly, respected authority, obeyed the rules, and practiced self-discipline. After all, you felt this was the moral way to behave. These dispositions didn't help you on the soccer field or in tryouts for the school play or even on the SAT, but they did help you in the classroom. Unbeknownst to you, schools reward particular dispositions. And it happens that schools reward students with the kinds of dispositions that your religious beliefs and practices inculcated within you. The classroom was yet another social institution where being kind, respecting authority, following the rules, and being self-disciplined paid off. Not only did the adults in your church like you, but now your teachers rewarded you for being well-behaved. You exuded conscientious and cooperative behavior.

You also steered clear of kids who partied and got in trouble at school—the detention dwellers. When you walked home from school, you took a longer route to avoid walking through the park where drugs and alcohol were readily available. Your peers likely saw you as one of the "goody two-shoes" kids, but you were okay with that. You didn't talk back to the teacher, you did your work, and you were nice to your classmates. You may not have been the smartest kid, but you were the kind of kid that made it easier for the teacher to do their job. And when your teachers sat down to fill out your report card, they gave you good grades because you at least were trying. It turns out that good behavior is half the battle in getting good grades, and your religious upbringing ensured that you won that battle before it even started. And those grades had a self-reinforcing effect on you: the more positive feedback you received on your good behavior, the more you wanted to repeat it.

In short, the academic advantage of religious restraint does not stem from simply praying or reading scripture. God does not appear to answer the prayers of children who crammed for the test. But religiously restrained adolescents do enjoy an academic advantage when they are so driven to please God that it fundamentally alters how they perceive themselves and how they behave. Neuroscientist Sam Harris, author of *The End of Faith*, writes about the power of belief in the following way: "belief is a lever that, once pulled, moves almost everything else in a person's life . . . Your beliefs define your vision of the world; they dictate your behavior; they determine your emotional responses to other human beings."[1]

Despite the legal separation of church and state ensuring that religious doctrine is not taught in public schools,[2] religion still finds its way into America's classrooms in surprising ways. As this book shows, teenagers who live their life for God do not shed their religious commitments once they pass through the schoolhouse doors. It doesn't matter to them that religion isn't formally in the public schools because kids believe that God is always with them. And because God is always watching, they always need to be on their best behavior. Emulating God is something kids strive to do no matter where they are or what they are doing. If you have any doubt of this, consider what 17-year-old Anthony said: "I don't care about the school rules, I just care about my religion's rules." The dispositions that teenagers learn through religious restraint are in many respects deeper than those taught to them at school. And it appears that teachers are fine with that, since they reward such students with higher grades.

~

In the beginning of this book, I described many of the long-term benefits of formal education. Americans who complete more education and do so at selective schools find higher-paying jobs, have better health, and live longer.

Who are the kinds of people who are most likely to succeed in our education system? We like to think that it's people who demonstrate ability and effort. But if that were true—if we really had a meritocratic education system—affluent kids wouldn't be four times more likely than poor kids to graduate college.

If we aren't rewarding merit, what are we rewarding? As this book suggests, one thing that is rewarded is compliance. In *The Case Against Education*, economist Bryan Caplan argues that education is the ultimate signal of people's willingness and ability to conform to social norms.[3] A college degree is valuable because it signals to employers that you will be a conscientious employee—it does not necessarily mean that you learned something in your classes that will help you do your job better. If education really did create useful skills and knowledge—which scholars call human capital—then people who are just one or two courses short of completing a bachelor's degree would be able to get jobs that were just as good as those who completed all their courses. But that isn't the case. If you don't finish those two courses, your job prospects are much lower. In Caplan's view, a college degree doesn't signal what you know but signals your conscientiousness. From an employer's perspective, an applicant who can't persevere through those final two courses may not be reliable on the job.

I don't bring up this point about education being a signal of compliance to condemn education. Given how many years of education I completed to get a PhD, I am certainly guilty of conforming to the social order. But when we view education as a signal of conformity, we can also understand why abiders have an academic advantage. One of the central points of this book is abiders' advantage in school stems from a synergy between schooling and religion: both institutions strive to maintain social order and reward children for behaviors that make order easier to maintain. Because religion and schooling promote the same ideals, the types of children who thrive in one institution are also likely to thrive in the other.

But the abiders' academic advantage may be more problematic than it seems at first glance. If we are rewarding children who are conscientious and cooperative—children who help teachers maintain social order—are we giving children a good education? What is the purpose of education anyway? Educational reformer and philosopher John Dewey believed that a good education was one that taught people how to live: "Education is a process of living and not a preparation of future living . . . to prepare him [a child] for the future life means to give him command of himself."[4] Dewey believed that the purpose of education was to help people realize their full potential and develop the ability to use those skills for the greater good. But even in the late 1800s and early 1900s, Dewey could see that schools were falling short on this type of education. Rather than preparing citizens for participation in society, schools were cultivating passive pupils by insisting that they master facts and discipline their bodies. Rather than preparing students to be reflective, autonomous, and ethical beings capable of arriving at social truths through critical and intersubjective discourse, schools were preparing students for docile compliance with authoritarian work and political structures. In short, Dewey saw the educational system of his day as stifling individual autonomy when learners were taught that knowledge is transmitted in one direction—from the expert to the learner.[5]

Have we come very far from this type of education? Maybe not. Although abiders' conscientious and cooperative nature may help them get better grades, this advantage may come at the expense of developing and encouraging critical thinking, creativity, and deeper engagement in the classroom. While abiders may have an academic advantage, it may be a result of an educational system that rewards dispositions for the sake of expediency rather than for the sake of learning. An educational system where knowledge is transmitted from teacher to compliant student is a system with little learner autonomy.

When I began working on this book, I wanted to know whether religion plays a role in academic performance and educational choices. My research shows that it does. An upbringing of religious restraint improves academic performance of kids from all social class backgrounds by boosting their grades and preparing them for college. However, an upbringing of religious restraint also limits educational opportunities, most markedly for professional-class kids. It does so by recalibrating their academic ambitions after graduation, leading them to rarely consider attending selective colleges despite their stellar grades in high school.

Scholars who study inequality in educational opportunity tend to focus on differences *between* social class groups. They ask, how do performance effects and choice effects differ for affluent students versus poor students? It is indisputable that, on average, children of professional-class backgrounds perform better in school and choose more selective colleges than do children from less affluent backgrounds. But rather than focusing on differences between social class groups, I was interested in how religious restraint creates differences for students within the *same* social class group. That is why throughout this book, I have compared abiders to nonabiders from similar social class groups. When it comes to performance, I found that religiously restrained students who live their life for God fare better because they are conscientious and cooperative. This is the case regardless of students' social class upbringing. Working-class abiders have better grades than working-class nonabiders. Middle-class abiders have better grades than middle-class nonabiders, and so on.

But this story changes when we look at their educational choices. Since abiders have better academic performance in high school, we would expect them to make more ambitious choices about higher education. This is generally the case, except in one social class group: kids from more affluent families—the professional class. Within the professional class, teens plan to go to college, but they don't seem to care where. When it comes to the transition to college, students from the professional class who live their life for God make less ambitious choices about college. The paradox of religious restraint is that, on average, it leads kids to complete more years of education, but at less selective schools than we would expect based on their grades—higher quantity but lower quality educational outcomes.

There are two popular theories about how students make choices about educational transitions. Some sociologists have argued that students make rational educational choices that allow them to minimize their chances of downward social mobility.[6] Other sociologists take a different view, seeing choices as largely social decisions influenced by the norms and values held by significant others in their social world.[7] My data suggest that the latter view is more accurate. God-centered students undermatch in the college selection process because they view educational decisions as social decisions that reflect their familial and social ties rather than a choice to optimize their economic position. Viewing matters this way allows us to see the effect of the home and community environment on norms and values surrounding education.

Some readers might be surprised that affluent abiders, who have more choices about college than their less affluent peers, attend nonselective colleges. I was. When I made decisions about college and graduate school, I went to the best school I could get into and could afford, and it didn't really matter to me that I had to move far away from home. But it's possible that high-achieving abiders don't even know about the range of colleges that exist. Selective colleges should consider what they can do to attract these highly religious applicants, many of whom are excellent students. This would require both better outreach to students outside of the traditional zip codes where admissions officers recruit from but also an openness by college admissions counselors to view religious and ideological diversity as valuable when admitting applicants.[8]

But increasing religious diversity is not just about recruitment. It is also about convincing religious Americans that higher education institutions are valuable. Right now, religious Americans do not think very highly of universities, especially the more selective ones. While there aren't data on how religious people feel about higher education institutions, we can look to studies of political groups as a clue, since there is a fair amount of overlap between political and religious views. A 2017 Pew study found that among Republicans (many of whom would describe themselves in ways that align with high religious intensity), only 30% felt warmly toward college professors.[9] Here is another grim indicator of how unpopular higher education is among right-leaning Americans: in 2017, a majority of Republicans and Republican-leaning independents (58%) said that colleges and universities have a negative effect on the country.[10]

This is problematic to say the least. We shouldn't be so divided on the value of higher education institutions, especially since so much of what happens in life depends on a college degree. Colleges are ideal contexts for emerging adults to develop ties across religious lines because universities are one of the only institutions left that bring Americans together who possess a diversity of ideas, perspectives, and cultures. Abiders and atheists don't need to agree on the truth about religion to share a common commitment to valuing civic engagement. Forging ties across religious lines is critically important because in civil society, members of different faiths need to get along. In other words, colleges need not be seen as places where the truth on religious matters is settled but rather as gathering points where civil comity is learned.[11]

It's hard to call someone a heretic to their face. Colleges can function as places where the next generation of Americans, including religiously committed individuals, can gather and learn to value the blessings of liberty—to believe what one wants, to practice one's faith freely, and to protect and value other civil obligations, duties, and freedoms protected and made possible by civil society. That's why while colleges are working hard to have more racial and class diversity, they also need to strive for more religious diversity: not merely students from different religious traditions but abiders who are religious.

As Diana Eck, scholar of religious studies and director of The Pluralism Project at Harvard University, puts it, "Diversity is a fact, but pluralism is an achievement—it means deliberate and positive engagement of diversity; it means building strong bonds between people of different backgrounds."[12] In the multireligious milieu that is America, diversity is an inescapable reality. Pluralism, however, is not. Colleges need to do their part to ensure pluralism.

~

Although my focus in this book has been on academic trajectories, I couldn't help but wonder how abiders' lives unfolded in other domains. First, I was interested in how they were faring economically, physically, and emotionally.

I wrote this book while working at the Stanford Center on Longevity and the economic, physical, and emotional facets of life are indicators of how long and how well Americans will live. If abiders were generally faring better academically by their mid- to late twenties, were they also earning more? Did they feel healthier? Were they more optimistic about life? What kinds of attitudes did they hold about social hierarchies and the social order, particularly those dealing with gender?

To figure this out, I used the survey data from the final wave of the National Study of Youth and Religion (NSYR) when respondents were between 23 and 27. First, I examined their earnings. This is an admittedly early point in life to evaluate one's earnings; however, it's an important point to do so because if differences have already emerged by this point, they are likely to become exacerbated over the life course. When I did this analysis, I controlled for important characteristics that are also associated with one's earnings, such as gender, race, age, social class upbringing, and the geographical region where they were living in their mid-twenties.

Already by this point, I could see patterns that I would have predicted: men earned more than women, White respondents earned more than Black respondents, respondents who grew up in the professional class earned more than those who grew up middle class, working class, or poor, older respondents earned more than younger respondents, respondents living in the Northeast earned more than those living in the South, Midwest, and West, and those with more formal schooling were earning more than those with less formal schooling. The fact that these results align with general stratification patterns should give us some confidence in the data, even though the respondents were only in their mid-twenties.

As expected, given their additional years of schooling, most abiders were faring better economically than their nonabider peers. But one group was bringing down the average: abiders who grew up in the professional class. These more affluent abiders were actually faring worse economically than nonabiders who grew up in the professional class. For professional-class kids, an upbringing of religious restraint not only constrains their educational opportunities but also their earnings. Part of this is explained by the undermatching process that I described in Chapter 5. Abiders from the professional class attend less selective schools than they could get into, which appears to have downstream effects in the labor market. Employers commonly recruit at colleges, so when they choose which schools to recruit from, they prioritize more selective schools where they assume students are more competent.[13] If you aren't attending those selective schools, it is more difficult to access those higher-paying jobs.

Another reason why abiders from the professional class earn less is because they pursue jobs that maximize their time with family even if they aren't as prestigious or lucrative. As a result, abiders were living in the same area in their mid-twenties as when they were as adolescents. Oftentimes they choose where to live not for economic reasons but to stay close to their family. Family ties are of the utmost importance for religious Americans. For most abiders, this means living in areas where religious talk is in the air people breathe—the South, the Midwest, and some states in the West. But these are also areas where higher-paying job opportunities are more limited, and where earnings are lower even for similar jobs.

~

Earnings are not all that matter in life. As emerging adults, abiders experienced fewer symptoms of emotional, physical, and cognitive despair. In the final round of NSYR surveys when respondents were between 23 and 27, they were asked a battery of questions about their emotional, social, and physical well-being. The first set of questions assessed common indicators of emotional despair, including frequency of struggling with sleep, trouble concentrating, loss of appetite, feeling lethargic, and thoughts of hurting yourself. The second set of questions assessed common indicators of physical despair, such as frequency of dizziness, hot/cold spells, numb body parts, and aching throughout the body. The third set of questions assessed common indicators of anxiety and cognitive despair, such as frequency of worrying about your health, feeling suddenly scared for no reason, nervousness or shakiness inside, feeling worthless, or feeling fearful. There was also a question where respondents provided an assessment of their own health, and another question that assessed respondents' optimism about life compared to 5 years earlier.

On all the indicators, abiders across social class groups fared better than nonabiders. This held true even after controlling for gender, age, race, educational attainment, school selectivity, and even earnings at the time. The pattern was clear: abiders are significantly less likely to experience emotional, cognitive, or physical despair. They feel less anxious, healthier, and more optimistic about life. Without a doubt, their deep relationship with God helps them overcome several challenges they bump up against. Abiders are simply more resilient. This is driven by their involvement in a religious social community but also their steadfast belief in God. Here are just a few snippets of how abiders talk that reveals why they are so optimistic about life and emotionally resilient: "I am living a life for God" (purpose), "God will make things better" (hope), "God is looking over me" (comfort), "God is watching, church people are watching" (accountability), "Church feels like home, keeps me out of trouble" (community), "God has a plan, things happen for a reason" (acceptance of bad situations), and "I will pray for something better" (sense of control).

Teddy was one of several abiders who found solace and joy in living for God throughout all 10 years of the study. At 16, Teddy describes the importance of looking beyond himself to find happiness: "[Nonreligious people] think too much about themselves. They're their own God. They're the center of their own universe so they want to be the best and look good." Teddy says he is less concerned with looking good and more concerned with pleasing God. He does not waver on this view as he gets older. At age 22, Teddy continues to find happiness in God: "The way I find happiness is in God. God is happiness. . . . And what God demands of us is that we find our happiness in Him." At age 26, Teddy said there is "joy" in his "daily living" and he continues to feel that God will get him through the challenges he will face in his life: "I think there's lots of joy in my daily living . . . there's lots of fears about the future but I just feel confident that it's gonna continue to be a good journey and that the Lord will be with me."

Nowhere was abiders' resiliency more evident than in interviews with Cameron, a Black abider we met earlier in the book. Cameron experienced trauma early in life and his faith in God played a key role in how he dealt with it. At 22, his wife died and left him widowed with their daughter. At 25, Cameron describes how her death caused him to wrestle with God but ultimately reaffirmed his faith.

After my wife passed away . . . I was pissed. 'S like, oh damn it, you know, just reaching up in the sky, it's like, fuck you! . . . Then I gained my composure and was like, okay I'm sorry. I'm sorry, I-I know, I'm just human, I know I'm not perfect. It just hurts. . . . But then again, the situations that I feel God has put me in have made me stronger, better. . . .[There's] really nothing [that would stop me from believing in my religious faith]. . . . I've suffered through a lot a pain, and . . . at this point in my life, it's like, yeah, I've gotten kinda used to it. . . . I'd say, I'm on the right path. Being good ain't easy. 'S never gonna be easy. I don't care how much money I get. It ain't be easy . . . so that means there's always going to be something bad happening in my life at that certain time whether it be sickness within myself or my family . . . or financial issues . . . so there's really nothing [that would cause me to move away from God]."

~

And yet while abiders are happier and healthier, survey data suggest that abiders overall—women and men—are also very content with the social order, including traditional gender norms. In the last wave of survey data, respondents who were abiders in adolescence were much more likely to espouse beliefs that are not consistent with gender egalitarianism. For example, even after holding constant respondents' gender, race, and age, abiders were more likely to believe that it is "better for everyone if the man earns the main living and the woman takes care of the home and family," that "most of the important decisions in the life of the family should be made by the man of the house," and that "men and women each have different roles to play in society."

Adhering to traditional gender norms is an indicator of a desire to maintain social order. From the perspective of religious conservatives, feminism is a threat to family stability.[14] And it's not just men who think that women's place is in the home. Religious women agree that men and women play different roles in society, with women being more responsible for the private domestic sphere. Sally was one of the women who wanted to stay home to raise her children while her husband was the "patriarch" and the "breadwinner." But her traditional gender views come alongside a desire to not just preserve traditional gender norms but also preserve a traditional social order. We can see this in her 2013 interview, where she laments the United States becoming too liberal and yearning to go back to the "good old days":

Our society today—things are very much changing. Families are not really families anymore. They're just broken homes, and I feel like the situation that we bring children into is poor. I feel like the wonderful foundation that our founding fathers created in our nation, I think it's being lost. They say that the times are changing, so the laws must change, [but] I don't feel that way. And I think we've seen through history what happens to nations when they change and they don't follow those laws that we have set down, and our nation has been so free and wonderful. . . . It's just, people want it to be a certain way and so they'll try to change it to be happy. I feel like this thing about gay rights, they're taking God out of the schools and trying to create it just so as if He was never there, just so the people that don't believe in Him would be happy. I feel that they're just doing it just so they don't feel guilty. Uh, and it's so selfish to go so far as to take it away from other people.

For Sally, contemporary society is one in which social order is not effectively maintained, partly because she understands patriarchal social institutions as in decline during a time when "things are very much changing." She draws on a mythical past American society of "our founding fathers" as a utopia of righteousness, without considering how such a society might appear from the perspective of marginalized groups. In her view, families that fall out-side of the patriarchal heteronormative model espoused by conservative Christianity are "not really families," but "broken homes" that one should not "bring children into."

Sally's comments also reveal her perceptions of the importance given to the concerns of religious people in the United States. Sally decries efforts to "take God out of the schools . . . as if He was never there." She understands those who do believe in God as part of a minority group whose concerns are not taken seriously, stating that God was removed from schools "so the people who don't believe in Him would be happy," while religious believers' wants and needs are presumably not taken into account.

These sentiments are likely to be at odds with some readers' views of social progress. How can religion be good if it places limits on people's autonomy and endorses traditional gender roles? But the religious views of abiders prioritize the group and not the individual. They exalt families and com-munities and assume that people should be treated differently according to social role or status—elders should be honored, and subordinates should be protected. They suppress forms of self-expression that might weaken the social fabric. They prize order, not equality, and value interdependence over autonomy. As a result, the prospects of progressives and conservatives reaching philosophical agreement on this issue seem unlikely—making the need to ensure that all parties embrace the democratic political process where these issues are hashed out peacefully at the voting box all the more important.

~

There is no doubt that in America education matters. But for about one-quarter of American teens and their families today, God matters, too. If social reproduction theory holds true, those numbers are likely to persist as the abider teens encountered in this book begin to have children themselves and raise their children following the logic of religious restraint. It would appear, then, that religious restraint will continue to play a significant role in the American educational system for the foreseeable future.

A Methodological Overview

The empirical evidence in this book is primarily based on my secondary analysis of the survey and interview data from the National Study of Youth and Religion (NSYR), the largest and most current study of the religious lives of US teens. The NSYR was directed by Christian Smith, Professor in the Department of Sociology at the University of Notre Dame, and Lisa Pearce, Professor in the Department of Sociology at the University of North Carolina at Chapel Hill. This project was supported by the Lilly Endowment, Inc. and the John Templeton Foundation. The project was designed to better understand the religious lives of American youth from adolescence into young adulthood.

The NSYR is longitudinal, meaning that the same cohort of individuals were followed for 10 years. The NSYR is also nationally representative, which means that the teenagers in this study closely reflect the broader US population (based on the 2002 Census) based on age, gender, race/ethnicity, household type, region, and household income. The NSYR initially surveyed 3,290 adolescents who were in grades 7–12 during the 2002/2003 school year. These teenagers were between 13 and 17 years old at the time of the first survey and are seen as "millennials" (the generation of Americans born between 1981 and 1996). I was not part of the initial NSYR data collection team, but the NSYR team generously shared all of their data with me.

NSYR Survey Data

The first wave of the study was conducted between July 2002 and April 2003 in English or Spanish.[1] The survey was conducted by researchers at the University of North Carolina at Chapel Hill using a random-digit-dial (RDD) method, employing a sample of randomly generated telephone numbers representative of all household telephones in the 50 United States, including Alaska and Hawaii. The national survey sample was arranged in replicates based on the proportion of working household telephone exchanges nationwide. This RDD method ensures equal representation of listed, unlisted, and not-yet-listed household telephone numbers. Eligible households included at least one teenager between the age of 13 and 17 living in the household for at least 6 months of the year. To randomize responses within households, and so to help attain representativeness of age and gender, interviewers asked to conduct the survey with the teenager in the household who had the most recent birthday. Teenagers and parents were offered cash to incentivize participation at each wave and for interviews. Parents didn't participate in subsequent surveys. At the time of the second wave of the survey (June–November 2005), respondents were between the ages of 16 and 21. At the time of the third survey (September 2007–April 2008), respondents were between the ages of 18 and 24. At the time of the fourth survey (February–December 2013), respondents were between the ages of 23 and 28. In wave 4, only 15% of surveys were conducted on the phone; the rest were completed online.

Throughout my survey analyses, I accounted for several other factors that influence one's academic outcomes, including parents' income and education level, the prestige of parents' occupations, the adolescents' racial and ethnic background, gender, geographic location, family structure, and whether the adolescent attended private or public school. I used survey weights to adjust for probability of sample selection and potential sampling bias.

NSYR Parent Surveys

Through the book, I use several pieces of data from the NSYR parent survey, which was conducted in wave 1. Parent interviews were conducted with either a mother or father, as they were available, although the survey asked to speak with mothers first, believing that they may be better qualified to answer questions about their families and teenagers. Stepparents, resident grandparents, resident partners of parents, and other resident parent-like figures were also eligible to complete the parent portion of the survey. The variables I use most commonly include the mother's and father's education levels, their combined income, their occupations (an open-ended answer), whether they own or rent their house, how much savings or debt they have, how closely they monitor their children, how close they feel to their children, how important it is to them that their children participate in certain activities, how important it is to them that their children graduate college, how they and their spouse identify religiously, how important their faith is to them, what kind of religious congregations they belong to, and how often they attend their religious organizations. Parents spent an average of 30 minutes completing the wave 1 phone survey.

Jewish Oversample

The NSYR also oversampled an additional 80 Jewish respondents in order to obtain a large enough number of cases with which to conduct meaningful statistical analyses of Jewish youth.[2] The Jewish oversample is not nationally representative and was excluded from most analyses in this book. The only time it was used was for the analysis about the educational attainment of children raised with Jewish parents described in Chapter 5.

NSYR Interview Data

The NSYR also includes in-person semistructured interviews with a subset of the youth survey participants.[3] Wave 1 interview participants were selected using stratified quota sampling to ensure diversity in race and ethnicity, gender, social class, rural and urban residence, region of the country, and religious affiliation. The interviews averaged about 2 hours in length and allowed for less structured and more in-depth discussions of topics the survey covered. Interviews were audio recorded and transcribed verbatim. Whenever possible, teenagers and interviewers were of the same racial and gender backgrounds.

My analytic sample consists of all the respondents who were interviewed in wave 1 and had at least one additional wave of interview data. This amounts to 216 respondents. These respondents were interviewed an average of three times over 10 years, which resulted in 675 transcripts (about 1,000 hours of recordings). Between 2017 and 2020, I hired 23 Stanford undergraduates, one postbaccalaureate student, and two doctoral students as research assistants (RAs) to help code and analyze the interview data. I intentionally took this team-based approach for two reasons. First, reading and analyzing these data was an enormous undertaking, and I needed help. Second, and perhaps more importantly, this team-based approach helped me assess the reliability and validity of the data by considering the data from multiple angles.

To facilitate a systematic review of the 216 NSYR interviews, I treated each person as a case and conducted a cross-case analysis by developing memos to track each respondent over time. I created a memo template that consisted of 18 questions based on the aforementioned themes I identified. In these memos, the RAs answered the template questions and provided quotes from the interviews as evidence for their answers. Each research assistant was responsible for coding and writing a detailed memo for each of the 216 respondents. The coding was conducted using Dedoose, a web-based qualitative analysis tool. I held regular group meetings with the RAs, during which they reported on their person and we discussed similarities and differences that were emerging from the interviews. These discussions proved to be hugely valuable and advanced my analysis of the data.

Positionality

Working with my RAs also helped me feel more confident about my interpretation of the data. My upbringing is quite different from the teenagers I highlight in this book and I was very concerned about how my personal experience would color my analysis. As I described in the Preface, I have a very different religious upbringing than the teenagers in this book. I also had a relatively unique upbringing in terms of social class because of my immigrant background. My parents were highly educated but worked as janitors—a very typical experience for immigrants, but less typical for the average American teenager. In some ways, I could relate to the struggles of working-class kids in the book. Like many of them, I lost a parent as a teenager after my father died in a car accident when I was 14, which left my mother as the sole income provider. In this respect, I could relate to the class struggle that so many NSYR interviewees described and how much they yearned to achieve the American dream. But in some respects, I also grew up with a lot of privilege and could relate to the kids in this book from the professional class. I attended private Jewish schools (with high amounts of financial aid), which meant that I accrued a tremendous amount of social and cultural capital. I spent countless evenings and weekends hanging out with my friends whose parents were mostly upper-middle-class professionals. My peers all went to college, and most went to highly selective colleges. There is no doubt that my social worlds catapulted me up the socioeconomic ladder. I went to a selective college, followed by two elite universities for graduate school. I am what Joan Williams calls a "class migrant,"[4] which is not the case for most NSYR participants. My interpretation of the data is also limited by the fact that, unlike many NSYR interviewees, I have always lived in suburban and urban areas near large cities.

My RAs helped me overcome my own limitations in interpreting the data. They were incredibly diverse in terms of religious upbringing (both in terms of religious tradition and religiosity), race, class, and geographic upbringing. Their religious backgrounds included Muslim, members of the Church of Jesus Christ of Latter-day Saints, Protestant, Catholic, Atheist, Buddhist, and other affiliations. Some grew up very religious and some grew up completely nonreligious. Several were first-generation and/or low-income college students, and several were students of color.

NSC Match

With help from Sara Skiles of the Notre Dame research team, I linked the NSYR to the National Student Clearinghouse (NSC) to obtain detailed records on college attendance and graduation. The NSC tracks data for most students enrolled in US higher education institutions, including whether they transfer and whether they complete a degree. Matching the NSYR to the NSC helped me overcome a common limitation of longitudinal research: respondents who dropped out of the study after wave 1 or who graduated from a postsecondary institution after the study ended lack complete educational outcome data. Because of the NSC match, I could identify all the higher education institutions that an individual ever attended or graduated from. The NSC match occurred in September 2016 when respondents were between 26 and 31 years old. By this age, most people who will complete their bachelor's degree have done so. Thus, I have college-going data even for respondents who dropped out after the first NSYR wave or completed college after the last wave of data collection.

I use SAT scores of enrolled students as a proxy for institutional selectivity, which is a common measure of quality. I obtain SAT score data from IPEDS, which reports 25th and 75th percentiles of a given cohort's SAT scores. I use the average of these parameters to construct a measure of central tendency for colleges' SAT scores.

National Longitudinal Study of Adolescent to Adult Health

I supplement my analyses of the NSYR with analyses of the National Longitudinal Study of Adolescent to Adult Health (Add Health).[5] The analyses of the Add Health were a collaborative effort between myself, Dr. Ben Domingue, and Dr. Kathleen Mullan Harris. We wanted to examine whether (and to what extent) observed associations between academic outcomes and religiosity were due to (potentially unmeasured) features of the family. We used family fixed-effects models to account for unobserved family factors that jointly contribute to a child's level of religiosity and his or her academic success. As family-level factors are netted out in the sibling models, the lack of observed measures regarding the families of children becomes less salient. The full version of this study was published in 2020 in *Social Science Research*.[6]

Add Health is a nationally representative cohort drawn from a probability sample of 80 US high schools and 52 US middle schools, representative of US schools in 1994–1995 with respect to region, urban setting, school size, school type, and race or ethnic background. Beginning with an in-school questionnaire administered to a nationally representative sample of 20,745 students in grades 7 through 12 in 1994–1995, the study follows up with a series of in-home interviews of students timed approximately 1 year, 6 years, and 13 years later. In wave 1, a parent, usually the resident mother, also completed a survey. Although these Add Health teenagers were born about 10 years earlier than the NSYR teenagers, I have no reason to expect that the relationship between religiosity and academic outcomes observed for teenagers in Add Health would be substantially different than for teenagers in the NSYR.

Of the 20,745 students surveyed during wave 1, more than 15,000 were followed longitudinally in the wave 4 survey, when the respondents were in their late twenties. In addition to the "full sample" of nearly 15,000 individuals, the Add Health also contains a sibling subsample of individuals that we used to control for shared family environment that may be associated with religiosity and academic outcomes. We only analyze the data on full siblings (not half siblings or unrelated siblings). Because these pairs were collected using all design features of Add Health, the subsample is also nationally representative.

Religiosity was our main explanatory variable. We used three variables from wave 1 (self-reported importance of religion, frequency of individual prayer, and frequency of religious service attendance over the prior 12 months) to construct a composite score of religiosity. Grade point average (GPA), college aspirations/expectations, and educational attainment were our main outcome variables. GPA was based on high school transcript data collected at wave 3 once all adolescents had finished high school. GPA is the average of the respondent's grades in mathematics, English, history or social studies, and science (on a 4-point scale).[7] College aspirations/expectations was based on the following question from wave 1: "On a scale of 1 to 5, where 1 is low and 5 is high, how much do you want to go to college?" Educational attainment was a measure of the highest degree completed by the time of interview at wave 4 when respondents were asked, "What is the highest level of education that you have achieved to date?"

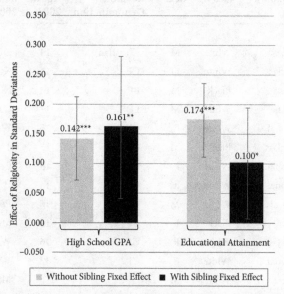

Note: Error bars represent the 95% confidence interval. All outcomes are reported in standard deviations; *p < .05. **p < .01. ***p < .001.

Figure A.1 Religiosity predicts higher GPA and higher educational attainment, even after including sibling fixed effects.

We found that the effect of religiosity on high school GPA, college aspirations/expecta-
tions, and educational attainment was not driven purely by shared family characteristics.
As Figure A.1 shows, adding the sibling fixed effect did not attenuate the effect of religiosity on GPA or one's desire to attend college. In other words, a sibling who is more religious earns better grades, has higher educational aspirations, and completes more years
of higher education than their less religious sibling. The effect of religiosity persists even
after controlling for individuals' verbal ability, meaning that the more religious siblings
don't appear to be more intelligent (based on this particular measure). The key takeaway
of this study is that highly religious adolescents earned higher GPAs in high school and
were generally more academically prepared for college. Thus, more religious adolescents
had higher educational attainment 14 years after their original religiosity was measured.

We were also curious whether adolescents who were more religious in wave 1 had
higher educational attainment in wave 4 because they had higher GPAs in high school.
That is, do more religious students get more years of education because they are better
able to get into college in the first place? Our findings suggest students who were more
religious during adolescence had higher rates of educational attainment largely because
they have better GPAs in high school.

Finally, Table A.1 offers a summary of the various teens who appear in this book.

Table A.1 NSYR Respondents Highlighted in This Book

Name	Socioeconomic Status	Race	Sex	Religious Denomination	Age in 2003	State in 2003
Abiders						
AJ	Professional	White	M	Christian	14	DE
Alex	Middle-class	White	M	CP	14	NC
Andrew	Middle-class	Black	M	BP	16	NC
Anthony	Professional	White	M	LDS	17	UT
Brittany	Professional	White	F	CP	15	WA
Cameron	Middle-class	Black	M	BP	15	TX
Caroline	Professional	White	F	CP	15	CA
Chase	Professional	White	M	Catholic	14	IL
Jacob	Working-class	White	M	Catholic	16	PA
Daisy	Poor	Black	F	CP	14	MD
Elise	Middle-class	White	F	CP	16	WA
Gina	Professional	White	F	CP	17	VA
John	Working-class	White	M	CP	16	MS
Lara	Middle-class	White	F	CP	16	ID
Lindsey	Middle-class	White	F	LDS	14	ID
Mia	Professional	Black	F	BP	14	MD
Michael	Poor	Black	M	BP	15	TX

Table A.1 *Continued*

Name	Socioeconomic Status	Race	Sex	Religious Denomination	Age in 2003	State in 2003
Nadia	Working-class	Hispanic	F	Christian	14	CA
Sally	Professional	White	F	LDS	17	UT
Sean	Professional	White	M	Catholic	14	OH
Susanna	Professional	White	F	Christian	16	AZ
Tim	Poor	White	M	CP	15	NC
Tyah	Poor	Black	F	BP	14	MD
Nonabiders						
Amy	Professional	White	F	Jewish	14	CA
Bret	Working-class	Black	M	Catholic	16	NY
Debbie	Professional	White	F	Jewish	17	MD
Ethan	Working-class	White	M	CP	16	TX
Janet	Middle-class	White	F	Not religious	15	ID
Jessica	Professional	White	F	Jewish	15	PA
Kyle	Professional	White	M	Not religious	14	CA
Laurence	Professional	White	M	Jewish	13	MD
Leah	Professional	White	F	Jewish	13	NH
Luca	Working-class	White	M	Catholic	16	NY
Nicholas	Working-class	White	M	Not religious	14	LA
Quinn	Working-class	White	F	CP	16	VA
Sage	Middle-class	Black	F	MP	17	NY
Simon	Professional	White	M	Catholic	16	WI
Stacy	Professional	White	F	Jewish	13	GA
Vanessa	Professional	White	F	Not religious	15	MI

CP=Conservative Protestant

BP= Black Protestant

MP= Mainline Protestant

Notes

Introduction

1. "Health, United States, 2011: With Special Feature on Socioeconomic Status and Health," 2012, https://www.cdc.gov/nchs/data/hus/hus11.pdf.
2. Anne Case and Angus Deaton, *Deaths of Despair and the Future of Capitalism* (Princeton, NJ: Princeton University Press, 2020).
3. US Bureau of Labor Statistics, "Median Weekly Earnings $606 for High School Dropouts, $1,559 for Advanced Degree Holders," 2019, https://www.bls.gov/opub/ted/2019/median-weekly-earnings-606-for-high-school-dropouts-1559-for-advanced-degree-holders.htm.
4. These rates were calculated as life expectancies for 25-year-old men in 2006. Women live about 5 years longer at each stage, but the educational gap remains. The rates for women are as follows: 77 years (high school dropouts), 82 (high school diploma), 83 (some college education), and 85 (bachelor's degree or more). See figure 32 in *Health, United States, 2011: With Special Feature on Socioeconomic Status and Health* (2012). National Center for Health Statistics. https://www.cdc.gov/nchs/data/hus/hus11.pdf.
5. Throughout this book, I use a college's selectivity as an indicator of the college quality. I measure selectivity by the mean SAT score of its incoming students. For a comprehensive discussion on college quality, see Liang Zhang, *Does Quality Pay?: Benefits of Attending a High-Cost, Prestigious College* (New York: Routledge, 2012).
6. Ibid., 148.
7. Ibid.
8. Scholars refer to this as subjective social status (SSS). See Jeremy E. Uecker and Lindsay R. Wilkinson, "College Selectivity, Subjective Social Status, and Mental Health in Young Adulthood," *Society and Mental Health* 10, no. 3 (2020): 257–75, doi:10.1177/2156869319869401.
9. Ibid.
10. Catherine E. Ross and John Mirowsky, "Refining the Association between Education and Health: The Effects of Quantity, Credential, and Selectivity," *Demography* 36, no. 4 (1999): 445–60, doi:10.2307/2648083.
11. In this book, I use the terms "social class" and "socioeconomic status (SES)" interchangeably, though I recognize that SES refers more to one's current social and economic situation and is relatively mutable, whereas social class refers to one's sociocultural background and is more stable, typically remaining static across generations.
12. The US education system is also stratified by race and gender. Asian Americans (71%) and Whites (44%) are much more likely to earn bachelor's degrees than Blacks (23%), Hispanics (21%), and American Indian/Pacific Islanders (16%). Forty-two percent

of women earned at least a bachelor's degree, compared with 36% of men: National Center for Education Statistics, "Table 104.20: Percentage of Persons 25 to 29 Years Old with Selected Levels of Educational Attainment, by Race/Ethnicity and Sex: Selected Years, 1920 through 2019," 2019, https://nces.ed.gov/programs/digest/d19/tables/dt19_104.20.asp.

13. For more information about the correlation between children's socioeconomic status and their educational outcomes, see Margaret W. Cahalan et al., "Indicators of Higher Education Equity in the United States," 2020, 147–49.

14. For-profit colleges, which do not have much payoff in the labor market, have exploited people for whom higher education has always been a long shot: poor people, single parents, the socially isolated, African Americans, and the working class. See Tressie McMillan Cottom, *Lower Ed: The Troubling Rise of for-Profit Colleges in the New Economy* (New York: The New Press, 2017).

15. Robert D. Putnam, *Our Kids: The American Dream in Crisis* (New York: Simon and Schuster, 2016).

16. Anne Fernald, Virginia A. Marchman, and Adriana Weisleder, "SES Differences in Language Processing Skill and Vocabulary Are Evident at 18 Months," *Developmental Science* 16, no. 2 (2013): 234–48, doi:10.1111/desc.12019.

17. Eric Klinenberg, *Palaces for the People: How Social Infrastructure Can Help Fight Inequality, Polarization, and the Decline of Civic Life* (New York: Broadway Books, 2018).

18. Fernald, Marchman, and Weisleder, "SES Differences in Language Processing Skill and Vocabulary Are Evident at 18 Months."

19. Case and Deaton, *Deaths of Despair and the Future of Capitalism*.

20. Annette Lareau, *Home Advantage: Social Class and Parental Intervention in Elementary Education*, 2nd ed. (Lanham, MD: Rowman & Littlefield, 2000); Annette Lareau, *Unequal Childhoods: Class, Race, and Family Life* (Berkeley: University of California Press, 2011).

21. Jessica McCrory Calarco, *Negotiating Opportunities: How the Middle Class Secures Advantages in School* (New York: Oxford University Press, 2018).

22. Calarco, *Negotiating Opportunities*.

23. Dalia Fahmy, "Americans Are Far More Religious Than Adults in Other Wealthy Nations," *Pew Research Center*, July 31, 2018, https://pewrsr.ch/2LPGypJ; Landon Schnabel and Sean Bock, "The Persistent and Exceptional Intensity of American Religion: A Response to Recent Research," *Sociological Science* 4 (2017): 686–700, doi:10.15195/v4.a28; Robert Putnam and David Campbell, *American Grace: How Religion Divides and Unites Us* (New York: Simon and Schuster, 2010).

24. I also focus on Christianity because surveys tend to phrase questions about religion in ways that reflect a Christian-centric view of religion. For example, notions of "individual prayer" and "faith" are more prevalent in Christianity than in non-Christian denominations. Thus, in nationally representative surveys like the ones I am using in this book, Christian respondents are more likely to appear as highly religious than non-Christian respondents simply based on the wording of the questions.

25. Some readers might bristle at this amalgamation, particularly the inclusion of the Church of Jesus Christ of Latter-day Saints alongside other Christian groups. (The Church of Jesus Christ of Latter-day Saints was formerly referred to as "LDS" and its members "Mormons," but in 2018 the church President said that these labels were no longer appropriate: https://www.nbcnews.com/news/us-news/don-t-use-mormon-or-lds-church-name-president-says-n901491.) Evangelicals generally do not view the Church of Jesus Christ of Latter-day Saints as Christians because of significant theological differences, but in terms of religiosity they share many of the same conservative commitments.

26. Putnam and Campbell, *American Grace*, 3.

27. While this book focuses on Christians, religious intensity is not unique to them, and Orthodox Jews describe a very similar relationship with God. Indeed, in many respects Orthodox Jews are closer to Evangelical Christians in terms of religious intensity than their reform brethren.

28. Pew Research Center, "When Americans Say They Believe in God, What Do They Mean?," 2018, https://www.pewforum.org/wp-content/uploads/sites/7/2018/04/Beliefs-about-God-FOR-WEB-FULL-REPORT.pdf.

29. I adopt this term from Arlie Russell Hochschild, *Strangers in Their Own Land: Anger and Mourning on the American Right* (New York: The New Press, 2018).

30. "How Religious Is Your State?," *Pew Research Center*, accessed December 21, 2020, https://www.pewresearch.org/fact-tank/2016/02/29/how-religious-is-your-state/?state=alabama.

31. Pew Research Center, "In U.S., Decline of Christianity Continues at Rapid Pace," 2019, https://www.pewforum.org/2019/10/17/in-u-s-decline-of-christianity-continues-at-rapid-pace/.

32. Landon Schnabel and Sean Bock use slightly different measures to describe the persistence of "intense religion." They identify people as intensely religious if they strongly affiliate with their religious group, attend religious services more than once a week, believe in biblical literalism, and identify as Evangelicals. See Schnabel and Bock, "The Persistent and Exceptional Intensity of American Religion."

33. Biblical literalists believe that the Bible is the literal word of God as opposed to (1) being inspired by God, but not a literal word of God, or (2) a book of fables. See Schnabel and Bock, "The Persistent and Exceptional Intensity of American Religion."

34. James Wellman Jr., Katie Corcoran, and Kate Stockly, *High on God: How Megachurches Won the Heart of America* (New York: Oxford University Press, 2020).

35. Michael O. Emerson and Christian Smith, *Divided by Faith: Evangelical Religion and the Problem of Race in America* (New York: Oxford University Press, 2001); Putnam and Campbell, *American Grace*; Chaeyoon Lim and Robert D. Putnam, "Religion, Social Networks, and Life Satisfaction," *American Sociological Review* 75, no. 6 (2010): 914–33, doi:10.1177/0003122410386686; Troy C. Blanchard, "Conservative Protestant Congregations and Racial Residential Segregation: Evaluating the Closed Community Thesis in Metropolitan and Nonmetropolitan Counties," *American Sociological Review* 72, no. 3 (2007): 416–33, doi:10.1177/000312240707200305.

36. Christian Smith, Bridget Ritz, and Michael Rotolo, *Religious Parenting: Transmitting Faith and Values in Contemporary America* (Princeton, NJ: Princeton University Press, 2019); Vern L. Bengtson, Norrella Putney, and Susan Harris, *Families and Faith: How Religion Is Passed down across Generations* (New York: Oxford University Press, 2013).

37. While this survey is not meant to be representative of US adults overall, it is weighted to be representative of two different populations: (1) parents with teens ages 13 to 17; and (2) teens ages 13 to 17. It is weighted to be representative by age and gender, race, ethnicity, education, and other categories.

38. Pew calculated that 34% of teenagers have a "high" level of religious commitment, meaning they see religion as very important in their life, attend religious services at least once a week, pray at least once a day, and believe in God with absolute certainty.

39. Smith, Ritz, and Rotolo make a similar observation that when it comes to religious parenting, parents across different social class groups share the same cultural models and describe similar strategies and practices. Though they didn't observe parents, they see how cultural models of religious parenting combine Lareau's strategies: parents in their study were intentional about arranging religious activities in a way that seemed reminiscent of "concerted cultivation," yet they also took a more "natural growth" approach in expecting children to absorb religion by observing and following their parents. See pages 263–64, footnote 1.

40. My research is based on surveys and interviews, whereas Lareau's research is based on ethnography. Thus, the insights I offer about what an upbringing of religious restraint looks like differ from the kinds of insights that Lareau offered about class-based child-rearing strategies. An ethnographic study of what religious restraints looks like across social class groups is an important next step in refining this theory.

41. Lisa D. Pearce, Michael Foster, and Jessica Halliday Hardie, "A Person-Centered Examination of Adolescent Religiosity Using Latent Class Analysis," *Journal for the Scientific Study of Religion* 52, no. 1 (March 1, 2013): 57–79, doi:10.1111/jssr.12001; Ingrid Storm, "Halfway to Heaven: Four Types of Fuzzy Fidelity in Europe," *Journal for the Scientific Study of Religion* 48, no. 4 (2009): 702–18, doi:10.1111/j.1468-5906.2009.01474.x.

42. I take a Durkheimian view of religion, in which religious beliefs work with religious practices to create a religious community. See chapter 11 in Jonathan Haidt, *The Righteous Mind: Why Good People Are Divided by Politics and Religion* (New York: Pantheon Books, 2012).

43. Ilana M. Horwitz, "Religion and Academic Achievement: A Research Review Spanning Secondary School and Higher Education," *Review of Religious Research* (2020), doi:10.1007/s13644-020-00433-y.

44. For more information, see Michelle Jackson, *Determined to Succeed?: Performance versus Choice in Educational Attainment* (Palo Alto, CA: Stanford University Press, 2013).

45. Scholars also refer to performance effects as a "primary effect," whereas choice effects are "secondary effects."

46. Colleges and universities are now increasingly offering merit-based aid, meaning they offer scholarships to students with high GPAs to improve the institutions' prestige. See Ron Lieber, *The Price You Pay for College: An Entirely New Roadmap for the Biggest Financial Decision Your Family Will Ever Make* (New York: HarperCollins, 2021).

47. This is why sociologists use the term "inequality of educational opportunity" when studying performance and choice effects. The fact that students perform at different levels is not a problem—as long as everyone has an equal shot of success at the starting line. But inequality in our schools is a problem because students' performance is tied to their social origins—students do not have an equal shot at success. When students from poor families or students of color systemically do worse in school, it means there is unjust inequality.

48. Emile Durkheim, *The Elementary Forms of Religious Life: A Study in Religious Sociology* (New York: Free Press, 1912); Karl Marx and Friedrich Engels, *The Economic and Philosophic Manuscripts of 1844 and the Communist Manifesto* (Buffalo, NY: Prometheus Books, 2009).

49. Gerhard Emmanuel Lenski, *The Religious Factor: A Sociological Study of Religion's Impact on Politics, Economics, and Family Life* (Garden City, NY: Doubleday & Company, 1961).

50. See Will Herberg, *Protestant—Catholic—Jew: An Essay in American Religious Sociology* (Chicago: University of Chicago Press, 1955).

51. David L. Featherman, "The Socioeconomic Achievement of White Religio-Ethnic Subgroups: Social and Psychological Explanations," *American Sociological Review* 36, no. 2 (1971): 207–22.

52. Lisa A. Keister and Darren E. Sherkat, *Religion and Inequality in America: Research and Theory on Religion's Role in Stratification* (Cambridge: Cambridge University Press, 2014).

53. Pippa Norris and Ronald Inglehart, *Sacred and Secular: Religion and Politics Worldwide* (Cambridge: Cambridge University Press, 2011).

54. Neil Gross, *Why Are Professors Liberal and Why Do Conservatives Care?* (Cambridge, MA: Harvard University Press, 2013).

55. Darren E. Sherkat and Christopher G. Ellison, "Recent Developments and Current Controversies in the Sociology of Religion," *Annual Review of Sociology* 25, no. 1 (1999): 363–94, doi:10.1146/annurev.soc.25.1.363.

56. Horwitz, "Religion and Academic Achievement."

57. Natasha Warikoo and Prudence Carter, "Cultural Explanations for Racial and Ethnic Stratification in Academic Achievement: A Call for a New and Improved Theory," *Review of Educational Research* 79, no. 1 (2009): 366–94, doi:10.3102/0034654308326162; Grace Kao and Jennifer S. Thompson, "Racial and Ethnic Stratification in Educational Achievement and Attainment," *Annual Review of Sociology* 29, no. 1 (2003): 417–42, doi:10.1146/annurev.soc.29.010202.100019.

58. Selcuk R. Sirin, "Socioeconomic Status and Academic Achievement: A Meta-Analytic Review of Research," *Review of Educational Research* 75, no. 3 (2005): 417–53, doi:10.3102/00346543075003417.

59. Claudia Buchmann, Thomas A. Diprete, and Anne Mcdaniel, "Gender Inequalities in Education," *Annual Review of Sociology*, no. 34 (2008): 19–37, doi:10.1146/annurev.soc.34.040507.134719.

60. Tim Clydesdale and Garces-Foley Kathleen, "Nones," in *The Twentysomething Soul: Understanding the Religious and Secular Lives of American Young Adults* (New York: Oxford University Press, 2019), 1–20, doi:10.1093/oso/9780190931353.001.0001; Christian Smith and Patricia Snell, *Souls in Transition: The Religious and Spiritual Lives of Emerging Adults* (Oxford University Press, 2009).

61. Lauren A. Rivera and Mitchell L. Stevens, "Why Economic Sociologists Should Care about Education," *Accounts: ASA Economic Sociology Newsletter* 12, no. 3 (2013): 5–8.

62. See Melissa Wilde and Lindsay Glassman, "How Complex Religion Can Improve Our Understanding of American Politics," *Annual Review of Sociology*, no. 42 (2016): 407–25, doi:10.1146/annurev-soc-081715-074420; Melissa J. Wilde, "Editorial: 'Complex Religion: Intersections of Religion and Inequality,'" *Social Inclusion* 6 (2018): 83–86, doi:10.17645/si.v6i2.1606.

63. See Melissa J. Wilde and Patricia Tevington, "Complex Religion: Toward a Better Understanding of the Ways in Which Religion Intersects with Inequality," *Emerging Trends in the Social and Behavioral Sciences* (2017): 1–14, doi.org/10.1002/9781118900772.etrds0440.

64. As I explain throughout the book, theological belief on its own is not enough to influence how children behave—adolescents have to believe *and* belong. The social nature of a religious community plays a central role in why religious Americans fare better in several aspects of life. See, for example, Chaeyoon Lim and Robert D. Putnam, "Religion, Social Networks, and Life Satisfaction," *American Sociological Review* 75, no. 6 (2010): 914–33, doi.org/10.1177/0003122410386686.

65. I linked the NSYR records of parents' occupation with O*Net to obtain their occupational prestige score (https://www.onetonline.org/).

Chapter 1

1. For a discussion of social class, see Richard V. Reeves, Katherine Guyot, and Eleanor Krause, "Defining the Middle Class: Cash, Credentials, or Culture?," The Brookings Institution, 2018, https://www.brookings.edu/research/defining-the-middle-class-cash-credentials-or-culture/; Joan C. Williams, *White Working Class: Overcoming Class Cluelessness in America* (Cambridge, MA: Harvard Business Press, 2020).

2. Lareau defined working-class children as those who live in households in which neither parent is employed in a middle-class position and at least one parent is employed in a position with little or no managerial authority and does not draw on highly complex, educationally certified skills. This category includes lower-level white-collar workers. She defined middle-class children as those who live in households in which at least one parent is employed in a position that either entails substantial managerial authority or that centrally draws upon highly complex, educationally certified (i.e.,

college-level) skills (Table C1, p. 365 in Annette Lareau, *Unequal Childhoods: Class, Race, and Family Life* [Berkeley: University of California Press, 2011]). Using Lareau's terms, Alex's family is probably working class, but based on my categories of class, I refer to his family as middle class.

3. Andrew, who was raised as a Black Protestant, might have been even more compliant than other abiders because Black Protestants might take an even stronger view on the issue of parental and God's authority. Smith, Ritz, and Rotolo (2020) observed that Black Protestant parents expressed more authority over their children, compared to other parents who tread more lightly when it comes to their authority to teach, command, and discipline their children. Importantly, their sample was limited and they urge more research in this area. See pages 139–42.

4. Bengtson, Putney, and Harris, *Families and Faith*.

5. Smith, Ritz, and Rotolo, *Religious Parenting*.

6. See Barbara Rogoff, Rebeca Mejia-Arauz, and Maricela Correa-Chávez, "A Cultural Paradigm—Learning by Observing and Pitching in," in *Advances in Child Development and Behavior*, vol. 49 (New York: Elsevier, 2015), 1–22; Barbara Rogoff et al., "Firsthand Learning through Intent Participation," *Annual Review of Psychology* 54 (2003): 175–203, doi:10.1146/annurev.psych.54.101601.145118.

7. Christian Smith, "Religious Participation and Network Closure among American Adolescents," *Journal for the Scientific Study of Religion* 42, no. 2 (2003): 259–67, doi:https://10.1111/1468-5906.00177.

8. Shirley Brice Heath, *Ways with Words: Language, Life and Work in Communities and Classrooms* (Cambridge: Cambridge University Press, 1983).

9. Tanya M. Luhrmann, *When God Talks Back: Understanding the American Evangelical Relationship with God* (New York: Alfred A. Knopf, 2012).

10. God is almost always referred to as male in these contexts.

11. See Chapter 2.

12. According to a 2018 Pew study, this type of reciprocal relationship with God is most common among Evangelicals, 45% of whom say that they talk with God and God talks back. But this is not just an Evangelical perspective: 60% of Black Protestants have a reciprocal relationship with God, and about a quarter of Catholics (23%) and Mainline Protestants (25%) share this viewpoint. The view that God is responsible for "all" things that happen in life is also prevalent across different religious traditions: it peaks at 61% among those in the historically Black Protestant tradition, and it is shared by 46% of Evangelical Protestants. One-quarter of Catholics (24%) also see God's hand at work in all or most things that happen to them, as do 29% of Mainline Protestants. See Pew Research Center 2018.

13. Wellman Jr., Corcoran, and Stockly, *High on God*.

14. Ann E. Jones and Marta Elliott, "Examining Social Desirability in Measures of Religion and Spirituality Using the Bogus Pipeline," *Review of Religious Research* 59, no. 1 (2017): 47–64, doi:10.1007/s13644-016-0261-6.

15. Steven Hitlin and Sarah K. Harkness, *Unequal Foundations: Inequality, Morality, and Emotions across Cultures* (New York: Oxford University Press, 2018).

16. Charles S. Carver and Michael F. Scheier, "The Self-Attention-Induced Feedback Loop and Social Facilitation," *Journal of Experimental Social Psychology* 17, no. 6 (1981): 545–68, doi:10.1016/0022-1031(81)90039-1.

17. Hitlin and Harkness, *Unequal Foundations*, 121.

18. Ayelet Fishbach, Tal Eyal, and Stacey R. Finkelstein, "How Positive and Negative Feedback Motivate Goal Pursuit," *Social and Personality Psychology Compass* 4, no. 8 (2010): 517–30, doi:10.1111/j.1751-9004.2010.00285.x.

19. Sheldon Stryker, "Identity Salience and Role Performance: The Relevance of Symbolic Interaction Theory for Family Research," *Journal of Marriage and Family* 30, no. 4 (1968): 558–64. doi:10.2307/349494

20. Edward L. Deci and Richard M. Ryan, "Self-Determination Theory: When Mind Mediates Behavior," *Journal of Mind and Behavior* 1, no. 1 (1980): 33–43. Retrieved July 1, 2021, from http://www.jstor.org/stable/43852807

21. Carl Ransom Rogers, *A Theory of Therapy, Personality, and Interpersonal Relationships: As Developed in the Client-Centered Framework*, vol. 3 (New York: McGraw-Hill, 1959).

22. Deci and Ryan, "Self-Determination Theory."

Chapter 2

1. Evan Schofer, "Schooling in Global Perspective," in *Education and Society: An Introduction to Key Issues in the Sociology of Education*, ed. Thurston Domina et al. (Berkeley: University of California Press, 2019), 7–22.

2. David F. Labaree, "Struggle Over Educational Goals," *American Educational Research Journal* 34, no. 1 (1997): 39–81, doi:10.3102/00028312034001039.

3. Lisa Nunn, "First-Generation College Students," in *Education and Society: An Introduction to Key Issues in the Sociology of Education*, ed. Thurston Domina et al. (Berkeley: University of California Press, 2019), 110–28.

4. Chetty et al., "Mobility Report Cards."

5. Bryan Caplan, *The Case against Education: Why the Education System Is a Waste of Time and Money* (Princeton, NJ: Princeton University Press, 2018).

6. Jeffrey Guhin, "Why Study Schools?," in *The Handbook of Classical Sociological Theory*, ed. Omar A. Lizardo and Seth Abrutyn (New York: Springer, 2021).

7. Jeanne H. Ballantine, Floyd M. Hammack, and Jenny Stuber, *The Sociology of Education: A Systematic Analysis* (New York: Routledge, 2017), doi:10.4324/9781315408545-8.; Emile Durkheim, *Moral Education: A Study in the Theory and Application of the Sociology of Education*, ed. and trans. Everett K. Wilson and Herman Schnurer (New York: Free Press, 1961).

8. Randall Collins, "Functional and Conflict Theories of Educational Stratification," *American Sociological Review* 36, no. 6 (1971): 1012.

9. Collins, "Functional and Conflict Theories of Educational Stratification"; David P. Baker, "The Great Antagonism That Never Was: Unexpected Affinities between

Religion and Education in Post-Secular Society," *Theory and Society* 48 (2019): 39–65, doi:https://10.1007/s11186-018-09338-w.

10. Tony Bryk, Valerie E. Lee, and Peter Blakeley Holland, *Catholic Schools and the Common Good* (Cambridge, MA: Harvard University Press, 1993); Charles L. Glenn, *The Myth of the Common School* (PhD diss., Boston University, 1987); David Labaree, *Someone Has to Fail* (Cambridge, MA: Harvard University Press, 2012).

11. Also see Baker, "The Great Antagonism That Never Was."

12. James W. Fraser, *Between Church and State: Religion and Public Education in a Multicultural America* (Baltimore: Johns Hopkins University Press, 2016).

13. Ibid., 9.

14. Ibid., 3.

15. While schooling grew significantly in all regions of the nation between 1870 and 1930, it developed exceptionally rapidly where evangelical Protestantism populations were prevalent. See John W. Meyer et al., "Public Education as Nation-Building in America: Enrollments and Bureaucratization in the American States, 1870–1930," *American Journal of Sociology* 85, no. 3 (1979): 591–613, doi:10.1086/227051.

16. Fraser, *Between Church and State*.

17. Baker, "The Great Antagonism That Never Was," 53–54.

18. David K. Cohen, 1987. "Educational Technology, Policy, and Practice," *Educational Evaluation and Policy Analysis* 9, no. 2 (1987): 153–70. https://doi:10.3102/01623737009002153

19. Cohen, "Educational Technology, Policy, and Practice," 161.

20. See Labaree, *Someone Has to Fail*, 64. Sociologist David Baker has gone so far to suggest that there is a reciprocal and mutually beneficial relationship between religion and schooling: "The worldwide spread of education could be partially sustained by its affinity with religious ideas. The evidence suggests a symbiosis that is distinct from the more common sociological image of blunt opposition and opens support for theorizing the two institutions as a nuanced synergy" (Baker, "The Great Antagonism That Never Was," 57).

21. Emile Durkheim, *Moral Education: A Study in the Theory and Application of the Sociology of Education*, ed. and trans. Everett K. Wilson and Herman Schnurer (New York: Free Press, 1961), 148.

22. Durkheim, *Moral Education*, 150.

23. Rebecca Raby, *School Rules: Obedience, Discipline, and Elusive Democracy* (Toronto: University of Toronto Press, 2012).

24. Philip Wesley Jackson, *Life in Classrooms* (New York: Holt, Rinehart, and Winston, 1968).

25. Ibid., 29.

26. Benson R. Snyder, *The Hidden Curriculum* (New York: Alfred A. Knopf, 1971).

27. Harry L. Gracey, "Learning the Student Role: Kindergarten as Academic Boot Camp," in *Readings in Introductory Sociology*, ed. Dennis Wrong and Harry Gracey (New York: The Macmillan Company, 1967), 8.

28. See discussion of Durkheim in Richard Arum, *Judging School Discipline* (Cambridge, MA: Harvard University Press, 2005), 33.

29. Ibid., 165.

30. See Mitchell L. Stevens, *Kingdom of Children: Culture and Controversy in the Homeschooling Movement* (Princeton, NJ: Princeton University Press, 2009).

31. Christopher G. Ellison and Darren E. Sherkat, "Obedience and Autonomy: Religion and Parental Values Reconsidered," *Journal for the Scientific Study of Religion* 32, no. 4 (1993): 313–29; Christopher G. Ellison and Xiaohe Xu, "Religion and Families," in *The Wiley Blackwell Companion to the Sociology of Families* (Hoboken, NJ: John Wiley & Sons, 2014), 277–99, doi:10.1002/9781118374085.ch14; Dennis E. Owen, Kenneth D. Wald, and Samuel S. Hill, "Authoritarian or Authority-Minded? The Cognitive Commitments of Fundamentalists and the Christian Right," *Religion and American Culture: A Journal of Interpretation* 1, no. 1 (1991): 73–100.

32. Penny Edgell, "In Rhetoric and Practice: Defining 'The Good Family' in Local Congregations," in *Handbook of the Sociology of Religion*, ed. Michele Dillon (New York: Cambridge University Press, 2003), 164–78.

33. Haidt, *The Righteous Mind*.

34. John P. Bartkowski, Xiaohe Xu, and Melinda L. Denton, *Mormon to the Core: Religion in the Lives of Latter-day Saint Teens and Young Adults*. Working manuscript.

35. Pew Research Center, "U.S. Teens Take after Their Parents Religiously, Attend Services Together and Enjoy Family Rituals," 2020, 91, https://www.pewforum.org/wp-content/uploads/sites/7/2020/09/PF_20.09.10_teens.religion.full_.report.pdf.

36. Christian Smith, "Theorizing Religious Effects among American Adolescents," *Journal for the Scientific Study of Religion* 42, no. 1 (2003): 17–30, doi:https://10.1111/1468-5906.t01-1-00158.

37. Nancy T. Ammerman, *Golden Rule Christianity: Lived Religion in the American Mainstream* (Princeton, NJ: Princeton University Press, 1997).

38. Kevin J. Burke and Avner Segall, "Teaching as Jesus Making: The Hidden Curriculum of Christ in Schooling," *Teachers College Record* 117, no. 3 (2015): 1–27.

39. Fraser, *Between Church and State*.

40. Baker, "The Great Antagonism That Never Was," 1.

41. Michael J. Cawley III, James E. Martin, and John A. Johnson, "A Virtues Approach to Personality," *Personality and Individual Differences* 28, no. 2000 (2009): 997–1013.

42. Michael E. Mccullough and Brian L. B. Willoughby, "Religion, Self-Regulation, and Self-Control: Associations, Explanations, and Implications," *Psychological Bulletin* 135, no. 1 (2009): 69–93, doi:https://10.1037/a0014213.

43. Vassilis Saroglou, "Religion and the Five Factors of Personality: A Meta-Analytic Review," *Personality and Individual Differences* 32, no. 1 (2002): 15–25, doi:https://10.1016/S0191-8869(00)00233-6.

44. Michael A. Hogg, Janice R. Adelman, and Robert D. Blagg, "Religion in the Face of Uncertainty: An Uncertainty-Identity Theory Account of Religiousness," *Personality and Social Psychology Review* 14, no. 1 (2010): 72–83, doi:https://10.1177/1088868309349692.

45. Crystal L. Park, "Religion and Meaning," in *Handbook of the Psychology of Religion and Spirituality*, ed. Raymond F. Paloutzian and Crystal L. Park (New York: The Guilford Press, 2005), 295–314.

46. Brent W. Roberts et al., "Conscientiousness," in *Handbook of Individual Differences in Social Behavior* (New York: The Guilford Press, 2009), 369–81. Also see Joshua J. Jackson et al., "What Do Conscientious People Do? Development and Validation of the Behavioral Indicators of Conscientiousness," *Journal of Research in Personality* 44, no. 4 (2010): 501–11, doi:10.1016/j.jrp.2010.06.005.

47. Mohammed Chowdhury and Mohammed Amin, "Personality and Students' Academic Achievement: Interactive Effects of Conscientiousness and Agreeableness on Students' Performance in Principles of Economics," *Social Behavior and Personality* 34, no. 4 (2006): 381–88.

48. Jesse Graham and Jonathan Haidt, "Beyond Beliefs: Religions Bind Individuals into Moral Communities," *Personality and Social Psychology Review* 14, no. 1 (2010): 140–50, doi:10.1177/1088868309353415.

49. Lee A. Kirkpatrick, *Attachment, Evolution, and the Psychology of Religion* (New York: Guilford Press, 2005).

50. Pehr Granqvist, Mario Mikulincer, and Phillip R. Shaver, "Religion as Attachment: Normative Processes and Individual Differences," *Personality and Social Psychology Review* 14, no. 1 (2010): 49–59, doi:10.1177/1088868309348618; Vassilis Saroglou, "Religiousness as a Cultural Adaptation of Basic Traits: A Five-Factor Model Perspective," *Personality and Social Psychology Review* 14, no. 1 (2010): 108–25, doi:10.1177/1088868309352322.

51. Soraya Hakimi, Elaheh Hejazi, and Masoud Gholamali Lavasani, "The Relationships between Personality Traits and Students' Academic Achievement," *Procedia—Social and Behavioral Sciences* 29 (2011): 836–45; Arthur E. Poropat, "A Meta-Analysis of the Five-Factor Model of Personality and Academic Performance," *Psychological Bulletin* 135, no. 2 (2009): 322–38.

52. Sam A. Hardy and Gustavo Carlo, "Religiosity and Prosocial Behaviours in Adolescence: The Mediating Role of Prosocial Values," *Journal of Moral Education* 34, no. 2 (2005): 231–49, doi:10.1080/03057240500127210; Saroglou, "Religiousness as a Cultural Adaptation of Basic Traits."

53. Ibid.

54. Chowdhury and Amin, "Personality and Students' Academic Achievement"; Christy Lleras, "Do Skills and Behaviors in High School Matter? The Contribution of Noncognitive Factors in Explaining Differences in Educational Attainment and Earnings," *Social Science Research* 37, no. 3 (2008): 888–902; Maureen A. Conard, "Aptitude Is Not Enough: How Personality and Behavior Predict Academic Performance," *Journal of Research in Personality* 40, no. 3 (2006): 339–46.

55. George Farkas, "Cognitive Skills and Noncognitive Traits and Behaviors in Stratification Processes," *Annual Review of Sociology* 29, no. 1 (2003): 547.

56. Chowdhury and Amin, "Personality and Students' Academic Achievement."

57. William Tirre, "Conscientiousness Provides High School Students an Advantage in Achieving Good Grades Incrementally to General Cognitive Ability," *North American Journal of Psychology* 19, no. 2 (2017): 303–24.

58. Conscientiousness appears to be an especially strong predictor of GPA for students who are the least intrinsically motivated to learn. For more on the compensatory

function of conscientiousness for students with low levels of intrinsic motivation, see Stefano I. Di Domenico and Marc A. Fournier, "Able, Ready, and Willing: Examining the Additive and Interactive Effects of Intelligence, Conscientiousness, and Autonomous Motivation on Undergraduate Academic Performance," *Learning and Individual Differences* 40 (2015): 156–62, doi:10.1016/j.lindif.2015.03.016.

59. For more on the link between religiosity and self-regulation, see Sam A. Hardy et al., "Adolescent Religiousness as a Protective Factor against Pornography Use," *Journal of Applied Developmental Psychology* 34, no. 3 (2013): 131–39, doi:10.1016/j.appdev.2012.12.002. For more on why delayed gratification and self-regulation are linked with academic success, see Yuichi Shoda, Walter Mischel, and Philip K. Peake, "Predicting Adolescent Cognitive and Self-Regulatory Competencies From Preschool Delay of Gratification: Identifying Diagnostic Conditions," *Developmental Psychology* 26, no. 6 (1990): 978–86, doi:10.1037/0012-1649.26.6.978.

60. When people think God is watching, they modify their behavior to be more prosocial and less selfish. See Azim F. Shariff and Ara Norenzayan, "God Is Watching You," *Psychological Science* 18, no. 9 (2007): 803–09, doi:10.1111/j.1467-9280.2007.01983.x.

61. As Ari Y. Kelman argues, people who make music for worship also make worship from music. See Ari Y. Kelman, *Shout to the Lord: Making Worship Music in Evangelical America* (New York: NYU Press, 2018).

62. See discussion of Basil Bernstein in Paul DiMaggio, "Sociological Perspectives on the Face-to-Face Enactment of Class Distinction," in *Facing Social Class: How Societal Rank Influences Interaction*, ed. Susan T Fiske and Hazel Rose Markus (Thousand Oaks, CA: Russell Sage Foundation, 2012), 15–38.

63. Ibid.

64. Ibid.

65. Ibid.

66. Three studies in which test scores are the outcome yield different results. Will J. Jordan and Saundra Murray Nettles, "How Students Invest Their Time Outside of School: Effects on School-Related Outcomes," *Social Psychology of Education* 3, no. 4 (2000): 217–43, doi:10.1023/A:1009655611694; Mark D. Regnerus, "Shaping Schooling Success: Religious Socialization and Educational Outcomes in Metropolitan Public Schools," *Journal for the Scientific Study of Religion* 39, no. 3 (2000): 363–70, http://dx.doi.org/10.1111/0021-8294.00030; William H. Jeynes, "The Effects of Religious Commitment on the Academic Achievement of Urban and Other Children," *Education and Urban Society* 36, no. 1 (2003): 44–62, doi:10.1177/0013124503257206. For a discussion, see Horwitz, "Religion and Academic Achievement."

67. Nine studies based on analyses of large-scale data sets of middle and high school adolescents consistently show that individual religiosity is associated with better grades. The effect of religiosity persists in all studies even after controls for background factors such as race, socioeconomic status, and gender. See Jennifer L. Glanville, David Sikkink, and Edwin I. Hernández, "Religious Involvement and Educational Outcomes: The Role of Social Capital and Extracurricular

Participation," *The Sociological Quarterly* 49, no. 1 (2008): 105–37, doi:10.1111/
j.1533-8525.2007.00108.x; Benjamin McKune and John P. Hoffmann, "Religion
and Academic Religion and Academic Achievement Among Adolescents,"
Interdisciplinary Journal of Research on Religion 5 (2009): 1–21; Alyssa S. Milot and
Alison Bryant Ludden, "The Effects of Religion and Gender on Well-Being, Substance
Use, and Academic Engagement Among Rural Adolescents," *Youth & Society* 40, no.
3 (2009): 403–25, doi:https://doi.org/10.1177/0044118X08316668; Mark D. Regnerus
and Glen Elder, "Staying on Track in School: Religious Influences in High- and Low-
Risk Settings," *Journal for the Scientific Study of Religion* 42, no. 4 (2003): 633–49; Tirre,
"Conscientiousness Provides High School Students an Advantage in Achieving Good
Grades Incrementally to General Cognitive Ability"; Ivory Toldson and Kenneth
Anderson, "Editor's Comment: The Role of Religion in Promoting Academic Success
for Black Students," *Journal of Negro Education* 79, no. 3 (2010): 205–13; Jerry Trusty
and Richard E. Watts, "Relationship of High School Seniors' Religious Perceptions
and Behavior to Educational, Career, and Leisure Variables," *Counseling and Values*
44, no. 1 (1999): 30–39, doi:10.1002/j.2161-007X.1999.tb00150.x. For a discussion,
see Horwitz, "Religion and Academic Achievement."

68. Buchmann, Diprete, and Mcdaniel, "Gender Inequalities in Education."
69. Gloria Ladson-Billings, "From the Achievement Gap to the Education
Debt: Understanding Achievement in U.S. Schools," *Educational Researcher* 35, no. 7
(2006): 3–12, doi:10.3102/0013189x035007003.
70. Warikoo and Carter, "Cultural Explanations for Racial and Ethnic Stratification in
Academic Achievement."
71. Sirin, "Socioeconomic Status and Academic Achievement."
72. All the existing studies that have used samples of US students to examine the relationship between religiosity and grades use regression frameworks that verify the presence of a correlation between dependent and independent variables.
73. Ilana Horwitz, Benjamin W. Domingue, and Kathleen Mullan Harris, "Not a Family
Matter: The Effects of Religiosity on Academic Outcomes Based on Evidence
From Siblings," *Social Science Research* 88–89 (2020), doi:https://doi.org/10.1016/
j.ssresearch.2020.102426.
74. It is still quite possible that the effect we observe is driven by personality less than
by religion. In other words, religious adolescents could be the type of kids who are
naturally self-disciplined and prefer structure. These adolescents would also be more
likely to do well in school, which would mean that religious adolescents earn better
grades because of personality differences and not because of religion. Unfortunately,
this is hard to test.
75. It is unclear whether increased religious engagement leads young people to be more
conscientious and agreeable, or if people who are conscientious and agreeable are
more drawn to religion. See Mark D. Regnerus and Christian Smith, "Selection Effects
in Studies of Religious Influence," *Review of Religious Research* 47, no. 1 (2005): 23–
50, doi:10.1093/socrel/68.2.145; Saroglou, "Religiousness as a Cultural Adaptation of
Basic Traits."

76. Annette Lareau and Erin Horvat, "Moments of Social Inclusion and Exclusion Race, Class, and Cultural Capital in Family-School Relationships," *Sociology of Education* 72, no. 1 (1999): 42.

Chapter 3

1. Saul Geiser and Maria Veronica Santelices, "Validity of High-School Grades in Predicting Student Success beyond the Freshman Year: High-School Record vs. Standardized Tests as Indicators of Four-Year College Outcomes: Research & Occasional Paper Series: CSHE. 6.07," 2007, https://escholarship.org/uc/item/7306z0zf; Rebecca Zwick and Jeffrey C. Sklar, "Predicting College Grades and Degree Completion Using High School Grades and SAT Scores: The Role of Student Ethnicity and First Language," *American Educational Research Journal* 42, no. 3 (2005): 439–64, doi:10.3102/00028312042003439.

2. Several longitudinal studies using large national data sets show a consistent and positive relationship between religiosity during adolescence and educational attainment. See Bo Hyeong J. Lee and Lisa D. Pearce, "Understanding Why Religious Involvement's Relationship with Education Varies by Social Class," *Journal of Research on Adolescence* 29, no. 2 (2019): 369–89, doi:10.1111/jora.12457; Sang Min Lee, Ana Puig, and Mary Ann Clark, "The Role of Religiosity on Postsecondary Degree Attainment," *Counseling & Values* 52, no. 1 (2007): 25–39, doi:10.1002/j.2161-007X.2007.tb00085.x; Evelyn L. Lehrer, "Religiosity as a Determinant of Educational Attainment: The Case of Conservative Protestant Women in the United States," *Review of Economics of the Household* 2 (2004): 203–19, doi:10.1023/B:REHO.0000031614.84035.8e; Evelyn L. Lehrer, "Religious Affiliation and Participation as Determinants of Women's Educational Attainment and Wages," in *Religion, Families, and Health: Population-Based Research in the United States*, ed. Robert Hummer and Christopher G. Ellison, 186–205 (Ithaca, NY: Rutgers University Press, 2010); Linda D. Loury, "Does Church Attendance Really Increase Schooling?," *Source Journal for the Scientific Study of Religion* 43, no. 1 (2004): 119–27, doi:10.1111/j.1468-5906.2004.00221.x; Charles E. Stokes, "The Role of Parental Religiosity in High School Completion," *Sociological Spectrum* 28, no. 5 (2008): 531–55, doi:10.1080/02732170802206153. These early studies of individual religiosity and educational attainment suffered from concerns about spuriousness versus causality, but methodological advancements in recent studies that use propensity score matching are helping to illuminate the causal pathways. See Madhu S. Mohanty, "Effect of Religious Attendance on Years of Schooling in the USA," *Education Economics* 24, no. 4 (2016): 411–26, doi:https://doi.org/10.1080/09645292.2015.1111866; Jeannie Kim, "The Academic Advantage of Devotion: Measuring Variation in the Value of Weekly Worship in Late Adolescence on Educational Attainment Using Propensity Score Matching," *Journal for the Scientific Study of Religion* 54, no. 3 (2015): 555–74, doi:10.1111/jssr.12219.

3. Hirokazu Yoshikawa et al., "Investing in Our Future: The Evidence Base on Preschool Education," 2013, https://www.fcd-us.org/the-evidence-base-on-preschool.

4. The definition of "proficient" varies from state to state as well as within states. For example, in California, educators apply a five-tier configuration: Far Below Basic, Below Basic, Basic, Proficient, and Advanced, to classify a student's performance level on the California Standards Tests. Attached to each tier are cut points ranging from 150 to 600. The cut point for proficiency on the California Standards Tests in both English language arts (ELA) and mathematics is 350 for grades two through eight. For more details, see Cheryl James-Ward, "No Child Left Behind and the Definition of Proficient: What Should School Leaders in California Know about the Definition of Proficient?," *Educational Leadership and Administration: Teaching and Program Development* 20 (2008): 109–15.

5. Bill Hussar et al., "The Condition of Education 2020," *Institute of Education Science*, vol. 5, 2020, https://nces.ed.gov/pubs2017/2017144.pdf.

6. Donald Hernandez, "Double Jeopardy: How Third-Grade Reading Skills and Poverty Influence High School Graduation," 2012, https://www.aecf.org/resources/double-jeopardy/.

7. Andrew Sum, Ishwar Khatiwada, and Joseph McLaughlin, "The Consequences of Dropping out of High School: Joblessness and Jailing for High School Dropouts and the High Cost for Taxpayers" (Boston, MA, 2009), https://www.prisonpolicy.org/scans/The_Consequences_of_Dropping_Out_of_High_School.pdf.

8. Case and Deaton, *Deaths of Despair and the Future of Capitalism.*

9. Claudia Goldin, "Human Capital," in *Handbook of Cliometrics*, ed. Claude Diebolt and Michael Haupert, 55–86 (Heidelberg, Germany: Springer Verlag, 2016).

10. Laura Carstensen, *A Long Bright Future: Happiness, Health, and Financial Security in an Age of Increased Longevity* (New York: Broadway Books, 2011).

11. Ellen R. Meara, Seth Richards, and David M. Cutler, "The Gap Gets Bigger: Changes in Mortality and Life Expectancy, by Education, 1981–2000," *Health Affairs* 27, no. 2 (2008): 350–60, doi:https://doi.org/10.1377/hlthaff.27.2.350.

12. "Health, United States, 2011: With Special Feature on Socioeconomic Status and Health."

13. Catherine E. Ross and Chia-ling Wu, "Education, Age, and the Cumulative Advantage in Health," *American Sociological Review* 37, no. 1 (1996): 104–20; David M. Cutler and Adriana Lleras-Muney, "Understanding Differences in Health Behaviors by Education," *Journal of Health Economics* 29, no. 1 (2010): 1–28, doi:10.1016/j.jhealeco.2009.10.003; James S. House, Paula M. Lantz, and Pamela Herd, "Continuity and Change in the Social Stratification of Aging and Health over the Life Course: Evidence from a Nationally Representative Longitudinal Study from 1986 to 2001/2002," *The Journals of Gerontology: Series B* 60, no. 2 (Special issue, October 1, 2005): S15–26, doi:10.1093/geronb/60.Special_Issue_2.S15.

14. Rita Hamad et al., "Educational Attainment and Cardiovascular Disease in the United States: A Quasi-Experimental Instrumental Variables Analysis," *PLoS Medicine* 16, no. 6 (2019): 1–19, doi:10.1371/journal.pmed.1002834.

15. Ichiro Kawachi, Nancy E. Adler, and William H. Dow, "Money, Schooling, and Health: Mechanisms and Causal Evidence," *Annals of the New York Academy of Sciences* 1186 (2010): 56–68, doi:10.1111/j.1749-6632.2009.05340.x.

16. Anne Jamieson, "Higher Education Study in Later Life: What Is the Point?," *Ageing and Society* 27, no. 3 (2007): 363–84, doi:10.1017/S0144686X06005745.

17. Horwitz, Domingue, and Harris, "Not a Family Matter."

18. United States Census Bureau. *Educational Attainment* (2019). Retrieved from https://www.census.gov/topics/education/educational-attainment.html.

19. National Center for Education Statistics, "Table 104.20: Percentage of Persons 25 to 29 Years Old with Selected Levels of Educational Attainment, by Race/Ethnicity and Sex: Selected Years, 1920 through 2019."

20. The rates vary slightly depending on how degree attainment is measured. See discussion of equity indicator 5 in M. Cahalan et al., "Indicators of Higher Education Equity in the United States: 2018 Historical Trend Report," 2018, www.pellinstitute.org.

21. Putnam points out that high-scoring poor kids are slightly less likely to get a college degree than low-scoring rich kids. See chapter 4 in Putnam, *Our Kids: The American Dream in Crisis*.

22. See Paul Tough, *The Inequality Machine: How College Divides Us* (New York: Houghton Mifflin Harcourt, 2019); Paul Tough, "What College Admissions Offices Really Want," *New York Times*, 2019, https://www.nytimes.com/interactive/2019/09/10/magazine/college-admissions-paul-tough.html.

Chapter 4

1. James Coleman, "Social Capital in the Creation of Human Capital," *American Journal of Sociology* 94 (1988), 95–110, doi:10.1086/228943; Alejandro Portes, "The Two Meanings of Social Capital Author," *Sociological Forum* 15, no. 1 (2000): 1–12.

2. See, for example, William J. Carbonaro, "A Little Help from My Friend's Parents: Intergenerational Closure and Educational Outcomes," *Sociology of Education* 71, no. 4 (1998): 295–313.

3. Smith, "Religious Participation and Network Closure among American Adolescents."

4. Smith, "Theorizing Religious Effects among American Adolescents."

5. The negative effects of family moves are significantly more pronounced in families with uninvolved fathers and unsupportive mothers. See John Hagan, Ross Macmillan, and Blair Wheaton, "New Kid in Town: Social Capital and the Life Course Effects of Family Migration on Children," *American Sociological Review* 61, no. 3 (1996): 368–85.

6. Klinenberg, *Palaces for the People*.

7. Timothy P. Carney, *Alienated America: Why Some Places Thrive While Others Collapse* (New York: HarperCollins, 2019).

8. Case and Deaton, *Deaths of Despair and the Future of Capitalism*.

9. Paul Tough documents this well, especially his illustration of Ned Johnson, the DC college counselor who helps children, mostly from affluent homes, psychologically prepare for the SAT: *The Inequality Machine: How College Divides Us* (Houghton Mifflin Harcourt, 2019).

10. US Department of Education, "Chronic Absenteeism in the Nation's Schools: A Hidden Educational Crisis," n.d., https://www2.ed.gov/datastory/chronicabsenteeism.html.

11. Stacy B. Ehrlich et al., "Preschool Attendance in Chicago Public Schools: Relationships with Learning Outcomes and Reasons for Absences," 2013, https://consortium.uchicago.edu/sites/default/files/2018-10/Pre-K Attendance Report.pdf.

12. Hernandez, "Double Jeopardy."

13. Maryam Adamu and Lauren Hogan, "Point of Entry: The Preschool-to-Prison Pipeline," 2015, https://cdn.americanprogress.org/wp-content/uploads/2015/10/08000111/PointOfEntry-reportUPDATE.pdf.

14. Russell J. Skiba et al., "The Color of Discipline: Sources of Racial and Gender Disproportionality in School Punishment," *The Urban Review* 34, no. 4 (2002): 317–42, doi:10.1023/A:1021320817372.

15. Ericka S. Weathers, "Bias or Empathy in Universal Screening? The Effect of Teacher–Student Racial Matching on Teacher Perceptions of Student Behavior," *Urban Education* (2019), doi:10.1177/0042085919873691.

16. Alexis Oscar, *Church Drill Team Member's Manual* (R.H. Boyd Company, 1997).

17. National Center for Education Statistics, table 237: Graduation rates of previous year's 12th-graders and college attendance rates of those who graduated, by selected high school characteristics: 1999–2000, 2003–2004, and 2007–2008, https://nces.ed.gov/programs/digest/d12/tables/dt12_237.asp.

18. In 2005, the year Cameron was graduating from high school, 12% of Black men ages 16–24 had dropped out of high school, compared with only 6.6% of White men. See table 105, U.S. Department of Commerce, Census Bureau, Current Population Survey (CPS), October 1967 through October 2006, https://nces.ed.gov/programs/digest/d07/tables/dt07_105.asp. Black adults are also less likely to start college, and they complete fewer years of education: Cristobal de Brey et al., "Status and Trends in the Education of Racial and Ethnic Groups 2018 (NCES 2019-038)" (Washington, DC, 2019), https://nces.ed.gov/pubs2019/2019038.pdf.

19. Horwitz, "Religion and Academic Achievement."

Chapter 5

1. Although selectivity is the most common measure of college quality, college quality is multidimensional. In a comprehensive study of college quality, Liang Zhang shows that using different measures of quality yields different results about the effect of quality, though all the effects are generally positive and statistically significant regardless of the measure. For example, the estimated earnings advantage of graduating from high-quality institutions is about 20% relative to graduating from low-quality

institutions when Barron's selectivity rankings are used, but the figure reduces by half when SAT score in used. He concludes that it pays to attend high-quality colleges, regardless of how selectivity is measured. See Zhang, *Does Quality Pay?*

2. When it comes to earnings, the benefits vary by demographic characteristics. Non-White students, students from low-SES and middle-SES families, and males who graduate from high-quality college see a bigger earnings boost than do White students, high-SES students, and females (respectively). See ibid.

3. Scholars have debated whether institutional quality yields higher wages, but recent studies by Zhang (2012) and Witteveen and Attewell (2017) show that graduates from high-quality institutions do earn higher wages. See Theodore P. Gerber and Sin Yi Cheung, "Horizontal Stratification in Postsecondary Education: Forms, Explanations, and Implications," *Annual Review of Sociology* 34, no. 1 (2008): 299–318, doi:10.1146/annurev.soc.34.040507.134604; Dirk Witteveen and Paul Attewell, "The Earnings Payoff from Attending a Selective College," *Social Science Research* 66 (2017): 154–69, doi:10.1016/j.ssresearch.2017.01.005; Zhang, *Does Quality Pay?*

4. Zhang, *Does Quality Pay?*, 148.

5. Zhang, *Does Quality Pay?*

6. Scholars refer to this as subjective social status (SSS). See Uecker and Wilkinson, "College Selectivity, Subjective Social Status, and Mental Health in Young Adulthood

7. Ibid.

8. Ross and Mirowsky, "Refining the Association between Education and Health."

9. M. Cahalan et al., "Indicators of Higher Education Equity in the United States: 2018 Historical Trend Report," 2018. www.pellinstitute.org.

10. Chetty et al., "Mobility Report Cards."

11. Denise Clark Pope, *Doing School: How We Are Creating a Generation of Stressed out, Materialistic, and Miseducated Students* (New Haven, CT: Yale University Press, 2008).

12. This quote is from a Q&A with Tough that appears on his website, https://www.paultough.com/books/years-that-matter-most/; see the book for the full explanation.

13. Geiser and Santelices, "Validity of High-School Grades in Predicting Student Success beyond the Freshman Year: High-School Record vs. Standardized Tests as Indicators of Four-Year College Outcomes: Research & Occasional Paper Series: CSHE. 6.07."

14. Many people intend to complete a bachelor's degree but get derailed. According to the National Center for Education Statistics, 74% of people who earn a bachelor's degree do so within 6 years; see National Center for Education Statistics, "Time to Degree," n.d., https://nces.ed.gov/fastfacts/display.asp?id=569.

15. Zhang, *Does Quality Pay?*

16. Based on a max SAT scores of 1600.

17. Pierre Bourdieu and Jean-Claude Passeron, *Reproduction in Education, Culture and Society* (London: Sage, 1977); Jay MacLeod, *Ain't No Makin' It: Aspirations and Attainment in a Low-Income Neighborhood*, 3rd ed. (Boulder, CO: Westview Press, 2009); Paul Willis, *Learning to Labour: How Working Class Kids Get Working Class Jobs* (New York: Columbia University Press, 1977).

18. Pierre Bourdieu, *Outline of a Theory of Practice* (Cambridge: Cambridge University Press, 1977).

19. Terry Rey, "Bourdieu's Writings on Religion," in *Bourdieu on Religion: Imposing Faith and Legitimacy* (New York: Routledge, 2007).

20. Bourdieu, *Outline of a Theory of Practice*.

21. Although religion is not overtly prevalent in Bourdieu's writing, Bourdieu was heavily influenced by Durkheim's sociological study of religion. See Erwan Dianteill, "Pierre Bourdieu and the Sociology of Religion: A Central and Peripheral Concern," *Theory and Society* 32 (2003): 529–49.

22. Peter J. Burke, "Identity Processes and Social Stress," *American Sociological Review* 56, no. 6 (1991): 836–49.

23. Gross, *Why Are Professors Liberal and Why Do Conservatives Care?*, 109–10.

24. Ibid.

25. According to churchofjesuschrist.org, a patriarchal blessing provides inspired direction from the Lord. Patriarchal blessings include a declaration of a person's lineage in the house of Israel and contain personal counsel from the Lord. As a person studies his or her patriarchal blessing and follows the counsel it contains, it will provide guidance, comfort, and protection.

26. Shannon N. Davis, "Gender Ideology Construction from Adolescence to Young Adulthood," *Social Science Research* 36 (2006): 1021–41, doi:10.1016/j.ssresearch.2006.08.001; Andrew L. Whitehead, "Gender Ideology and Religion: Does a Masculine Image of God Matter?" *Review of Religious Research* 54, no. 2 (2012): 139–56, doi:10.1007/s13644-012-0056-3.

27. Samantha K. Ammons and Penny Edgell, "Religious Influences on Work-Family Trade-Offs," *Journal of Family Issues* 28, no. 6 (2007): 794–826, doi:10.1177/0192513X07299682; Elizabeth A. Corrigall and Alison M. Konrad, "Gender Role Attitudes and Careers: A Longitudinal Study," *Sex Roles* 56, no. 11–12 (2007): 847–55, doi:10.1007/s11199-007-9242-0; Shannon N. Davis and Lisa D. Pearce, "Adolescents' Work-Family Gender Ideologies and Educational Expectations," *Sociological Perspectives* 50, no. 2 (2007): 249–71, doi:10.1525/sop.2007.50.2.249.250.

28. Ilana M. Horwitz et al., "From Bat Mitzvah to the Bar: Religious Habitus, Self-Concept, and Women's Educational Outcomes," *American Sociological Review*, under review.

Chapter 6

1. Self-determination theory distinguishes between autonomous and controlled motivation. Autonomous motivation is defined as engaging in a behavior because it is perceived to be consistent with intrinsic goals or outcomes and emanates from the self. In other words, the behavior is self-determined. Individuals engaging in behaviors feel a sense of choice, personal endorsement, interest, and satisfaction and, as a consequence, are likely to persist with the behavior. The behavior is consistent with

and supports the individuals' innate needs for autonomy, the need to feel like a personal agent in one's environment, competence, and the need to experience a sense of control and efficacy in one's actions. Individuals acting for autonomous reasons are more likely to initiate and persist with a behavior without any external reinforcement and contingency. Autonomously motivated individuals are, therefore, more likely to be effective in self-regulation of behavior. Controlled motivation, in contrast, reflects engaging in behaviors for externally referenced reasons such as to gain rewards or perceived approval from others or to avoid punishment or feelings of guilt. See M. S. Hagger et al., "Autonomous and Controlled Motivational Regulations for Multiple Health-Related Behaviors: Between- and Within-Participants Analyses," *Health Psychology and Behavioral Medicine* 2, no. 1 (2014): 565–601, doi:10.1080/21642850.2014.912945; Sara Manganelli et al., "The Interplay between Self-Determined Motivation, Self-Regulated Cognitive Strategies, and Prior Achievement in Predicting Academic Performance," *Educational Psychology* 39, no. 4 (2019): 470–88, doi:10.1080/01443410.2019.1572104.

2. Components of openness to experience, such as intellectual curiosity, creativity, and self-confidence, are more important in predicting differences in reading and mathematics ability than self-discipline, conscientiousness, and diligence. See Margherita Malanchini et al., "'Same but Different': Associations between Multiple Aspects of Self-Regulation, Cognition, and Academic Abilities," *Journal of Personality and Social Psychology* 117, no. 6 (2018): 1164–88, doi:10.1037/pspp0000224.

3. In this chapter, I compare atheists, nonreligious theists, and abiders. As Christel Manning points out, earlier studies have mostly compared those who are religiously committed to those who are disengaged from religion, and not paying attention to those who were never interested in religion in the first place—the atheists. See Christel Manning, *Losing Our Religion: How Unaffiliated Parents Are Raising Their Children* (New York: New York University Press, 2015).

4. A 2020 meta-analysis of 83 studies showed a significant negative association between religiosity and intelligence (defined as the ability to reason, plan, solve problems, think abstractly, comprehend complex ideas, learn quickly, and learn from experience). See Miron Zuckerman et al., "The Negative Intelligence–Religiosity Relation: New and Confirming Evidence," *Personality and Social Psychology Bulletin* 46, no. 6 (2020): 856–68, doi:10.1177/0146167219879122.

5. No prior research that I am aware of has examined the academic outcomes of atheists. Nonreligious people tend to get lumped together, so previous studies do not distinguish between atheists and nonreligious theists when looking at academic success. Because religiosity is generally measured on a continuum of low to high, respondents who appear religiously disengaged (i.e., they do not pray, do not attend religious services, and do not see religion as salient to their life) are typically pooled into one homogenous group. But nonreligious adolescents are not a homogenous group. Pearce and Denton (2011) point this out based on a latent class analysis of the NSYR survey data. They identified two types of nonreligious adolescents: atheists and avoiders. Atheists do not believe in God. Avoiders (whom I refer to as nonreligious theists) believe in God but avoid all forms of religious practices. They are not dismissive of

religion, but they are uninterested in having religion be a part of their life. I ran OLS regressions and found that atheists' grades were not statistically different from those of abiders, even after I included a full set of control variables for demographics. I also found that, compared to abiders, atheists care less about doing well in school and skip class more frequently. This suggests that atheists' good grades are not the result of conscientious and cooperative behavior, as is the case with abiders. The lack of statistical difference between atheists and abiders could reflect the small sample of atheists in the NYSR (3%, $n = 90$), which means there is not enough power to detect a difference (standard errors for these parameters were high, suggesting a lot of noise).

6. Pew Research Center, "U.S. Teens Take after Their Parents Religiously, Attend Services Together and Enjoy Family Rituals."

7. This aligns with other studies. For example, Zuckerman finds that people who move away from religion (i.e., apostates) are more likely to be better educated, to get higher grades, and to describe themselves as having an "intellectual orientation" than their religious peers. See Phil Zuckerman, *Faith No More: Why People Reject Religion* (New York: Oxford University Press, 2015).

8. Alan Cooperman, Cary Funk, and Gregory A Smith, "'Nones' on the Rise: One-in-Five Adults Have No Religious Affiliation," 2012, http://www.pewforum.org/Unaffiliated/nones-on-the-rise.aspx.

9. Malanchini et al., "'Same But Different': Associations between Multiple Aspects of Self-Regulation, Cognition, and Academic Abilities," 1184. Several other studies also link openness to academic achievement. See Yaman Köseoğlu, "To What Extent Can the Big Five and Learning Styles Predict Academic Achievement," *Journal of Education and Practice* 7, no. 30 (2016): 43–51.

10. Penny Edgell, Joseph Gerteis, and Douglas Hartmann, "Atheists as 'Other': Moral Boundaries and Cultural Membership in American Society," *American Sociological Review* 71, no. 2 (2006): 211–34.

11. Lisa D. Pearce and Melinda Denton, *A Faith of Their Own: Stability and Change in the Religiosity of America's Adolescents* (New York: Oxford University Press, 2011), 67.

12. Ibid., 10.

13. Other studies also show that cognitive processing on the part of the nonreligious reflects a preference toward intellectualism, an interest in science. They also tend to be analytic and rational as opposed to intuitive and emotional, and have personalities marked by openness to new experiences. See chapter 6 in Phil Zuckerman, Luke W. Galen, and Frank L. Pasquale, *The Nonreligious: Understanding Secular People and Societies* (New York: Oxford University Press, 2016), doi:10.1093/acprof. Psychologists are also actively researching a theory of *analytical atheism*, which suggests that the extent to which one believes in God may be influenced by one's tendency to rely on intuition versus reflection. See Amitai Shenhav, David G. Rand, and Joshua D. Greene, "Divine Intuition: Cognitive Style Influences Belief in God," *Journal of Experimental Psychology: General* 141, no. 3 (2012): 423–28, doi:10.1037/a0025391; Will M. Gervais et al., "Analytic Atheism: A Cross-Culturally Weak and Fickle Phenomenon?," *Judgment and Decision Making* 13 (2018), https://osf.io/v53c4/.;

Will M. Gervais and Ara Norenzayan, "Analytic Thinking Promotes Religious Disbelief," *Science* 336, no. 6080 (2012): 493–96, doi:10.1126/science.1215647.

14. Also see Manning, *Losing Our Religion: How Unaffiliated Parents Are Raising Their Children*; Phil Zuckerman, *Living the Secular Life: New Answers to Old Questions* (New York: Penguin Books, 2015).

15. Parents and teenagers were instructed to take the survey separately to avoid being influenced by each other's answers. See Pew Research Center, "U.S. Teens Take After Their Parents Religiously, Attend Services Together and Enjoy Family Rituals," 6.

16. Lisa D. Pearce and William G. Axinn, "The Impact of Family Religious Life on the Quality of Mother-Child Relations," *American Sociological Review* 63, no. 6 (1998): 810–28.

17. Zuckerman found a similar pattern. See Zuckerman, *Faith No More*.

18. For an example of this, see Tara Westover, *Educated: A Memoir* (New York: Random House, 2018).

19. Jeremy E. Uecker, M. Regnerus, and Margaret L. Vaaler, "Losing My Religion: The Social Sources of Religious Decline in Early Adulthood," *Social Forces* 85, no. 4 (2007): 1667–92.

20. This aligns with previous research. See Bob Altemeyer and Bruce E. Hunsberger, *Amazing Conversions: Why Some Turn to Faith & Others Abandon Religion* (Buffalo, NY: Prometheus Books, 2010).

21. Key pieces of legislation were being passed just as the NSYR participants were coming of age. For example, in 2004, Massachusetts became the first state to legalize gay marriage. In the following 6 years, four states (New Hampshire, Vermont, Connecticut, and Iowa) along with Washington, DC, all followed suit. Just 6 months before Jacob's interview in May 2008, presidential candidates were invited to participate in a forum focusing specifically on LGBTQ+ issues. The years between Jacob's 2008 interview and his final interview in August 2013 were marked by various pieces of legislation to further the case for marriage equality. It is clear that gay rights issues weighed heavily on Jacob and many NSYR participants.

22. Philip Schwadel, "Does Higher Education Cause Religious Decline?: A Longitudinal Analysis of the Within- and Between-Person Effects of Higher Education on Religiosity," *Sociological Quarterly* 57, no. 4 (2016): 761–62, doi:10.1111/tsq.12153.

23. Damon Mayrl and Jeremy E. Uecker, "Higher Education and Religious Liberalization among Young Adults," *Social Forces* 6, no. 9 (2011): 2166–71, doi:10.1093/sf/90.1.181.

24. William Deresiewicz, *Excellent Sheep: The Miseducation of the American Elite and the Way to a Meaningful Life* (New York: Simon and Schuster, 2015).

Conclusion

1. See Sam Harris, *The End of Faith: Religion, Terror, and the Future of Reason* (New York: WW Norton & Company, 2005), 12.

2. For more on the history of religion in public schools, see Pew Research Center, "Religion in the Public Schools," 2019, https://www.pewforum.org/2019/10/03/religion-in-the-public-schools-2019-update/.

3. Caplan, *The Case against Education*.

4. John Dewey, *My Pedagogic Creed* (New York: EL Kellogg & Company, 1897).

5. Kandan Talebi, "John Dewey—Philosopher and Educational Reformer," *European Journal of Education Studies* 1, no. 1 (2016): 1–13, http://oapub.org/edu/index.php/ejes/article/view/1.

6. Richard Breen and John Goldthorpe, "Explaining Educational Differentials: Towards a Formal Rational Action Theory," *Rationality and Society* 9 (1997): 275–305.

7. William H. Sewell, Arhchibald O. Haller, and Alejandro Portes, "The Educational and Early Occupational Attainment Process," *American Sociological Review* 34, no. 1 (1969): 82–92, doi:https://doi.org/10.2307/2092789.

8. For more on how selective college admissions counselors do their work, and what criteria they use to admit students, see Mitchell L. Stevens, *Creating a Class: College Admissions and the Education of Elites* (Cambridge, MA: Harvard University Press, 2007).

9. Pew Research Center, "Partisans Differ Widely in Views of Police Officers, College Professors," 2017, https://www.pewresearch.org/politics/2017/09/13/partisans-differ-widely-in-views-of-police-officers-college-professors/. By comparison, more than twice as many Democrats—66%—felt warmly toward college professors.

10. Pew Research Center, "Sharp Partisan Divisions in Views of National Institutions," 2017, https://www.pewresearch.org/politics/2017/07/10/sharp-partisan-divisions-in-views-of-national-institutions/#positive-views-of-colleges-decline-across-most-gop-groups. By contrast, most Democrats and Democratic leaners (72%) say colleges and universities have a positive effect.

11. Ilana M. Horwitz, "Are Universities Contributing to Religious Polarization?" *Inside Higher Ed*, May 18, 2021. https://www.insidehighered.com/views/2021/05/18/problems-come-colleges-sweeping-religion-under-rug-opinion.

12. Diana Eck, *Encountering God: A spiritual journey from Bozeman to Banaras* (Boston, MA: Beacon Press, 1993).

13. See Lauren A. Rivera, *Pedigree: How Elite Students Get Elite Jobs* (Princeton, NJ: Princeton University Press, 2016).

14. Haidt, *The Righteous Mind*.

Appendix

1. Additional details about the methodological design and procedures for the NSYR can be found at https://youthandreligion.nd.edu/assets/102496/master_just_methods_11_12_2008.pdf. The data files and code books can be found and downloaded from the Association of Religion Data Archives: https://www.thearda.com/Archive/Files/Descriptions/NSYRW1.asp.

2. For further details about the Jewish oversample, see pages 6 and 7 of the methodological design and procedures document (https://youthandreligion.nd.edu/assets/102496/master_just_methods_11_12_2008.pdf) and the "Methodological Design and Procedures for the National Survey of Youth and Religion (NSYR)" (Smith and Denton 2003).

3. Copies of the survey instruments and semistructured interview guides can be found at http://youthandreligion.nd.edu; also see Smith and Denton 2004. Details on the interviews can be accessed at https://youthandreligion.nd.edu/assets/102495/personalivmethods.pdf and https://youthandreligion.nd.edu/assets/102494/w2_iv_guide.pdf.

4. Williams, *White Working Class*.

5. Add Health is directed by Kathleen Mullan Harris. It was designed by J. Richard Udry, Peter S. Bearman, and Kathleen Mullan Harris at the University of North Carolina at Chapel Hill, and it was funded by grant P01-HD31921 from the Eunice Kennedy Shriver National Institute of Child Health and Human Development, with cooperative funding from 23 other federal agencies and foundations. Information about the Add Health study design, types of data, data documentation, codebooks, and access is available on our website (www.cpc.unc.edu/addhealth).

6. Horwitz, Domingue, and Harris, "Not a Family Matter."

7. More information about the AHAA can be found at http://www.prc.utexas.edu/ahaa/.

Bibliography

Adamu, Maryam, and Lauren Hogan. "Point of Entry: The Preschool-to-Prison Pipeline." 2015. https://cdn.americanprogress.org/wp-content/uploads/2015/10/08000111/PointOfEntry-reportUPDATE.pdf.

Alexis, Oscar. *Church Drill Team Member's Manual*. R.H. Boyd Company, 1997.

Altemeyer, Bob, and Bruce E. Hunsberger. *Amazing Conversions: Why Some Turn to Faith & Others Abandon Religion*. Buffalo, NY: Prometheus Books, 2010.

Ammerman, Nancy T. *Golden Rule Christianity: Lived Religion in the American Mainstream*. Princeton, NJ: Princeton University Press, 1997.

Ammons, Samantha K., and Penny Edgell. "Religious Influences on Work-Family Trade-Offs." *Journal of Family Issues* 28, no. 6 (2007): 794–826. doi:10.1177/0192513X07299682.

Arum, Richard. *Judging School Discipline*. Cambridge, MA: Harvard University Press, 2005.

Baker, David P. "The Great Antagonism That Never Was: Unexpected Affinities between Religion and Education in Post-Secular Society." *Theory and Society* 48 (2019): 39–65. doi:https://10.1007/s11186-018-09338-w.

Ballantine, Jeanne H., Floyd M. Hammack, and Jenny Stuber. *The Sociology of Education: A Systematic Analysis*. New York: Routledge, 2017. doi:10.4324/9781315408545-8.

Bengtson, Vern L, Norrella Putney, and Susan Harris. *Families and Faith: How Religion Is Passed down across Generations*. New York: Oxford University Press, 2013.

Blanchard, Troy C. "Conservative Protestant Congregations and Racial Residential Segregation: Evaluating the Closed Community Thesis in Metropolitan and Nonmetropolitan Counties." *American Sociological Review* 72, no. 3 (2007): 416–33. doi:10.1177/000312240707200305.

Bourdieu, Pierre. *Outline of a Theory of Practice*. Cambridge: Cambridge University Press, 1977.

Bourdieu, Pierre, and Jean-Claude Passeron. *Reproduction in Education, Culture and Society*. London: Sage, 1977.

Breen, Richard, and John Goldthorpe. "Explaining Educational Differentials: Towards a Formal Rational Action Theory." *Rationality and Society* 9, no. 3 (1997): 275–305.

Bryk, Tony, Valerie E. Lee, and Peter Blakeley Holland. *Catholic Schools and the Common Good*. Cambridge, MA: Harvard University Press, 1993.

Buchmann, Claudia, Thomas A. Diprete, and Anne McDaniel. "Gender Inequalities in Education." *Annual Review of Sociology* 34 (2008): 19–37. doi:10.1146/annurev.soc.34.040507.134719.

Burke, Kevin J., and Avner Segall. "Teaching as Jesus Making: The Hidden Curriculum of Christ in Schooling." *Teachers College Record* 117, no. 3 (2015): 1–27.

Burke, Peter J. "Identity Processes and Social Stress." *American Sociological Review* 56, no. 6 (1991): 836–49.

Cahalan, M., L. W. Perna, M. Yamashita, J. Wright, and S. Santillan. *Indicators of Higher Education Equity in the United States: Historical Trend Report.* Washington, DC: The Pell Institute, 2018. www.pellinstitute.org.

Cahalan, Margaret W., Laura W. Perna, Marisha Addison, Chelsea Murray, Pooja R. Patel, and Nathan Jiang. *Indicators of Higher Education Equity in the United States.* Washington, DC: The Pell Institute, 2020.

Calarco, Jessica McCrory. *Negotiating Opportunities: How the Middle Class Secures Advantages in School.* New York: Oxford University Press, 2018.

Caplan, Bryan. *The Case against Education: Why the Education System Is a Waste of Time and Money.* Princeton, NJ: Princeton University Press, 2018.

Carbonaro, William J. "A Little Help from My Friend's Parents: Intergenerational Closure and Educational Outcomes." *Sociology of Education* 71, no. 4 (1998): 295–313.

Carney, Timothy P. *Alienated America: Why Some Places Thrive While Others Collapse.* New York: HarperCollins, 2019.

Carstensen, Laura. *A Long Bright Future: Happiness, Health, and Financial Security in an Age of Increased Longevity.* New York: Broadway Books, 2011.

Carver, Charles S., and Michael F. Scheier. "The Self-Attention-Induced Feedback Loop and Social Facilitation." *Journal of Experimental Social Psychology* 17, no. 6 (1981): 545–68. doi:10.1016/0022-1031(81)90039-1.

Case, Anne, and Angus Deaton. *Deaths of Despair and the Future of Capitalism.* Princeton, NJ: Princeton University Press, 2020.

Cawley, Michael J. III, James E. Martin, and John A. Johnson. "A Virtues Approach to Personality." *Personality and Individual Differences* 28, no. 2000 (2009): 997–1013.

Chetty, Raj, John N. Friedman, Emmanuel Saez, Nicholas Turner, and Danny Yagan. "Mobility Report Cards: The Role of Colleges in Intergenerational Mobility." No. w23618. Washington, DC: National Bureau of Economic Research, 2017.

Chowdhury, Mohammed, and Mohammed Amin. "Personality and Students' Academic Achievement: Interactive Effects of Conscientiousness and Agreeableness on Students' Performance in Principles of Economics." *Social Behavior and Personality* 34, no. 4 (2006): 381–88.

Clydesdale, Tim, and Garces-Foley Kathleen. "Nones." In *The Twentysomething Soul: Understanding the Religious and Secular Lives of American Young Adults*, 1–20. New York: Oxford University Press, 2019. doi:10.1093/oso/9780190931353.001.0001.

Cohen, David K. "Educational Technology, Policy, and Practice." *Educational Evaluation and Policy Analysis* 9, no. 2 (1987): 153–70. doi:https://10.3102/01623737009002153.

Coleman, James. "Social Capital in the Creation of Human Capital." *American Journal of Sociology* 94, no. 95–110 (1988). doi:10.1086/228943.

Collins, Randall. "Functional and Conflict Theories of Educational Stratification." *American Sociological Review* 36, no. 6 (1971): 1002–19.

Conard, Maureen A. "Aptitude Is Not Enough: How Personality and Behavior Predict Academic Performance." *Journal of Research in Personality* 40, no. 3 (2006): 339–46.

Cooperman, Alan, Cary Funk, and Gregory A. Smith. "'Nones' on the Rise: One-in-Five Adults Have No Religious Affiliation." 2012. http://www.pewforum.org/Unaffiliated/nones-on-the-rise.aspx.

Corrigall, Elizabeth A., and Alison M. Konrad. "Gender Role Attitudes and Careers: A Longitudinal Study." *Sex Roles* 56, no. 11–12 (2007): 847–55. doi:10.1007/s11199-007-9242-0.

Cottom, Tressie McMillan. *Lower Ed: The Troubling Rise of For-Profit Colleges in the New Economy*. New York: The New Press, 2017.

Cutler, David M., and Adriana Lleras-Muney. "Understanding Differences in Health Behaviors by Education." *Journal of Health Economics* 29, no. 1 (2010): 1–28. doi:10.1016/j.jhealeco.2009.10.003.

Davis, Shannon N. "Gender Ideology Construction from Adolescence to Young Adulthood." *Social Science Research* 36 (2006): 1021–41. doi:10.1016/j.ssresearch.2006.08.001.

Davis, Shannon N., and Lisa D. Pearce. "Adolescents' Work-Family Gender Ideologies and Educational Expectations." *Sociological Perspectives* 50, no. 2 (2007): 249–71. doi:10.1525/sop.2007.50.2.249.250.

De Brey, Cristobal de, Lauren Musu, Joel McFarland, Sidney Wilkinson-Flicker, Melissa Diliberti, Anlan Zhang, Claire Branstetter, and Xialei Wang. "Status and Trends in the Education of Racial and Ethnic Groups 2018 (NCES 2019-038)." Washington, DC: National Center for Education Statistics, 2019. https://nces.ed.gov/pubs2019/2019038.pdf.

Deci, Edward L., and Richard M. Ryan. "Self-Determination Theory: When Mind Mediates Behavior." *Journal of Mind and Behavior* 1, no. 1 (1980): 33–43. http://www.jstor.org/stable/43852807.

Deresiewicz, William. *Excellent Sheep: The Miseducation of the American Elite and the Way to a Meaningful Life*. New York: Simon and Schuster, 2015.

Dewey, John. *My Pedagogic Creed*. New York: EL Kellogg & Company, 1897.

Dianteill, Erwan. "Pierre Bourdieu and the Sociology of Religion: A Central and Peripheral Concern." *Theory and Society* 32 (2003): 529–49.

DiMaggio, Paul. "Sociological Perspectives on the Face-to-Face Enactment of Class Distinction." In *Facing Social Class: How Societal Rank Influences Interaction*, edited by Susan T. Fiske and Hazel Rose Markus, 15–38. Thousand Oaks, CA: Russell Sage Foundation, 2012.

Domenico, Stefano I. Di, and Marc A. Fournier. "Able, Ready, and Willing: Examining the Additive and Interactive Effects of Intelligence, Conscientiousness, And Autonomous Motivation on Undergraduate Academic Performance." *Learning and Individual Differences* 40 (2015): 156–62. doi:10.1016/j.lindif.2015.03.016.

Durkheim, Emile. *The Elementary Forms of Religious Life: A Study in Religious Sociology*. New York: Free Press, 1912.

Durkheim, Emile. *Moral Education: A Study in the Theory and Application of the Sociology of Education*. Edited and translated by Everett K. Wilson and Herman Schnurer. New York: Free Press, 1961.

Eck, D. L. *Encountering God: A Spiritual Journey from Bozeman to Banaras*. Boston: Beacon Press.

Edgell, Penny. "In Rhetoric and Practice: Defining 'The Good Family' in Local Congregations." In *Handbook of the Sociology of Religion*, editd by Michele Dillon, 164–78. New York: Cambridge University Press, 2003.

Edgell, Penny, Joseph Gerteis, and Douglas Hartmann. "Atheists as 'Other': Moral Boundaries and Cultural Membership in American Society." *American Sociological Review* 71, no. 2 (2006): 211–34.

Ehrlich, Stacy B., Julia A. Gwynne, Amber Stitziel Pareja, Elaine M. Allensworth, Paul Moore, Sanja Jagesic, and Elizabeth Sorice. "Preschool Attendance in Chicago Public

Schools: Relationships with Learning Outcomes and Reasons for Absences." 2013. https://consortium.uchicago.edu/sites/default/files/2018-10/Pre-K Attendance Report.pdf.

Ellison, Christopher G., and Darren E. Sherkat. "Obedience and Autonomy: Religion and Parental Values Reconsidered." *Journal for the Scientific Study of Religion* 32, no. 4 (1993): 313–29.

Ellison, Christopher G., and Xiaohe Xu. "Religion and Families." In *The Wiley Blackwell Companion to the Sociology of Families*, edited by Judith Treas, Jacqueline Scott, and Martin Richards, 277–99. Hoboken, NJ: John Wiley & Sons, 2017. doi:10.1002/9781118374085.ch14.

Emerson, Michael O., and Christian Smith. *Divided by Faith: Evangelical Religion and the Problem of Race in America*. New York: Oxford University Press, 2001.

Fahmy, Dalia. "Americans Are Far More Religious Than Adults in Other Wealthy Nations." *Pew Research Center*. Washington, DC, July 31, 2018. https://pewrsr.ch/2LPGypJ.

Farkas, George. "Cognitive Skills and Noncognitive Traits and Behaviors in Stratification Processes." *Annual Review of Sociology* 29, no. 1 (2003): 541–62.

Featherman, David L. "The Socioeconomic Achievement of White Religio-Ethnic Subgroups: Social and Psychological Explanations." *American Sociological Review* 36, no. 2 (1971): 207–22.

Fernald, Anne, Virginia A. Marchman, and Adriana Weisleder. "SES Differences in Language Processing Skill and Vocabulary Are Evident at 18 Months." *Developmental Science* 16, no. 2 (2013): 234–48. doi:10.1111/desc.12019.

Fishbach, Ayelet, Tal Eyal, and Stacey R. Finkelstein. "How Positive and Negative Feedback Motivate Goal Pursuit." *Social and Personality Psychology Compass* 4, no. 8 (2010): 517–30. doi:10.1111/j.1751-9004.2010.00285.x.

Fraser, James W. *Between Church and State: Religion and Public Education in a Multicultural America*. Baltimore: Johns Hopkins University Press, 2016.

Geiser, Saul, and Maria Veronica Santelices. "Validity of High-School Grades in Predicting Student Success beyond the Freshman Year: High-School Record vs. Standardized Tests as Indicators of Four-Year College Outcomes: Research & Occasional Paper Series: CSHE. 6.07." Center for Studies in Higher Education, University of California, Berkeley, 2007. https://escholarship.org/uc/item/7306z0zf.

Gerber, Theodore P., and Sin Yi Cheung. "Horizontal Stratification in Postsecondary Education: Forms, Explanations, and Implications." *Annual Review of Sociology* 34, no. 1 (2008): 299–318. doi:10.1146/annurev.soc.34.040507.134604.

Gervais, Will M., and Ara Norenzayan. "Analytic Thinking Promotes Religious Disbelief." *Science* 336, no. 6080 (2012): 493–96. doi:10.1126/science.1215647.

Gervais, Will M., Michiel Van Elk, Dimitris Xygalatas, Ryan T. McKay, Mark Aveyard, Emma E. Buchtel, Ilan Dar-Nimrod, et al. "Analytic Atheism: A Cross-Culturally Weak and Fickle Phenomenon?" *Judgment and Decision Making* 13 (2018): 268–74. https://osf.io/v53c4/.

Glanville, Jennifer L., David Sikkink, and Edwin I. Hernández. "Religious Involvement and Educational Outcomes: The Role of Social Capital and Extracurricular Participation." *The Sociological Quarterly* 49, no. 1 (2008): 105–37. doi:10.1111/j.1533-8525.2007.00108.x.

Glenn, Charles L. *The Myth of the Common School*. PhD diss., Boston University, 1987.

Goldin, Claudia. "Human Capital." In *Handbook of Cliometrics*, edited by Claude Diebolt and Michael Haupert, 55–86. Heidelberg: Springer Verlag, 2016. doi:10.1007/978-3-642-40458-0_23-1.

Gracey, Harry L. "Learning the Student Role: Kindergarten as Academic Boot Camp." In *Readings in Introductory Sociology*, edited by Dennis Wrong and Harry Gracey, 82–95. New York: MacMillan, 1967.

Graham, Jesse, and Jonathan Haidt. "Beyond Beliefs: Religions Bind Individuals into Moral Communities." *Personality and Social Psychology Review* 14, no. 1 (2010): 140–50. doi:10.1177/1088868309353415.

Granqvist, Pehr, Mario Mikulincer, and Phillip R. Shaver. "Religion as Attachment: Normative Processes and Individual Differences." *Personality and Social Psychology Review* 14, no. 1 (2010): 49–59. doi:10.1177/1088868309348618.

Gross, Neil. *Why Are Professors Liberal and Why Do Conservatives Care?* Cambridge, MA: Harvard University Press, 2013.

Guhin, Jeffrey. "Why Study Schools?" In *The Handbook of Classical Sociological Theory*, edited by Omar A. Lizardo and Seth Abrutyn. Heidelberg: Springer, 2021.

Hagan, John, Ross Macmillan, and Blair Wheaton. "New Kid in Town: Social Capital and the Life Course Effects of Family Migration on Children." *American Sociological Review* 61, no. 3 (1996): 368–85.

Hagger, M. S., S. J. Hardcastle, A. Chater, C. Mallett, S. Pal, and N. L. D. Chatzisarantis. "Autonomous and Controlled Motivational Regulations for Multiple Health-Related Behaviors: Between- and Within-Participants Analyses." *Health Psychology and Behavioral Medicine* 2, no. 1 (2014): 565–601. doi:10.1080/21642850.2014.912945.

Haidt, Jonathan. *The Righteous Mind: Why Good People Are Divided by Politics and Religion*. New York: Pantheon Books, 2012.

Hakimi, Soraya, Elaheh Hejazi, and Masoud Gholamali Lavasani. "The Relationships between Personality Traits and Students' Academic Achievement." *Procedia—Social and Behavioral Sciences* 29 (2011): 836–45.

Hamad, Rita, Thu T. Nguyen, Jay Bhattacharya, M. Maria Glymour, and David H. Rehkopf. "Educational Attainment and Cardiovascular Disease in the United States: A Quasi-Experimental Instrumental Variables Analysis." *PLoS Medicine* 16, no. 6 (2019): 1–19. doi:10.1371/journal.pmed.1002834.

Hardy, Sam A., and Gustavo Carlo. "Religiosity and Prosocial Behaviours in Adolescence: The Mediating Role of Prosocial Values." *Journal of Moral Education* 34, no. 2 (2005): 231–49. doi:10.1080/03057240500127210.

Hardy, Sam A., Michael A. Steelman, Sarah M. Coyne, and Robert D. Ridge. "Adolescent Religiousness as a Protective Factor against Pornography Use." *Journal of Applied Developmental Psychology* 34, no. 3 (2013): 131–39. doi:10.1016/j.appdev.2012.12.002.

Harris, Sam. *The End of Faith: Religion, Terror, and the Future of Reason*. New York: WW Norton & Company, 2005.

"Health, United States, 2011: With Special Feature on Socioeconomic Status and Health." 2012. https://www.cdc.gov/nchs/data/hus/hus11.pdf.

Heath, Shirley Brice. *Ways with Words: Language, Life and Work in Communities and Classrooms*. Cambridge: Cambridge University Press, 1983.

Herberg, Will. *Protestant—Catholic—Jew: An Essay in American Religious Sociology*. Chicago: University of Chicago Press, 1955.

Hernandez, Donald. "Double Jeopardy: How Third-Grade Reading Skills and Poverty Influence High School Graduation." Baltimore: Annie E. Casey Foundation, 2012. https://www.aecf.org/resources/double-jeopardy/.

Hitlin, Steven, and Sarah K. Harkness. *Unequal Foundations: Inequality, Morality, and Emotions across Cultures*. New York: Oxford University Press, 2018.

Hochschild, Arlie Russell. *Strangers in Their Own Land: Anger and Mourning on the American Right*. New York: The New Press, 2018.

Hogg, Michael A., Janice R. Adelman, and Robert D. Blagg. "Religion in the Face of Uncertainty: An Uncertainty-Identity Theory Account of Religiousness." *Personality and Social Psychology Review* 14, no. 1 (2010): 72–83. doi:https://10.1177/1088868309349692.

Horwitz, Ilana M. "Are Universities Contributing to Religious Polarization?" *Inside Higher Ed*, May 18, 2021. https://www.insidehighered.com/views/2021/05/18/problems-come-colleges-sweeping-religion-under-rug-opinion.

Horwitz, Ilana M. "Religion and Academic Achievement: A Research Review Spanning Secondary School and Higher Education." *Review of Religious Research* 63, no. 1 (2020): 107–54.

Horwitz, Ilana M., Benjamin W. Domingue, and Kathleen Mullan Harris. "Not a Family Matter: The Effects of Religiosity on Academic Outcomes Based on Evidence from Siblings." *Social Science Research* 88–89 (2020). doi:https://doi.org/10.1016/j.ssresearch.2020.102426.

Horwitz, Ilana M., Kaylee Matheny, Krystal Laryea, and Landon Schnabel. "From Bat Mitzvah to the Bar: Religious Habitus, Self-Concept, and Women's Educational Outcomes." *American Sociological Review*, Forthcoming.

House, James S., Paula M. Lantz, and Pamela Herd. "Continuity and Change in the Social Stratification of Aging and Health over the Life Course: Evidence from a Nationally Representative Longitudinal Study from 1986 to 2001/2002." *The Journals of Gerontology: Series B* 60, no. Special Issue 2 (October 1, 2005): S15–26. doi:10.1093/geronb/60.Special_Issue_2.S15.

"How Religious Is Your State?" *Pew Research Center*. https://www.pewresearch.org/fact-tank/2016/02/29/how-religious-is-your-state/?state=alabama.

Hussar, Bill, Jijun Zhang, Sarah Hein, Ke Wang, Ashley Roberts, and Jiashan Cui Mary. "The Condition of Education 2020." *Institute of Education Science* 5 (2020). https://nces.ed.gov/pubs2017/2017144.pdf.

Jackson, Joshua J., Dustin Wood, Tim Bogg, Kate E. Walton, Peter D. Harms, and Brent W. Roberts. "What Do Conscientious People Do? Development and Validation of the Behavioral Indicators of Conscientiousness." *Journal of Research in Personality* 44, no. 4 (2010): 501–11. doi:10.1016/j.jrp.2010.06.005.

Jackson, Michelle. *Determined to Succeed?: Performance versus Choice in Educational Attainment*. Palo Alto, CA: Stanford University Press, 2013.

Jackson, Philip Wesley. *Life in Classrooms*. New York: Holt, Rheinhart, and Winston, 1968.

James-Ward, Cheryl. "No Child Left Behind and the Definition of Proficient: What Should School Leaders in California Know about the Definition of Proficient?" *Educational Leadership and Administration: Teaching and Program Development* 20 (2008): 109–15.

Jamieson, Anne. "Higher Education Study in Later Life: What Is the Point?" *Ageing and Society* 27, no. 3 (2007): 363–84. doi:10.1017/S0144686X06005745.

Jeynes, William H. "The Effects of Religious Commitment on the Academic Achievement of Urban and Other Children." *Education and Urban Society* 36, no. 1 (2003): 44–62. doi:10.1177/0013124503257206.

Jones, Ann E., and Marta Elliott. "Examining Social Desirability in Measures of Religion and Spirituality Using the Bogus Pipeline." *Review of Religious Research* 59, no. 1 (2017): 47–64. doi:10.1007/s13644-016-0261-6.

Jordan, Will J., and Saundra Murray Nettles. "How Students Invest Their Time Outside of School: Effects on School-Related Outcomes." *Social Psychology of Education* 3, no. 4 (2000): 217–43. doi:10.1023/A:1009655611694.

Kao, Grace, and Jennifer S. Thompson. "Racial and Ethnic Stratification in Educational Achievement and Attainment." *Annual Review of Sociology* 29, no. 1 (2003): 417–42. doi:10.1146/annurev.soc.29.010202.100019.

Kawachi, Ichiro, Nancy E. Adler, and William H. Dow. "Money, Schooling, and Health: Mechanisms and Causal Evidence." *Annals of the New York Academy of Sciences* 1186 (2010): 56–68. doi:10.1111/j.1749-6632.2009.05340.x.

Keister, Lisa A., and Darren E. Sherkat. *Religion and Inequality in America: Research and Theory on Religion's Role in Stratification.* Cambridge: Cambridge University Press, 2014.

Kelman, Ari Y. *Shout to the Lord: Making Worship Music in Evangelical America.* New York: NYU Press, 2018.

Kim, Jeannie. "The Academic Advantage of Devotion: Measuring Variation in the Value of Weekly Worship in Late Adolescence on Educational Attainment Using Propensity Score Matching." *Journal for the Scientific Study of Religion* 54, no. 3 (2015): 555–74. doi:10.1111/jssr.12219.

Kirkpatrick, Lee A. *Attachment, Evolution, and the Psychology of Religion.* New York: Guilford Press, 2005.

Klinenberg, Eric. *Palaces for the People: How Social Infrastructure Can Help Fight Inequality, Polarization, and the Decline of Civic Life.* New York: Broadway Books, 2018.

Köseoğlu, Yaman. "To What Extent Can the Big Five and Learning Styles Predict Academic Achievement." *Journal of Education and Practice* 7, no. 30 (2016): 43–51.

Labaree, David. *Someone Has to Fail.* Cambridge, MA: Harvard University Press, 2012.

Labaree, David F. "Struggle over Educational Goals." *American Educational Research Journal* 34, no. 1 (1997): 39–81. doi:10.3102/00028312034001039.

Ladson-Billings, Gloria. "From the Achievement Gap to the Education Debt: Understanding Achievement in U.S. Schools." *Educational Researcher* 35, no. 7 (2006): 3–12. doi:10.3102/0013189x035007003.

Lareau, Annette. *Home Advantage: Social Class and Parental Intervention in Elementary Education.* 2nd ed. Lanham, MD: Rowman & Littlefield, 2000.

Lareau, Annette. *Unequal Childhoods: Class, Race, and Family Life.* Berkeley: University of California Press, 2011.

Lareau, Annette, and Erin Horvat. "Moments of Social Inclusion and Exclusion Race, Class, and Cultural Capital in Family-School Relationships." *Sociology of Education* 72, no. 1 (1999): 37–53.

Lee, Bo Hyeong J., and Lisa D. Pearce. "Understanding Why Religious Involvement's Relationship with Education Varies by Social Class." *Journal of Research on Adolescence* 29, no. 2 (2019): 369–89. doi:10.1111/jora.12457.

Lee, Sang Min, Ana Puig, and Mary Ann Clark. "The Role of Religiosity on Postsecondary Degree Attainment." *Counseling & Values* 52, no. 1 (2007): 25–39. doi:10.1002/j.2161-007X.2007.tb00085.x.

Lehrer, Evelyn L. "Religiosity as a Determinant of Educational Attainment: The Case of Conservative Protestant Women in the United States." *Review of Economics of the Household* 2 (2004): 203–19. doi:10.1023/B:REHO.0000031614.84035.8e.

Lehrer, Evelyn L. "Religious Affiliation and Participation as Determinants of Women's Educational Attainment and Wages." In *Religion, Families, and Health: Population-Based*

Research in the United States, edited by Robert Hummer and Christopher G. Ellison, 186–205. Ithaca, NY: Rutgers University Press, 2010.

Lenski, Gerhard Emmanuel. *The Religious Factor: A Sociological Study of Religion's Impact on Politics, Economics, and Family Life*. Garden City, NY: Doubleday & Company, 1961.

Lieber, Ron. *The Price You Pay for College: An Entirely New Roadmap for the Biggest Financial Decision Your Family Will Ever Make*. New York: HarperCollins, 2021.

Lim, Chaeyoon, and Robert D. Putnam. "Religion, Social Networks, and Life Satisfaction." *American Sociological Review* 75, no. 6 (2010): 914–33. doi:10.1177/0003122410386686.

Lleras, Christy. "Do Skills and Behaviors in High School Matter? The Contribution of Noncognitive Factors in Explaining Differences in Educational Attainment and Earnings." *Social Science Research* 37, no. 3 (2008): 888–902.

Loury, Linda D. "Does Church Attendance Really Increase Schooling?" *Source Journal for the Scientific Study of Religion* 43, no. 1 (2004): 119–27. doi:10.1111/j.1468-5906.2004.00221.x.

Luhrmann, Tanya M. *When God Talks Back: Understanding the American Evangelical Relationship with God*. New York: Alfred A. Knopf, 2012.

MacLeod, Jay. *Ain't No Makin' It: Aspirations and Attainment in a Low-Income Neighborhood*. 3rd ed. Boulder, CO: Westview Press, 2009.

Malanchini, Margherita, Laura E. Engelhardt, Andrew D. Grotzinger, K. Paige Harden, and Elliot M. Tucker-Drob. "'Same but Different': Associations between Multiple Aspects of Self-Regulation, Cognition, and Academic Abilities." *Journal of Personality and Social Psychology* 117, no. 6 (2018): 1164–88. doi:10.1037/pspp0000224.

Manganelli, Sara, Elisa Cavicchiolo, Luca Mallia, Valeria Biasi, Fabio Lucidi, and Fabio Alivernini. "The Interplay between Self-Determined Motivation, Self-Regulated Cognitive Strategies, and Prior Achievement in Predicting Academic Performance." *Educational Psychology* 39, no. 4 (2019): 470–88. doi:10.1080/01443410.2019.1572104.

Manning, Christel. *Losing Our Religion: How Unaffiliated Parents Are Raising Their Children*. New York: New York University Press, 2015.

Marx, Karl, and Friedrich Engels. *The Economic and Philosophic Manuscripts of 1844 and the Communist Manifesto*. Buffalo, NY: Prometheus Books, 2009.

Mayrl, Damon, and Jeremy E. Uecker. "Higher Education and Religious Liberalization among Young Adults." *Social Forces* 6, no. 9 (2011): 2166–71. doi:10.1093/sf/90.1.181.

McCullough, Michael E., and Brian L. B. Willoughby. "Religion, Self-Regulation, and Self-Control: Associations, Explanations, and Implications." *Psychological Bulletin* 135, no. 1 (2009): 69–93. doi:https://10.1037/a0014213.

McKune, Benjamin, and John P. Hoffmann. "Religion and Academic Religion and Academic Achievement Among Adolescents." *Interdisciplinary Journal of Research on Religion* 5 (2009): 1–21.

Meara, Ellen R., Seth Richards, and David M. Cutler. "The Gap Gets Bigger: Changes in Mortality and Life Expectancy, By Education, 1981–2000." *Health Affairs* 27, no. 2 (2008): 350–60. doi:https://doi.org/10.1377/hlthaff.27.2.350.

Meyer, John W., David Tyack, Joane Nagel, and Audri Gordon. "Public Education as Nation-Building in America: Enrollments and Bureaucratization in the American States, 1870–1930." *American Journal of Sociology* 85, no. 3 (1979): 591–613. doi:10.1086/227051.

Milot, Alyssa S., and Alison Bryant Ludden. "The Effects of Religion and Gender on Well-Being, Substance Use, and Academic Engagement among Rural Adolescents." *Youth & Society* 40, no. 3 (2009): 403–25. doi:https://doi.org/10.1177/0044118X08316668.

Mohanty, Madhu S. "Effect of Religious Attendance on Years of Schooling in the USA." *Education Economics* 24, no. 4 (2016): 411–26. doi:https://doi.org/10.1080/09645292.2015.1111866.

National Center for Education Statistics. "Table 104.20 Percentage of Persons 25 to 29 Years Old with Selected Levels of Educational Attainment, by Race/Ethnicity and Sex: Selected Years, 1920 through 2019." 2019. https://nces.ed.gov/programs/digest/d19/tables/dt19_104.20.asp.

National Center for Education Statistics. "Time to Degree." n.d. https://nces.ed.gov/fastfacts/display.asp?id=569.

Norris, Pippa, and Ronald Inglehart. *Sacred and Secular: Religion and Politics Worldwide.* Cambridge: Cambridge University Press, 2011.

Nunn, Lisa. "First-Generation College Students." In *Education and Society: An Introduction to Key Issues in the Sociology of Education*, edited by Thurston Domina, Benjamin G. Gibbs, Lisa Nunn, and Andrew Penner, 110–28. Berkeley: University of California Press, 2019.

Owen, Dennis E., Kenneth D. Wald, and Samuel S. Hill. "Authoritarian or Authority-Minded? The Cognitive Commitments of Fundamentalists and the Christian Right." *Religion and American Culture: A Journal of Interpretation* 1, no. 1 (1991): 73–100.

Park, Crystal L. "Religion and Meaning." In *Handbook of the Psychology of Religion and Spirituality*, edited by Raymond F Paloutzian and Crystal L. Park, 295–314. New York: The Guilford Press, 2005.

Pearce, Lisa D., and William G. Axinn. "The Impact of Family Religious Life on the Quality of Mother-Child Relations." *American Sociological Review* 63, no. 6 (1998): 810–28.

Pearce, Lisa D., and Melinda Denton. *A Faith of Their Own: Stability and Change in the Religiosity of America's Adolescents.* New York: Oxford University Press, 2011.

Pearce, Lisa D., Michael Foster, and Jessica Halliday Hardie. "A Person-Centered Examination of Adolescent Religiosity Using Latent Class Analysis." *Journal for the Scientific Study of Religion* 52, no. 1 (March 1, 2013): 57–79. doi:10.1111/jssr.12001.

Pearce, Lisa D., Jeremy E. Uecker, and Melinda Lundquist Denton. "Religion and Adolescent Outcomes: How and Under What Conditions Religion Matters." *Annual Review of Sociology* 45, no. 1 (2019): 201–22. https://doi.org/10.1146/annurev-soc-073117-041317.

Pew Research Center. "In U.S., Decline of Christianity Continues at Rapid Pace." 2019. https://www.pewforum.org/2019/10/17/in-u-s-decline-of-christianity-continues-at-rapid-pace/.

Pew Research Center. "Partisans Differ Widely in Views of Police Officers, College Professors." 2017. https://www.pewresearch.org/politics/2017/09/13/partisans-differ-widely-in-views-of-police-officers-college-professors/.

Pew Research Center. "Religion in the Public Schools." 2019. https://www.pewforum.org/2019/10/03/religion-in-the-public-schools-2019-update/.

Pew Research Center. "Sharp Partisan Divisions in Views of National Institutions." 2017. https://www.pewresearch.org/politics/2017/07/10/sharp-partisan-divisions-in-views-of-national-institutions/#positive-views-of-colleges-decline-across-most-gop-groups.

Pew Research Center. "U.S. Teens Take after Their Parents Religiously, Attend Services Together and Enjoy Family Rituals." 2020. https://www.pewforum.org/wp-content/uploads/sites/7/2020/09/PF_20.09.10_teens.religion.full_.report.pdf.

Pew Research Center. "When Americans Say They Believe in God, What Do They Mean?" 2018. https://www.pewforum.org/wp-content/uploads/sites/7/2018/04/Beliefs-about-God-FOR-WEB-FULL-REPORT.pdf.

Pope, Denise Clark. *Doing School: How We Are Creating a Generation of Stressed out, Materialistic, and Miseducated Students*. New Haven, CT: Yale University Press, 2008.

Poropat, Arthur E. "A Meta-Analysis of the Five-Factor Model of Personality and Academic Performance." *Psychological Bulletin* 135, no. 2 (2009): 322–38.

Portes, Alejandro. "The Two Meanings of Social Capital Author." *Sociological Forum* 15, no. 1 (2000): 1–12.

Putnam, Robert D. *Our Kids: The American Dream in Crisis*. New York: Simon and Schuster, 2016.

Putnam, Robert, and David Campbell. *American Grace: How Religion Divides and Unites Us*. New York: Simon and Schuster, 2010.

Raby, Rebecca. *School Rules: Obedience, Discipline, and Elusive Democracy*. Toronto: University of Toronto Press, 2012.

Reeves, Richard V., Katherine Guyot, and Eleanor Krause. "Defining the Middle Class: Cash, Credentials, or Culture?" *The Brookings Institution*. 2018. https://www.brookings.edu/research/defining-the-middle-class-cash-credentials-or-culture/.

Regnerus, Mark D. "Shaping Schooling Success: Religious Socialization and Educational Outcomes in Metropolitan Public Schools." *Journal for the Scientific Study of Religion* 39, no. 3 (2000): 363–70. http://dx.doi.org/10.1111/0021-8294.00030.

Regnerus, Mark D., and Christian Smith. "Selection Effects in Studies of Religious Influence." *Review of Religious Research* 47, no. 1 (2005): 23–50. doi:10.1093/socrel/68.2.145.

Regnerus, Mark D., and Glen Elder. "Staying on Track in School: Religious Influences in High- and Low-Risk Settings." *Journal for the Scientific Study of Religion* 42, no. 4 (2003): 633–49.

Rey, Terry. "Bourdieu's Writings on Religion." In *Bourdieu on Religion: Imposing Faith and Legitimacy*, 57–80. New York: Routledge, 2007.

Rivera, Lauren A. *Pedigree: How Elite Students Get Elite Jobs*. Princeton, NJ: Princeton University Press, 2016.

Rivera, Lauren A., and Mitchell L. Stevens. "Why Economic Sociologists Should Care about Education." *Accounts: ASA Economic Sociology Newsletter* 12, no. 3 (2013): 5–8.

Roberts, Brent W., Joshua J. Jackson, Jennifer V. Fayard, Grant Edmonds, and Jenna Meints. "Conscientiousness." In *Handbook of Individual Differences in Social Behavior*, 369–81. New York: The Guilford Press, 2009.

Rogers, Carl Ransom. *A Theory of Therapy, Personality, and Interpersonal Relationships: As Developed in the Client-Centered Framework*. Vol. 3. New York: McGraw-Hill, 1959.

Rogoff, Barbara, Rebeca Mejia-Arauz, and Maricela Correa-Chávez. "A Cultural Paradigm—Learning by Observing and Pitching In." *Advances in Child Development and Behavior* 49 (2015): 1–22.

Rogoff, Barbara, Ruth Paradise, Rebeca Mejía Arauz, Maricela Correa-Chávez, and Cathy Angelillo. "Firsthand Learning through Intent Participation." *Annual Review of Psychology* 54 (2003): 175–203. doi:10.1146/annurev.psych.54.101601.145118.

Ross, Catherine E., and Chia-Ling Wu. "Education, Age, and the Cumulative Advantage in Health." *American Sociological Review* 37, no. 1 (1996): 104–20.

Ross, Catherine E., and John Mirowsky. "Refining the Association between Education and Health: The Effects of Quantity, Credential, and Selectivity." *Demography* 36, no. 4 (1999): 445–60. doi:10.2307/2648083.

Saroglou, Vassilis. "Religion and the Five Factors of Personality: A Meta-Analytic Review." *Personality and Individual Differences* 32, no. 1 (2002): 15–25. doi:https://10.1016/S0191-8869(00)00233-6.

Saroglou, Vassilis. "Religiousness as a Cultural Adaptation of Basic Traits: A Five-Factor Model Perspective." *Personality and Social Psychology Review* 14, no. 1 (2010): 108–25. doi:10.1177/1088868309352322.

Schnabel, Landon, and Sean Bock. "The Persistent and Exceptional Intensity of American Religion: A Response to Recent Research." *Sociological Science* 4 (2017): 686–700. doi:10.15195/v4.a28.

Schofer, Evan. "Schooling in Global Perspective." In *Education and Society: An Introduction to Key Issues in the Sociology of Education*, edited by Thurston Domina, Benjamin G. Gibbs, Lisa Nunn, and Andrew Penner, 7–22. Berkeley: University of California Press, 2019.

Schwadel, Philip. "Does Higher Education Cause Religious Decline?: A Longitudinal Analysis of the Within- and Between-Person Effects of Higher Education on Religiosity." *Sociological Quarterly* 57, no. 4 (2016): 759–86. doi:10.1111/tsq.12153.

Sewell, William H., Arhchibald O. Haller, and Alejandro Portes. "The Educational and Early Occupational Attainment Process." *American Sociological Review* 34, no. 1 (1969): 82–92. doi:https://doi.org/10.2307/2092789.

Shariff, Azim F., and Ara Norenzayan. "God Is Watching You." *Psychological Science* 18, no. 9 (2007): 803–09. doi:10.1111/j.1467-9280.2007.01983.x.

Shenhav, Amitai, David G. Rand, and Joshua D. Greene. "Divine Intuition: Cognitive Style Influences Belief in God." *Journal of Experimental Psychology: General* 141, no. 3 (2012): 423–28. doi:10.1037/a0025391.

Sherkat, Darren E., and Christopher G. Ellison. "Recent Developments and Current Controversies in the Sociology of Religion." *Annual Review of Sociology* 25, no. 1 (1999): 363–94. doi:10.1146/annurev.soc.25.1.363.

Shoda, Yuichi, Walter Mischel, and Philip K. Peake. "Predicting Adolescent Cognitive and Self-Regulatory Competencies from Preschool Delay of Gratification: Identifying Diagnostic Conditions." *Developmental Psychology* 26, no. 6 (1990): 978–86. doi:10.1037/0012-1649.26.6.978.

Sirin, Selcuk R. "Socioeconomic Status and Academic Achievement: A Meta-Analytic Review of Research." *Review of Educational Research* 75, no. 3 (2005): 417–53. doi:10.3102/00346543075003417.

Skiba, Russell J., Robert S. Michael, Nardo Abra Carroll, and Reece L. Peterson. "The Color of Discipline: Sources of Racial and Gender Disproportionality in School Punishment." *The Urban Review* 34, no. 4 (2002): 317–42. doi:10.1023/A:1021320817372.

Smith, Christian. "Religious Participation and Network Closure among American Adolescents." *Journal for the Scientific Study of Religion* 42, no. 2 (2003): 259–67. doi:https://10.1111/1468-5906.00177.

Smith, Christian. "Theorizing Religious Effects Among American Adolescents." *Journal for the Scientific Study of Religion* 42, no. 1 (2003): 17–30. doi:https://10.1111/1468-5906.t01-1-00158.

Smith, Christian, Bridget Ritz, and Michael Rotolo. *Religious Parenting: Transmitting Faith and Values in Contemporary America*. Princeton, NJ: Princeton University Press, 2019.

Smith, Christian, and Patricia Snell. *Souls in Transition: The Religious and Spiritual Lives of Emerging Adults*. New York: Oxford University Press, 2009.

Snyder, Benson R. *The Hidden Curriculum*. New York: Alfred A. Knopf, 1971.

Stevens, Mitchell L. *Creating a Class: College Admissions and the Education of Elites*. Cambridge, MA: Harvard University Press, 2007.

Stevens, Mitchell L. *Kingdom of Children: Culture and Controversy in the Homeschooling Movement*. Princeton, NJ: Princeton University Press, 2009.

Stokes, Charles E. "The Role of Parental Religiosity in High School Completion." *Sociological Spectrum* 28, no. 5 (2008): 531–55. doi:10.1080/02732170802206153.

Storm, Ingrid. "Halfway to Heaven: Four Types of Fuzzy Fidelity in Europe." *Journal for the Scientific Study of Religion* 48, no. 4 (2009): 702–18. doi:10.1111/j.1468-5906.2009.01474.x.

Stryker, Sheldon. "Identity Salience and Role Performance: The Relevance of Symbolic Interaction Theory for Family Research." *Journal of Marriage and Family* 30, no. 4 (1968): 558–64. doi:10.2307/349494.

Sum, Andrew, Ishwar Khatiwada, and Joseph McLaughlin. "The Consequences of Dropping out of High School: Joblessness and Jailing for High School Dropouts and the High Cost for Taxpayers." Boston, MA, 2009. https://www.prisonpolicy.org/scans/The_Consequences_of_Dropping_Out_of_High_School.pdf.

Talebi, Kandan. "John Dewey—Philosopher and Educational Reformer." *European Journal of Education Studies* 1, no. 1 (2016): 1–13. http://oapub.org/edu/index.php/ejes/article/view/1.

Tirre, William. "Conscientiousness Provides High School Students an Advantage in Achieving Good Grades Incrementally to General Cognitive Ability." *North American Journal of Psychology* 19, no. 2 (2017): 303–24.

Toldson, Ivory, and Kenneth Anderson. "Editor's Comment: The Role of Religion in Promoting Academic Success for Black Students." *The Journal of Negro Education* 79, no. 3 (2010): 205–13.

Tough, Paul. "What College Admissions Offices Really Want." *New York Times*, September 10, 2019. https://www.nytimes.com/interactive/2019/09/10/magazine/college-admissions-paul-tough.html.

Tough, Paul. *The Inequality Machine: How College Divides Us*. New York: Houghton Mifflin Harcourt, 2019.

Trusty, Jerry, and Richard E. Watts. "Relationship of High School Seniors' Religious Perceptions and Behavior to Educational, Career, and Leisure Variables." *Counseling and Values* 44, no. 1 (1999): 30–39. doi:10.1002/j.2161-007X.1999.tb00150.x.

Uecker, Jeremy E., M. Regnerus, and Margaret L. Vaaler. "Losing My Religion: The Social Sources of Religious Decline in Early Adulthood." *Social Forces* 85, no. 4 (2007): 1667–92.

Uecker, Jeremy E., and Lindsay R. Wilkinson. "College Selectivity, Subjective Social Status, and Mental Health in Young Adulthood." *Society and Mental Health* 10, no. 3 (2020): 257–75. doi:10.1177/2156869319869401.

US Bureau of Labor Statistics. "Median Weekly Earnings $606 for High School Dropouts, $1,559 for Advanced Degree Holders." 2019. https://www.bls.gov/opub/ted/2019/median-weekly-earnings-606-for-high-school-dropouts-1559-for-advanced-degree-holders.htm.

US Department of Education. "Chronic Absenteeism in the Nation's Schools: A Hidden Educational Crisis." n.d. https://www2.ed.gov/datastory/chronicabsenteeism.html.

Warikoo, Natasha, and Prudence Carter. "Cultural Explanations for Racial and Ethnic Stratification in Academic Achievement: A Call for a New and Improved Theory." *Review of Educational Research* 79, no. 1 (2009): 366–94. doi:10.3102/0034654308326162.

Weathers, Ericka S. "Bias or Empathy in Universal Screening? The Effect of Teacher–Student Racial Matching on Teacher Perceptions of Student Behavior." *Urban Education* (2019): 1–30. doi:10.1177/0042085919873691.

Wellman Jr., James, Katie Corcoran, and Kate Stockly. *High on God: How Megachurches Won the Heart of America*. New York: Oxford University Press, 2020.

Westover, Tara. *Educated: A Memoir*. New York: Random House, 2018.

Whitehead, Andrew L. "Gender Ideology and Religion: Does a Masculine Image of God Matter?," *Review of Religious Research* 54 (2012): 139–56. doi:10.1007/s13644-012-0056-3.

Wilde, Melissa J. "Editorial: 'Complex Religion: Intersections of Religion and Inequality.'" *Social Inclusion* 6 (2018): 83–86. doi:10.17645/si.v6i2.1606.

Wilde, Melissa, and Lindsay Glassman. "How Complex Religion Can Improve Our Understanding of American Politics." *Annual Review of Sociology* 42 (2016): 407–25. doi:10.1146/annurev-soc-081715-074420.

Wilde, Melissa J., and Patricia Tevington. "Complex Religion: Toward a Better Understanding of the Ways in Which Religion Intersects with Inequality." In *Emerging Trends in the Social and Behavioral Sciences*, edited by Robert Scott and Marlis Buchmann , 1–14. Hoboken, NJ: Wiley, 2017. https://doi.org/10.1002/9781118900772.etrds0440.

Williams, Joan C. *White Working Class: Overcoming Class Cluelessness in America*. Cambridge, MA: Harvard Business Press, 2020.

Willis, Paul. *Learning to Labour: How Working Class Kids Get Working Class Jobs*. New York: Columbia University Press, 1977.

Witteveen, Dirk, and Paul Attewell. "The Earnings Payoff from Attending a Selective College." *Social Science Research* 66 (2017): 154–69. doi:10.1016/j.ssresearch.2017.01.005.

Yoshikawa, Hirokazu, Christina Weiland, Jeanne Brooks-Gunn, Margaret R. Burchinal, Linda M. Espinosa, William T. Gormley, Jens Ludwig, et al. "Investing in Our Future: The Evidence Base on Preschool Education Investing in Our Future: The Evidence Base on Preschool Education." 2013. https://www.fcd-us.org/the-evidence-base-on-preschool.

Zhang, Liang. *Does Quality Pay?: Benefits of Attending a High-Cost, Prestigious College*. New York: Routledge, 2012.

Zuckerman, Miron, Chen Li, Shengxin Lin, and Judith A. Hall. "The Negative Intelligence–Religiosity Relation: New and Confirming Evidence." *Personality and Social Psychology Bulletin* 46, no. 6 (2020): 856–68. doi:10.1177/0146167219879122.

Zuckerman, Phil. *Faith No More: Why People Reject Religion*. New York: Oxford University Press, 2015.

Zuckerman, Phil. *Living the Secular Life: New Answers to Old Questions*. New York: Penguin Books, 2015.

Zuckerman, Phil, Luke W. Galen, and Frank L. Pasquale. *The Nonreligious: Understanding Secular People and Societies*. New York: Oxford University Press, 2016. doi:10.1093/acprof.

Zwick, Rebecca, and Jeffrey C. Sklar. "Predicting College Grades and Degree Completion Using High School Grades and SAT Scores: The Role of Student Ethnicity and First Language." *American Educational Research Journal* 42, no. 3 (2005): 439–64. doi:10.3102/00028312042003439.

Index